OUR
BEST
LIFE
TOGETHER

A Daily Devotional for Couples

OUR
BEST
LIFE
TOGETHER

A Daily Devotional for Couples

JOEL & VICTORIA OSTEEN

Faith
Words

New York • Nashville

FaithWords
Hachette Book Group
1290 Avenue of the Americas
New York, NY 10104
www.faithwords.com
twitter.com/faithwords

First Edition: March 2018

FaithWords is a division of Hachette Book Group, Inc.
The FaithWords name and logo are trademarks of Hachette Book Group, Inc.

The publisher is not responsible for websites (or their content) that are not owned by the publisher.

The Hachette Speakers Bureau provides a wide range of authors for speaking events. To find out more, go to www.hachettespeakersbureau.com or call (866) 376-6591.

Scripture quotations noted NKJV are taken from the *New King James Version* of the Bible. Copyright © 1982 by Thomas Nelson, Inc. Used by permission. All rights reserved.
    Scripture quotations noted NIV are taken from *The Holy Bible, New International Version*® NIV®. Copyright © 1973, 1978, 1984, 2011 by Biblica, Inc.™ Used by permission. All rights reserved worldwide.
    Scripture quotations noted NLT are taken from the *Holy Bible, New Living Translation*, copyright © 1996, 2004, 2007 by Tyndale House Foundation. Used by permission of Tyndale House Publishers, Inc., Carol Stream, Illinois 60188. All rights reserved.
    Scripture quotations noted AMP are taken from *The Amplified Bible*. Copyright © 2015 by The Lockman Foundation, La Habra, CA 90631. All rights reserved. For permission to quote information visit www.lockman.org.
    Scripture quotations noted AMPC are from *The Amplified Bible, Classic Edition*. Copyright © 1954, 1958, 1962, 1964, 1965, 1987 by The Lockman Foundation. All rights reserved. Used by permission. (www.Lockman.org)
    Scripture quotations noted ESV are from *The Holy Bible, English Standard Version*®. Copyright © 2001 by Crossway, a publishing ministry of Good News Publishers. All rights reserved.
    Scripture quotations noted TLB are taken from the *Living Bible*, copyright © 1971 by Tyndale House Foundation. Used by permission of Tyndale House Publishers, Inc., Carol Stream, Illinois 60188. All rights reserved.
    Scripture quotations noted MSG are taken from the *The Message*. Copyright © 1993, 1994, 1995, 1996, 2000, 2001, 2002. Used by permission of NavPress Publishing Group.
    Scripture quotations noted KJV are from the *King James Version* of the Holy Bible.

Literary development: Lance Wubbels Literary Services, LLC, Bloomington, Minnesota.

Printed in the United States of America

ISBN: 978-1-4555-9864-9

10 9 8 7 6 5 4 3 2 1

Introduction

Whether you're newly married or have been married for decades, you need regular, quiet moments together to renew your love and commitment to each other. Today, more than ever, we have to be proactive and do whatever we can to stand together for our relationship. Adversity comes. Disagreements happen. Too many homes are suffering with strife, lack of commitment, wrong priorities, and bad attitudes. If we're going to have a strong, healthy relationship, we must dig our heels in and press forward for our best life together as a couple.

Victoria and I want to encourage you in your marriage and remind you that God brought you together. He has a good plan for your marriage, and He has good things in store. He brought you together to help each other succeed and to become all He created you to be, to help each other reach your full potential. That means you have an assignment as a couple. Every day you should be encouraging each other, building each other up, challenging each other to reach for new heights. If you will do your part by being kind, respecting each other, treating each other the way you want to be treated, God will do His part, and you can live in love!

And even if you are living your best life together now, it's important that you do not become stagnant. God always wants to increase you, to do more in you and through you. He always wants to take you deeper into self-discovery and then wants to raise you to a higher level of living together. He didn't create your relationship to be average. He doesn't want you to settle for "good enough." He wants you to keep stretching, to keep pressing forward into the next level.

Now, in this devotional, we want to encourage you to do just that. We're hoping to help you discover and unlock the seeds of greatness that God has placed within each of you, allowing them to burst forth in an abundantly blessed life together. Too many couples settle for mediocrity in their thoughts, attitudes, or actions. It's time to put off those negative mind-sets and rise higher. Remember, God has put in you everything you need to live a victorious life and marriage. Now, it's up to you to draw it out.

Through these daily readings, the two of you will find inspiration and help to live your best life together. There's no better way to experience the fulfilling marriage God intends for you than to set aside a devotional time together each day and set your minds in the right direction. If you don't set the tone for your marriage, negative thoughts will set it for you. That's why we've created this devotional, to help you set your mind for a positive, happy, faith-filled marriage. When you take the time to be grateful together, thinking about God's goodness, expecting His favor, you're setting the tone for a blessed relationship. Take a few minutes for five days a week and read one devotional. It just takes a couple minutes, but it can make a big difference. When you live together in unity, you honor God and open the door for His blessings and favor to flow into every area of your lives.

Put God First

TODAY'S SCRIPTURE

In everything you do, put God first, and he will direct you and crown your efforts with success.

Proverbs 3:6 TLB

A lot of people are good at taking care of the physical part of their lives, watching their diets and working out. And many pay attention to taking care of their emotional needs. But most people today don't take care of the spiritual part of their lives. When there's no connection or minimal connection to God, you're not going to be your best. Your lives will be more rewarding, more fulfilling, when you're in relationship with your Creator. He breathed life into you. He knows what your purpose is, both individually and as a couple. He knows what you can accomplish.

When you make God a part of your lives, you'll go further than you can in just your own abilities and talents. God's favor on your lives will take you where your talents could not take you. He wants to give you the advantage for success. If you want to reach your highest potential, take care of the total you. Make your spiritual lives a priority. When you get up in the morning, take time to thank God for the day. Start the day off with a grateful attitude. Read the Scripture, meditate on His promises, and fill your minds with thoughts of faith, hope, and victory. Put God first, and He will crown your efforts with success.

A PRAYER FOR TODAY

Father, thank You that You invited us into a relationship with You. We want to put You first and have You direct our lives. Thank You for speaking to us through Your Word and giving us Your promises. We believe that You will bring fulfillment to our lives in Jesus' Name. Amen.

Becoming One Takes Time

TODAY'S SCRIPTURE

That is why a man leaves his father and mother and is united to his wife, and they become one flesh.

Genesis 2:24 NIV

Like any other couple, when we first got married, we had to work through some things. The Scripture says the two will become one, but you don't become one overnight. It takes some time. Thirty years later, we're still becoming. We're not perfect, but we made the decision early on to keep strife out of our home. It didn't happen automatically. We're two different people and have two different ways of doing things. We had to grow together, make allowances, and overlook some things. Had we not stayed on the offensive and worked to keep strife out, we wouldn't have the wonderful marriage we have today.

The two of us don't agree all the time, but that doesn't mean we have to argue. If things start to get heated, walk away. You don't have to engage. It's better to have peace than to have your own way. It is better to have a loving, kind, joyful atmosphere in your home than to win the battle and be so miserable that you don't want to be there. We've learned that when we leave it up to God, He'll change what needs to be changed. We can't change each other. Only God can.

A PRAYER FOR TODAY

Father, thank You that You brought us together to grow together into a oneness of heart and soul. Help us to overlook some things, to make allowances for our differences, and to stop trying to change each other. We declare that only You can change what needs to be changed in our lives in Jesus' Name. Amen.

Have Your Anchor Down

TODAY'S SCRIPTURE

Now faith is the substance of things hoped for,
the evidence of things not seen.

Hebrews 11:1 NKJV

The Scripture tells us, "We have this hope as an anchor for the soul, firm and secure." What's going to keep you together as a couple, what's going to cause you to overcome challenges and reach your dreams, is when you are anchored to hope. That means that no matter what you face, no matter how long it's taking, you know that God is still on the throne. You know that His plans for you are for good, that He's bigger than any obstacle, that His favor is surrounding you. When you are tied to this hope, the winds, the waves, and the storms cannot move you.

We've learned that there will always be something trying to get us to pull up our anchor—a bad medical report, bad breaks, delays, disappointments. In the tough times, when life doesn't make sense, when your prayers aren't answered, you have to make sure the two of you keep your anchor down. If you pull it up, you'll drift over into doubt, discouragement, and self-pity. When you're anchored by hope, you may think, *This problem is never going to work out*, but your faith will kick in. "No, we know the answer is already on the way." Every time negative thoughts come, trying to pull you away, your anchor kicks in.

A PRAYER FOR TODAY

Father, thank You that we have You as the anchor of our
relationship. Our hope and faith are firm and secure in You.
We believe that Your plans for us are good and that Your
favor is surrounding us. Help us to keep our anchor
down in Jesus' Name. Amen.

A Joyful Home

TODAY'S SCRIPTURE

Our mouths were filled with laughter, our tongues
with songs of joy. Then it was said among the nations,
"The LORD has done great things for them."

Psalm 126:2 NIV

F riends often ask us about the secret to a healthy marriage. We always tell them two things: number one, always be respectful, even when you disagree. And number two, don't ever stop laughing together. Make sure your house is full of joy and happiness. The enemy cannot stand the sound of husbands and wives and family members having fun together. He wants there to be so much strife, tension, and pressure that we never have any joy in our homes. Don't fall into that trap.

If your relationship isn't what you'd like it to be, we recommend a good dose of humor, laughter, and joy. We know the pressures of life can weigh on the best of marriages and test the love of even the most devoted, but it might help you to remember why you fell in love in the first place. Remember the things you enjoyed doing together, the fun and the laughter that made you want to go from being single to being a couple.

If you bring that joy back into the home, you will see a freshness in your relationship. Find the humor in everyday moments. Make laughter a lifestyle choice. Welcome joy into your home as a permanent resident.

A PRAYER FOR TODAY

Father, thank You for healthy, joy-filled relationships,
especially our relationship. Help us to always overlook offenses
and fill our home with laughter each and every day. Give us
opportunities to lighten the load of the people we love.
Let our joy be contagious in Jesus' Name. Amen.

OUR BEST LIFE TOGETHER

We Declare

God's incredible
blessings over our lives.
We will see an explosion
of God's goodness,
a sudden widespread
increase. We will experience
the surpassing greatness
of God's favor. It will elevate
us to a level higher than
we ever dreamed of.
Explosive blessings are
coming our way.

Turn It into Worship

TODAY'S SCRIPTURE

"And who of you by worrying and being anxious
can add one unit of measure (cubit) to his
stature or to the span of his life?"

Matthew 6:27 AMPC

f we could add inches to our lives by worrying, some of us would be twenty-three-feet tall. What do you worry about as a couple? What keeps you up at night? What's taking your joy? When you worry about your health or child or finances, you're making those your God. Do yourselves a favor: take that worry off the throne, and put God back on the throne. Use that same energy to thank God that He's in control.

Worry is not going to go away automatically. It's a decision you make. Every time you're tempted to worry, turn it around and thank God that He's taking care of that situation. Guard your mind. That's where the real battles take place. Most of the time, especially in difficult situations, the first thoughts that come are negative. *What if this doesn't work?* The easy thing to do is to start dwelling on it. *What if we can't make the payments?* Your life is going to follow your thoughts. Turn your worry into worship. Thank God that He's fighting your battles. Thank Him that no weapon formed against you will prosper.

A PRAYER FOR TODAY

Father, we praise and worship Your holy Name. Thank You
that in Your presence is fullness of joy, peace, and rest. We choose
to guard our minds from worrisome, anxious thoughts. We give
You thanks that You're in control, and we declare that You are
fighting our battles in Jesus' Name. Amen.

Happiness Is Your Choice

TODAY'S SCRIPTURE

This is the day that the LORD has made;
let us rejoice and be glad in it.

Psalm 118:24 ESV

t is a simple yet profound truth: happiness is a choice. You don't have to wait for everything to be perfect in your relationship or your family or with your business. You don't have to forgo happiness until you lose weight, break an unhealthy habit, or accomplish all your goals. If you want to enjoy your best life together, it is vital that you choose to be happy today and every day. It's up to you.

You might as well choose to enjoy your lives! When you do that, not only will you feel better, but your faith will cause God to show up and work wonders. To do so, you need to understand that God gives us the grace to live today. He has not yet given us tomorrow's grace, and you should not worry about it. Learn to live one day at a time. By an act of your will, choose to start enjoying your lives right now. Learn to enjoy each other, your family, friends, health, and work; enjoy everything in your lives. Happiness is a decision you make, not an emotion you feel. God gives us His peace on the inside, but it's up to us to tap into God's supernatural peace. Happiness is your choice.

A PRAYER FOR TODAY

Father, You alone are worthy of our praise. Thank You that
You have made this day, and every day, for us to choose to be
happy and enjoy our lives. We choose to live one day at a time.
We declare that we will walk together in Your supernatural peace
no matter what comes our way in Jesus' Name. Amen.

Constant Reminders

TODAY'S SCRIPTURE

...you who [are His servants and by your prayers]
put the Lord in remembrance [of His promises],
keep not silence, and give Him no rest...

Isaiah 62:6-7 AMPC

One of the most powerful ways to pray as a couple is to find a promise in the Scripture and remind God what He said about you. "God, You said we're blessed and cannot be cursed." "God, You said Your favor is not for a season but for a lifetime." When you can say, "God, You said...," all of heaven comes to attention. God is faithful to His Word.

Notice that it doesn't say, "Put God in remembrance of your *problems.*" Sometimes we use prayer as an excuse to complain. "God, our children are getting on our nerves. We can't take it anymore." You don't have to tell God your problems. He already knows your needs and every concern. It's okay to be open and honest and tell God how you feel, but don't turn that into a self-pity session. All that will do is make you more discouraged.

If you want God to turn it around, then instead of complaining, find a promise you can stand on. When God hears His promises, He sets the miracle into motion. He will change things in your favor. It may not happen overnight, but just stay in faith and keep reminding God what He promised you day in and day out.

A PRAYER FOR TODAY

Father, we praise You that You are the Lord our provider. You
said You would supply all our needs according to Your riches.
You said what is impossible with men is possible with You.
Thank You that You are faithful to Your Word and keeping
every promise to us in Jesus' Name. Amen.

Heart Matters

TODAY'S SCRIPTURE

"For the eyes of the Lord search back and forth across the whole earth, looking for people whose hearts are perfect toward him..."

2 Chronicles 16:9 TLB

All of us make mistakes and do things we know we shouldn't. We lose our tempers with each other, don't keep our word, let our guard down and compromise. It's easy to go around feeling guilty and condemned, beating ourselves up with shame. Voices will whisper, "God's never going to bless you as a couple. You don't deserve it." We think, *Once we overcome all these things we're struggling with, we'll have God's favor.*

But God is not looking for couples who have a perfect performance, who never make a mistake. He's looking for people who have perfect hearts toward Him. That means you may make mistakes, but you have a desire to please Him. Deep down you want to honor Him with your lives. It's your hearts that matter.

When Jesus chose His twelve disciples, He chose people who had lots of flaws. God looks beyond all that. He knows it's the heart that matters. He chose those whose hearts were turned toward Him. Your performance may not be perfect, and your behavior, attitude, and character may need some improvement, but just as with the disciples, God is saying, "I know your hearts are sincere. So I'm going to show Myself strong in your lives."

A PRAYER FOR TODAY

Father, we love You and humbly come to You with open and willing hearts. Search us. Know us. Our performance is far from perfect, and there is so much we need to improve on in our attitudes and characters, but our hearts are toward You. Our hearts are set to do the right thing in Jesus' Name. Amen.

Sharpen Each Other

TODAY'S SCRIPTURE

As iron sharpens iron, so a friend
sharpens a friend.

Proverbs 27:17 NLT

This principle is true in our relationships: if you see the good in your spouse, your children, your friends—focus on their strengths, praise them for what you like about them— that will draw out more good. People improve when you praise them for what's right, not when you nag them about what's wrong. Your spouse can have a hundred good qualities, but if you focus on the three things you don't like, it will become a source of frustration that drives a wedge between you. If you focus on their good qualities, your relationship will improve.

If you overlook the things you don't like and focus on the things you do like, it will change the atmosphere in your home. Here's a news flash: your spouse is not a finished product. God's still working on them. God has put you together so you would sharpen each other. Don't use your iron to say hurtful words that cut like a knife or use your iron to try to hammer out all the flaws and weaknesses. The way you sharpen each other is by bringing out their good qualities. Praise them for what you like, encourage them in what they're good at, cheer them on for what they're doing right. Be a voice that pushes them forward.

A PRAYER FOR TODAY

Father, we love You and praise You that You're working in our lives. Thank You that You brought us together so we would sharpen each other and bring out each other's good qualities in Jesus' Name. Amen.

Don't Rely on People

TODAY'S SCRIPTURE

"Your approval means nothing to me…"

John 5:41 NLT

t's great when people believe in us, cheer us on, and make us feel valuable. We love when our spouse compliments us, a friend gives encouragement, a coworker helps us on a project. God uses people to help move us toward our destiny. But here's the key: you can't become so dependent on people, including your spouse, that you're trying to get your worth and value from them. It's easy to begin to rely on them to keep you feeling good about yourself and make you feel approved. But if they don't meet your expectations, you'll feel discouraged and inferior. The problem is, you're trying to get from people what only God can give. Your value, your self-worth, doesn't come from another person—it comes from your Creator.

If you rely on people for your value, you'll be disappointed. People will let you down, won't always be there when you need them, and sometimes will turn on you. When Jesus was about to be crucified, when He needed His friends the most, Peter denied that he knew Him and others fled. Jesus knew better than to rely on people. What they do or don't do doesn't determine your worth and cannot stop your purpose. God breathed life into you and crowned you with favor. Quit depending on others' approval and start approving yourselves.

A PRAYER FOR TODAY

Father, we honor and glorify You. Thank You for the people You've placed in our lives to help us move to our destiny. Help us, though, to not become dependent upon their approval or try to get our value from them. We declare that we have Your approval and love and that's all we need in Jesus' Name. Amen.

Always Thankful

TODAY'S SCRIPTURE

And whatever you do, whether in word or deed,
do it all in the name of the Lord Jesus, giving thanks
to God the Father through him.

Colossians 3:17 NIV

D o you ever wonder how much more we would enjoy life if we chose a lifestyle of being thankful, constantly thinking about how blessed we are as couples and all the good things God has in store for us? Even in difficult times, we're thanking Him that He's bigger than our problems. We're thanking Him that what He started in our lives together He will finish. Every time you do that, you're not just being positive, you're getting filled back up. God is pouring strength, peace, and joy back into you.

It's easy to think about what's wrong in life and leak out your joy. You have to learn this principle of always being joyful. You can develop this new habit of being thankful in all circumstances by purposefully finding things to be grateful for. It's not complicated. When you're brushing your teeth, say, "Lord, thank You for this day." When you're making breakfast, say, "Lord, thank You for our children." When you're driving to work, say, "Lord, thank You for our jobs." When you're going to bed, say, "Lord, thank You for my spouse." In your thoughts, you're always meditating on God's goodness. That's how you have the continual joy that gives you the strength you need to achieve your dreams together.

A PRAYER FOR TODAY

Father, thank You that we can enter into Your gates with
thanksgiving and into Your courts with praise. We are thankful
that You are doing exceedingly abundantly beyond all we could
ever ask or imagine, and we bless Your Name. We choose to
meditate on Your goodness in Jesus' Name. Amen.

Crooked Floors

TODAY'S SCRIPTURE

The heart of man plans his way,
but the LORD establishes his steps.

Proverbs 16:9 ESV

When we first got married, we found a house that looked perfect for us. It was located on a beautiful lot in a neighborhood with young families, and it had a swimming pool. We made the best offer we could and prayed that the owners would accept it, but they didn't.

Then another property caught our attention. It was an old abandoned house with broken windows on a beautiful lot in a nice neighborhood. Despite a cracked foundation, we believed it was right for us—not based on how much sense it made in the natural, but based on the supernatural peace we had inside. Sure enough, our offer was accepted.

Friends and family made jokes about our crooked floors, but we grew to love that house. We knew God gave us that house, so we didn't look back and focus on what we didn't get, and God blessed us beyond our wildest dreams. We ended up dividing our lot and selling half of it for the same price we originally paid for the entire property.

Don't get stuck focusing on what didn't work out. Trust that God is guiding your steps. If you let go of what you had in mind, God can give you something better. If He can bless us through a crooked-floored house, there's no telling what He will do for you!

A PRAYER FOR TODAY

Father, we praise and worship Your holy Name. Thank You
that You are guiding our steps and orchestrating Your plan for
our lives. We declare that we will walk in Your supernatural
peace no matter what the circumstances. Help us to totally
trust in You always in Jesus' Name. Amen.

We Declare

we will experience God's
faithfulness. We will not worry.
We will not doubt. We will
keep our trust in Him,
knowing that He will not
fail us. We will give birth to
every promise God puts
in our hearts, and we will
become everything God
created us to be.

Overlook It

TODAY'S SCRIPTURE

Above all, have fervent and unfailing love for
one another, because love covers a multitude of sins
[it overlooks unkindness and unselfishly seeks
the best for others].

1 Peter 4:8 AMP

n relationships we all have conflicts and things we don't like.
We will have disagreements, tension, and stress. When we do,
we need to step back and not make hurtful comments in the
heat of the moment. That's going to damage our relationships.
Too often we say, "Well, if my spouse wouldn't push my buttons,
I wouldn't say things I shouldn't." No, these are tests that we all
have to pass. No one in your life, including your spouse, is ever
going to be perfect. You have to learn to tame your tongue. That
means you don't say everything you feel like saying. You may think
it, but you're disciplined enough to zip it up.

Love makes allowances for other people's weaknesses. Love
overlooks a wrong done to it. You have to rise above these petty
things that are pulling you apart. Give each other room to have a
bad day. Life is too short for you to live at odds, being contentious,
arguing over things that don't matter. Some people have to have
the last word in every argument. Don't be so hardheaded. Let it go.
Don't waste your valuable time on something that's not moving
you toward your purpose.

A PRAYER FOR TODAY

Father, thank You for loving, accepting, and approving of us
just as we are. Help us to do the same with each other and to
seek the best for each other. We ask You for the strength and the
confidence to overlook offenses and weaknesses so that we can
honor You in everything we do in Jesus' Name. Amen.

No Masks

TODAY'S SCRIPTURE

We refuse to wear masks and play games. We don't maneuver and manipulate behind the scenes.... Rather, we keep everything we do and say out in the open.

2 Corinthians 4:2 MSG

Facing the truth about ourselves and as a couple can be uncomfortable. It's hard to admit, "Maybe my motive wasn't right. Maybe the real reason that I was so nice to you was because I wanted to get something from you. Maybe I'm smiling on the outside, but on the inside I'm angry and resentful." If you pull back that mask, look inside and get honest with yourself, that's when you can deal with the hidden issues that will hold you back—the motives, the pride, the jealousy, the insecurity.

The apostle Paul said we have to refuse to wear masks and play games, but rather keep everything out in the open. Our lives should be open books with each other. We're not wearing any masks, thinking one thing and saying another. We're not perfect, but our motives are pure and we're dealing with the issues. We're not pretending, hiding behind a disguise. We're real. What you see is what you get. When you acknowledge that you need God's help, He'll make things happen that you could never make happen. When you live openly and honestly, God will make you and mold you into vessels of honor and use you for His highest purposes.

A PRAYER FOR TODAY

Father, we love You and humbly come to You. We invite You to search our hearts. Our desire is to please You and drop the masks and pretending in our relationship. We need Your help to be honest and open with each other and to change what we cannot change ourselves in Jesus' Name. Amen.

Deep Roots

TODAY'S SCRIPTURE

The root of the righteous cannot be moved.

Proverbs 12:3 NKJV

During a storm many years ago, a big sturdy oak tree in our yard was blown over by winds that were strong but not out of the ordinary. Although the oak tree has an extensive root system that extends beyond its canopy, its roots are shallow. Because the ground was so saturated with rain, the surface roots didn't have anything to anchor to. However, the pine trees in our yard that are much taller than the oak have roots that go down deep and hold tight against the saturated ground and high winds.

It's the same principle in our relationship. We all have things that come against us—a medical issue, a business downturn, a child gets in trouble. What's going to determine whether or not you stand strong and outlast these storms is the depth of your roots. The reason some couples are always upset, offended, and discouraged is that they only have surface roots. They're moved by each other's mistakes, the tone of one's voice, and the way one drives in traffic. They're always being tossed to and fro. But when you have deep roots, when you know that God has the two of you in the palms of His hands, the storms may come, but when it's all said and done, you know you'll still be standing strong.

A PRAYER FOR TODAY

Father, we praise and worship You. Thank You for giving us the promise that the root of the righteous cannot be moved. Help us to sink our roots of faith deep in You and to trust in Your faithfulness. We declare that we are strong in You and in the power of Your might in Jesus' Name. Amen.

Be Victors

TODAY'S SCRIPTURE

But he said to me, "My grace is sufficient for you,
for my power is made perfect in weakness."

2 Corinthians 12:9 NIV

When the Angel of the Lord told Gideon that God wanted him to save the people of Israel from the Midianites (see Judg. 7), the first words spoken were, "The Lord is with you, you mighty man of fearless courage." Gideon showed his true colors when he replied, "But Lord, how can I save Israel? My clan is the weakest in Manasseh, and I am the least in my family." Sound familiar? So often we sense God telling us that He has something big for us to do, but because of a poor self-image, we say, "God, we don't have what it takes."

It's interesting to note the difference between the way Gideon saw himself and the way God rewarded him. Gideon felt weak; God saw him as strong. Gideon felt unqualified; God saw him as competent to do the job. Gideon felt insecure and full of fear; God saw him as fearless and with enough courage and boldness to lead His people into battle and victory. And Gideon did!

Moreover, God sees the two of you as champions. He regards you as a strong, courageous, successful, overcoming couple. You may not see yourselves that way, but that doesn't change God's image of you. You may feel unqualified, insecure, or overwhelmed by life, but God sees you as victors!

A PRAYER FOR TODAY

Father, we give You all the praise and glory, and we receive
Your words of life, strength, and encouragement. Thank You
that You have equipped and are empowering us to be strong and
courageous where we feel weak and unqualified. We choose to
see ourselves as You see us in Jesus' Name. Amen.

"Fresh and Green"

TODAY'S SCRIPTURE

The righteous will flourish like a palm tree...
in the courts of our God. They will still bear fruit
in old age, they will stay fresh and green.

Psalm 92:12-14 NIV

f you want to stay "fresh and green" in your life together, you have to stay productive and engaged with each other. Perhaps you know some couples who went through disappointments, had some failures, or somebody did them wrong, and they lost their joy. They just settled and stopped enjoying life and each other. Some people quit living at fifty, but aren't buried until they are eighty. Even though they've been alive, they haven't been really living, and their relationship has suffered. When you're not producing, you're not growing and you won't flourish.

Don't get caught in that trap. God always has another victory in your future and something great in front of the two of you. You need to guard your passion for living. God is not finished with you and will complete what He started in your lives. The Scripture says God will bring us to a flourishing finish—not a fizzling finish. If you've gotten stuck, shake off what didn't work out and refuse to feel sorry for yourselves. God said He will take what was meant for your harm and not only bring you out, but also bring you out "fresh and green," better off than you were before.

A PRAYER FOR TODAY

Father, we praise You for the promise that You will cause us to stay fresh and green like a palm tree. Thank You that You will bring our lives to a flourishing finish no matter what we are going through today. We believe that You have something great that is still in front of us in Jesus' Name. Amen.

Magnify the Good

TODAY'S SCRIPTURE

*To the pure, all things are pure, but to those who are
corrupted and do not believe, nothing is pure.*

Titus 1:15 NIV

There was a man who asked his wife to fry him one egg
and scramble a second egg. She did exactly as he asked,
but when he saw the eggs, he said, "I knew this would
happen. You fried the wrong egg." Some people have
become so critical-minded that no matter what is done for them,
it's not right. They never see the good their spouse is doing, but
magnify the wrong things.

Everyone has faults and habits that can get on your nerves.
The key is to recognize what you are magnifying. You are magnifying
the wrong thing when you let the critical spirit take over and
complain about an egg. You can train yourselves to focus on the
things you like about your spouse and magnify the good qualities,
or you can focus on the things you don't like and magnify the
less-desirable characteristics.

If you struggle in this area, make a list of the qualities you like
about your spouse. He may not be a great communicator, but he's
a hard worker. Write it down. She may have some weaknesses, but
she's a great mother. Put that on your list and go over it every day.
Make a shift and start focusing on those good qualities and learn
to downplay the weaknesses.

A PRAYER FOR TODAY

*Father, we love You and praise You for accepting and approving
of us. Help us to not have a critical spirit but to always see the
best in each other and other people and overlook weaknesses.
Help us to train ourselves to see others' strengths and magnify
their good qualities in Jesus' Name. Amen.*

All Things

TODAY'S SCRIPTURE

And we know that all things work together for good to those who love God, to those who are the called according to His purpose.

Romans 8:28 NKJV

When other people do us wrong, or we have a bad break and it isn't our fault, we can have faith that God will restore, that He will pay us back. But when we bring the trouble on ourselves, when we blow it, it's easy to live in regrets, thinking that God will never help us. But here's the beauty: God didn't base His plan for your lives on you making perfect decisions. God has a plan even for your mistakes and failures. God has a way of making miracles out of mistakes. What should have set you back, He knows how to turn around and set you up to move into your destiny.

When we make mistakes, too often we get down on ourselves, not expecting anything good. Be encouraged. The apostle Paul said, "All things," even our mistakes, "work together for good to those who love God." You may be in a complicated situation that seems as though there's no way out. There are other people involved. God has it all figured out. He is saying, "I'm going to correct those complications. I'm going to cause good things to work out that you could never make happen on your own. I will make miracles out of your mistakes."

A PRAYER FOR TODAY

Father, we praise You for Your unconditional love for us. Thank You for Your promise that You make all things work together for our good, even our mistakes. We believe that nothing is too hard or too complicated for You and that You can even work miracles out of our mistakes in Jesus' Name. Amen.

Cups Running Over

TODAY'S SCRIPTURE

You anoint my head with oil;
my cup overflows.

Psalm 23:5 NKJV

When God laid out the plan for your lives together, He didn't just put into it what you need to get by and endure until the end. He put more than enough in it. He's a God of abundance. We see this all through the Scripture. After Jesus multiplied the little boy's lunch of five loaves and two fish, thousands of people ate, and yet there were basketfuls of leftovers. On purpose, He made more than enough. That's the God we serve.

David says, "My cup runs over." He had more than he needed. Yes, we should thank God that our needs are supplied, but don't settle there. He is a more-than-enough God. He wants you to have an abundance, so you can be a blessing to those around you.

Are you asking for the abundant, overflowing, more-than-enough life that God has for you? God says you are to reign in life together, that you are blessed and that whatever you touch will prosper and succeed. Don't pray to just get by. Dare to ask big. Ask for what God has promised you. If your dreams look impossible, remind Him: "God, You said Your blessings would chase us down, that we're surrounded by favor, and that You would give us the desires of our hearts." Ask Him for explosive blessings. Ask Him to propel you into your purpose.

A PRAYER FOR TODAY

Father, thank You for Your grace, favor, and mercy to us.
Thank You for being the God of overflow! We are asking You
for the more-than-enough life that You have promised. We believe
that You will give us the desires of our hearts, and we declare
that our cups will run over in Jesus' Name. Amen.

OUR
BEST
LIFE
TOGETHER

We Declare

we have the grace we
need for today.
We are full of power,
strength, and determination.
Nothing we face will be
too much for us. We will
overcome every obstacle,
outlast every challenge,
and come through every
difficulty better off than
we were before.

Something Better

TODAY'S SCRIPTURE

Then Jesus said, "Did I not tell you that if you believe,
you will see the glory of God?"

John 11:40 NIV

n the Scripture, Mary and Martha sent word to Jesus that their brother, Lazarus, was very sick. They thought He would come right away and heal Lazarus. But days passed, and Lazarus died. When Jesus showed up, Mary and Martha were so upset. They said, "Jesus, if You had been here, our brother would still be alive." Against all apparent odds, Jesus went to the tomb and raised Lazarus from the dead.

Sometimes God will wait on purpose till the odds look way against you. You're ready to bury that dream or promise. You don't see any way it could work out. But God's ways are not our ways. Mary and Martha prayed for a healing, but God had a resurrection in mind. Maybe God's not going to answer your prayers the way you thought. Maybe He has something better than you ever dreamed.

The odds may look totally against you, but the Most High God is totally for you. You've been asking and asking, but God didn't show up on time. Don't get discouraged. Trust Him. He knows what's best for both of you. When He speaks, dead things come back to life. He's not moved by the odds. God controls the universe. Odds don't determine what He can and cannot do.

A PRAYER FOR TODAY

Father, thank You that You are the Most High God and the keeper
of our dreams. We trust You that when all the odds are stacked
against us that You are totally for us. We declare that You are
working behind the scenes and bringing a resurrection to what
we thought was dead in Jesus' Name. Amen.

Really Alive

TODAY'S SCRIPTURE

*For this reason I remind you to fan into flame
the gift of God, which is in you.*

2 Timothy 1:6 NIV

Are you really alive as a couple? Are you passionate about your lives or are you stuck in a rut, letting the pressures of life weigh you down or taking for granted what you have together? You weren't created to simply exist or to go through the motions; you were created to be really alive. You have seeds of greatness on the inside. There's something more for you to accomplish. The day you quit being excited about your future together, you go from living to merely existing.

In the natural there may not be anything for you to be excited about. When you look into the future, all you see is more of the same. You have to be strong and say, "We refuse to drag through this day with no passion. We're not just alive—we're *really* alive." You have to do what Paul told Timothy: "Stir up the gift, fan the flame." When you stir up the passion, your faith will allow God to do amazing things.

When you fell in love, you knew it was the result of God's goodness. Don't take it for granted. Remember what God has done. If you want to remain passionate, you cannot let what was once a miracle become so common that it's ordinary.

A PRAYER FOR TODAY

Father, we praise You that You have placed seeds of greatness in us and created us to be truly alive. We are remembering the amazing things You have done for us. We declare that we are fanning into flames and stirring up our gifts, and we believe You are restoring our passion in Jesus' Name. Amen.

Stop the Blaming

TODAY'S SCRIPTURE

*"Rabbi," his disciples asked him, "why was
this man born blind? Was it because of
his own sins or his parents' sins?"*

John 9:2 NLT

n the Scripture, some people asked Jesus whose fault it was that this man was born blind. They were looking for somebody to blame. Jesus said, "It's nobody's fault. The reason he was born this way was so that the goodness of God could be displayed."

When something unfair, something negative, happens in your relationship, don't get stuck looking for a reason, trying to find someone or something to blame. You're not going to understand why everything happens. If you stay in faith, God will use it to show out in your lives. It's easy to want to blame someone for what happened, even each other. All the blaming is going to do is give you a reason to feel sorry for yourselves, and before long you'll have that as a crutch that holds you back.

Nothing that's happened to you is a surprise to God. You have to take the hand you've been dealt and make the most of it together. If you'll not use it as an excuse to get bitter and have a chip on your shoulder, He'll use it to your advantage. He will pay you back for the unfair things that have happened.

A PRAYER FOR TODAY

*Father, we love You and thank You for the abundance of Your
goodness in our lives. Thank You that nothing that's happened to
us is a surprise to You. Whatever we go through that might harm
us, we know You will use to our advantage. We declare that
You are a God of justice in Jesus' Name. Amen.*

Cut the Puppet Strings

TODAY'S SCRIPTURE

A hot-tempered person must pay the penalty;
rescue them, and you will have to do it again.

Proverbs 19:19 NIV

One of the greatest freedoms for some couples is when they get free from other controlling people. Some people are always having a crisis and in desperate need of something. It's good to help people who are in real need. But if it seems the emergencies never stop, you need to recognize that's a manipulator and you are their puppet. They know if they pull one string, you'll feel guilty, or another string and you'll bail them out.

If someone is playing one or both of you like a puppet, it's time to cut the strings. No more letting other people make you feel guilty. No more will you come running. If you feel you'll lose their friendship if you won't meet unreasonable demands, that person is a manipulator, not your friend. The sooner you break free, the better off you'll be.

Are you so good-hearted that you're sacrificing your time and happiness to keep everyone around you happy? You need to examine your relationships. They are out of balance. Don't waste your lives playing up to people, trying to meet all their demands. Cut the puppet strings. You have a destiny to fulfill together. Be bold, take charge of your lives, and pursue the dreams God has placed in your hearts.

A PRAYER FOR TODAY

Father, thank You that You did not make us to be other people's
puppets and try to please them by fulfilling their wishes and
demands. We want to be loving and kind and help others who are
in real need, but help us to be bold and cut the strings of those
who would manipulate and use us in Jesus' Name. Amen.

Love Yourself

TODAY'S SCRIPTURE

"Love your neighbor as yourself."

Matthew 22:39 NIV

Jesus said to love your neighbor as you love yourself. If you don't love yourself in a healthy way, you'll never be able to love others in the way that you should. If you don't get along with yourself, you'll never get along with others. We all have weaknesses, shortcomings, things we wish were different. But God never designed us to go through life being against our self. The opinion you have of yourself is the most important opinion that you have. If you see yourself as less-than, not talented, not valuable, you will become exactly that. And you constantly convey what you feel on the inside. If you feel unhappy with who you are on the inside, you will convey feelings of unhappiness. That's going to push people away, including your spouse. The problem is on the inside. You carry yourself the way you see yourself.

Here's a key: people see you the way you see yourself. Perhaps if you would change the opinion you have of yourself, if you would quit focusing on your flaws and everything you wish was different, if you would quit comparing yourself to somebody you think is better and start loving yourself in a healthy way, being proud of who God made you to be, then as you send out these different messages, it's going to bring new opportunities, new relationships, and new levels of God's favor.

A PRAYER FOR TODAY

Father, we love You and appreciate You. Thank You for uniquely designing us with gifts, talents, and abilities to enjoy life and accomplish Your will. Help us to love ourselves, with all our weaknesses and shortcomings and things we wish were different. We celebrate who we are in Jesus' Name. Amen.

Take Hold of God's Strength

TODAY'S SCRIPTURE

"Let him take hold of My strength, that he may make peace with Me; and he shall make peace with Me."

Isaiah 27:5 NKJV

One challenge we all face as couples is weariness. Everyone gets tired. *Weary* means to lose your sense of pleasure, to not feel the enjoyment you should with yourself or each other. You can be raising great children, but because you're weary, you're not enjoying them. You can have the job of your dreams, but fatigue sets in and you're not passionate about it anymore.

God knew weariness would come. When the apostle Paul says, "Don't get weary or become discouraged in doing good," he means that you're doing the right thing but not getting the right results. It doesn't seem as though it's making a difference. Let us encourage you: your time is coming to reap. Don't let seeming delays or discouragement or negative thoughts convince you to give up and settle where you are. If you dwell on those thoughts, you'll become more tired, discouraged, and negative. Weariness cannot automatically come in; you have to open the door.

Take hold of God's strength. When discouraging thoughts come in, just say, "No, thanks. God is on the throne. Our time is coming. We've been armed with strength for this battle. We can do all things through Christ. We are strong in the Lord." His strength is available, but you have to take hold of it.

A PRAYER FOR TODAY

Father, thank You that You are the Most High God and seated on Your throne. Help us to shake off our weariness and take hold of Your strength. We declare that You have armed us for the battle we are to fight and that we are strong in Jesus' Name. Amen.

Be a Peacemaker

TODAY'S SCRIPTURE

"Blessed are the peacemakers..."

Matthew 5:9 NIV

t's easy to think, *If my spouse wouldn't push my buttons, I wouldn't argue so often.* No, you have to be the bigger person. Just because they're doing wrong doesn't mean you have to engage. That's the enemy baiting you. That's the spirit of strife saying, "Come on, let me in. Argue, fight, set the record straight, prove you're right." Don't take the bait. It takes a mature person to overlook an insult and say, "No, I'm staying in peace." It takes maturity to walk away in silence when everything in you says, "Tell them off."

Jesus didn't say, "Blessed are those who are right." Sometimes you have to let the other person think they're right, even when you know they're wrong, just for the sake of peace. We think, *I'm right, and I'm not going to back down. I'm going to prove that I'm right. I'm going to win this fight.* Can we tell you that being right is overrated? You can be right, and be miserable. You can be right, and sleep on the couch. You can win every battle, prove your points, but what you don't realize is your relationship is being damaged. Take the high road and keep your mouth closed. Put your ego down and let them be right even though you think you're right. Be a peacemaker.

A PRAYER FOR TODAY

Father, thank You for the promise of blessedness when we take the high road and are peacemakers in our relationship. Give us wisdom to know when to keep our mouths closed and overlook something that bothers us. We believe that walking in peace is Your will for our lives in Jesus' Name. Amen.

Celebrate Yourselves

TODAY'S SCRIPTURE

As they danced, they sang: "Saul has slain his thousands,
and David his tens of thousands."

1 Samuel 18:7 NIV

King Saul had been happy on the throne until David started getting more praise than him. From that moment on, he never looked at David the same way and ended up losing his throne over it. What was his problem? He couldn't handle somebody getting ahead of him. He spent months and months trying to kill David, all because he wasn't comfortable with who he was.

It's easy to want what others have or to do what they do, but if that's not where you're called to be, if it's not where you're gifted, you'll have to constantly work to try to stay in that position. But where God takes you, He will keep you. And when you're not comparing, not trying to be something that you're not, it takes all the pressure off.

Don't get distracted with competing against other couples, friends, or coworkers. Just run your races. Here's a phrase we like: *Don't compare yourselves. Celebrate yourselves.* If somebody else has conquered ten thousand and you've conquered a thousand, a thousand is still good. Celebrate what you've accomplished. Very few people today can say, "We like ourselves. We are satisfied with who God made us to be." Remember, when you use what you have, God will breathe on it and do amazing things.

A PRAYER FOR TODAY

Father, thank You for the amazing people that You have brought into our lives, and thank You that You've made us amazing as well. Thank You that we are not competing against others. We declare that we refuse to compare ourselves, but we celebrate who You have made us to be in Jesus' Name. Amen.

OUR
BEST
LIFE
TOGETHER

We Declare

it is not too late to
accomplish everything God
has placed in our hearts.
We have not missed our
windows of opportunity.
God has moments of favor
in our future. He is preparing
us right now because He is
about to release a special
grace to help us accomplish
our dreams. This is our time.
This is our moment.
We receive it today!

Imperfect People

TODAY'S SCRIPTURE

*"While he was still a long way off, his father saw him
and was filled with compassion for him; he ran to his
son, threw his arms around him and kissed him."*

Luke 15:20 NIV

Most of the time we believe God loves us as long as
we're making good decisions, resisting temptation,
and treating people right. We know God is on our side.
But there will be times when we compromise, when we
have doubts, when we fail. When we don't perform perfectly, it's
easy to think, *God is far from us. If we make poor choices, we're
on our own.*

But the truth is that when you fall, God doesn't turn away. He
comes running toward you. When you blow it, He comes after you
with a greater passion. When you make a mistake, God loves you
so much that He pursues you. He won't leave you alone until He
sees you restored and back on the right course. He will send people
across your path to encourage you, to help reignite your faith.
That's the mercy of God coming after you, saying, "You may have
blown it, but you're still My child. You may have lost faith in Me,
but I haven't lost faith in you."

We don't have to have a perfect performance where we never
fail. Certainly, we should try our best each day to honor God. But
God loves imperfect people.

A PRAYER FOR TODAY

*Father, thank You that Your love and forgiveness of us is
not based on our performance but upon the fact that we are
Your children. Thank You that You love us, imperfect as we are,
and that every mistake we've made and ever will make has
already been paid in full in Jesus' Name. Amen.*

When You Don't Understand

TODAY'S SCRIPTURE

It is God's privilege to conceal things.

Proverbs 25:2 NLT

One night the teenage son of a couple we know was killed in a car accident. You can imagine how devastated and heartbroken they were. Many couples would get angry and perhaps blame God, letting the tragedy sour the rest of their lives. They went through a dark time, but they came through it and explained how: "We made the decision that we weren't going to exchange what we do know for what we don't know. We know that God is good, that He's loving, that He's merciful, that He's for us. We would not let one situation that we don't understand cancel all that out."

Maybe there's something you've gone through that doesn't make sense, and it's causing you to doubt, to live in discouragement. Quit trying to figure it out and go back to what you know. The Scripture says, "We see in part now, through a glass dimly, but one day we will see in full." The best thing you can do is to drop it. If God wants you to know why, He'll tell you why. But there are some things God doesn't want us to know. If we're going to trust God, we have to be mature enough to say, "God, we don't have to have all the answers. We trust that Your ways are better than ours."

A PRAYER FOR TODAY

Father, thank You that no matter what we go through, we know that You are good and that You love us. We leave the things we don't understand in Your hands and know that You will reveal or conceal things according to what's best for us. We trust that Your ways are better than ours in Jesus' Name. Amen.

Good and Beneficial Words

TODAY'S SCRIPTURE

*Let no...unwholesome or worthless talk [ever] come out
of your mouth, but only such [speech] as is good and
beneficial to the spiritual progress of others.*

Ephesians 4:29 AMPC

One reason couples get stuck in one place in their relationship is because they say hurtful things, put each other down, and argue. They don't realize their mouths are keeping them from rising higher. God won't promote you as a couple if you don't have the character in your relationship to back it up. You don't have to be perfect, but you should be improving. Pay attention to what you're saying to each other. Sometimes we've spoken to each other a certain way for so long that we don't realize that we're harsh, sarcastic, and condescending.

Words can leave scars, tear us apart, and make us feel insecure, inferior, and not valued. Before you say something, you need to ask yourself, "Is this going to be beneficial to my spouse? Is it going to build them up or put them down? Is this comment going to make them feel better about who they are or is it just going to feed my ego?" These are tests that you have to pass. For some couples, the only thing holding them back from a healthy marriage, a growing friendship, and their best life together is their words.

A PRAYER FOR TODAY

*Father, thank You that You have given us the gift of speaking
words that are good and beneficial. Help us to pay attention to
what we're actually saying to each other and to be honest about it.
We commit ourselves to taming our tongues and using our words
to build each other up in Jesus' Name. Amen.*

You Have Control

TODAY'S SCRIPTURE

*Do not give the devil an opportunity [to lead you into
sin by holding a grudge, or nurturing anger, or harboring
resentment, or cultivating bitterness].*

Ephesians 4:27 AMP

t's easy to go through life holding on to things that weigh us
down—guilt, resentment, worry, doubt. These things come
naturally in any relationship. The problem is that when we allow
them in, they take up space that should be reserved for good
things. Imagine your relationship as a container. God created it to
be filled with joy, peace, confidence, and creativity. But if you allow
worry in, it pushes out peace. If you allow guilt in, it pushes out the
confidence you need. Some couples don't enjoy their life together
because their relationship is filled and contaminated with so many
negatives—stress, bitterness, anger, regrets, jealousy. They wonder
why they don't have room for the strength, joy, passion, creativity,
and happiness they should have.

When the Scripture says to give no place to the enemy, that
includes guilt, worry, and bitterness. The negative can't come in
automatically and take over. You control what comes into your
relationship. You have control over negative thoughts and emotions.
You have to make the choice, "We're not going to give valuable
space to negativity and let it poison our relationship." When you
feel like being sour, bitter, holding a grudge, you have to be disciplined to say, "We're not giving any room for this offense." Take
inventory of what you're giving place to. Life is too short for you
to go through it with negative things holding you back.

A PRAYER FOR TODAY

*Father, we worship and praise Your holy Name. We come to
You in faith declaring that we are finished with giving any room
to negative thoughts and emotions in our relationship. Thank
You for setting us free. Fill us with Your joy and peace as we
move forward in victory in Jesus' Name. Amen.*

The Second Touch

TODAY'S SCRIPTURE

*Then Jesus placed his hands on the man's eyes again,
and his eyes were opened. His sight was completely
restored, and he could see everything clearly.*

Mark 8:25 NLT

n the Scripture, Jesus opened the eyes of a blind man for the first
time. You can imagine how thrilled he was. Then Jesus asked
him, "What do you see?" The man answered, "I see people, but
they look like trees walking." He could see, but everything was
out of focus. Then Jesus touched his eyes a second time, and his
eyes were completely healed.

Many of us are like this man. We've seen God's goodness in
our relationship. He's helped us get to where we are. We're grateful
even though we haven't accomplished our dreams. He's made us a
whole lot better together, but too often we settle for less than God's
best. God has a second touch coming your way.

The second touch is when you come totally out of debt, when
your whole family comes to know the Lord, when God opens
doors that you never dreamed would open, when God amazes you
with His goodness. Don't be satisfied with better. Be grateful for
what God has done, but keep your faith stirred up for the fullness
of your best life together. God didn't bring you together to partially
reach your destiny. What He started in your relationship, He's
going to complete.

A PRAYER FOR TODAY

*Father, we praise You for Your goodness and helping us to get to
where we are. Thank You for being the God of second touches.
We open ourselves to all You have for our future. We declare
we haven't seen anything yet because You promised to amaze
us with Your goodness in Jesus' Name. Amen.*

Talk about the Promise

TODAY'S SCRIPTURE

You are snared by the words of your mouth;
you are taken by the words of your mouth.

Proverbs 6:2 NKJV

To be *snared* means "to be trapped." Your words can trap you and keep you from your potential. You're not snared by what you think. Negative thoughts come to us all. But when you speak them out, you give them life. If you say, "We never get any good breaks," that stops the favor that was ordained to you. When you say, "We're not that talented or smart," that is calling in mediocrity. It's setting the limits for your lives.

You may think, *We'll never get better jobs. We'll never be able to afford that nice house.* Those thoughts come to all of us. You can't stop that. Our challenge is: don't give them life by speaking them out. Don't go call your friends and tell them how it's not going to happen. Let your report be: "God is supplying all our needs. It may look impossible, but with God all things are possible." If you keep prophesying the right things—increase, favor, more than enough—you will start moving toward it.

In the tough times, it's very tempting to vent your frustrations and continually talk about the problem. That's only going to make you more discouraged, and it gives that problem more life. Turn it around. Don't talk about the problem; talk about the promise.

A PRAYER FOR TODAY

Father, we praise You for Your faithfulness in our lives.
Thank You that we do not have to keep being snared by the
words of our mouths. We choose to not focus on or talk about
negative circumstances, but on Your faithful promises. Help us
to keep prophesying the right things in Jesus' Name. Amen.

A Commanded Blessing

TODAY'S SCRIPTURE

Behold, how good and how pleasant it is...
to dwell together in unity...for there the LORD has
commanded the blessing: life forevermore.

Psalm 133:1-3 AMP

The Scripture says, "One can chase a thousand, and two can put ten thousand to flight." When there's unity in your relationship, the favor on your marriage is increased. You are ten times more powerful when you're in agreement. That means you have ten times the strength to overcome obstacles, to withstand attacks. You can accomplish dreams that are ten times bigger, ten times more rewarding. You can go so much further and live much more fulfilled if you keep unity in your home. Perhaps there are obstacles that you can't seem to overcome and doors that are not opening because you're operating with the strength of one, because there's strife and division. That person God has put in your life is not just for companionship—there's a spiritual force that's released when you live together in peace and harmony. You need the ten-times power to reach the fullness of your destiny.

God has big things in store for you. It's going to take more than one of you having faith; you need the ten-times blessing that comes from unity in your home. Think about what your children can accomplish when you and your spouse are in unity. Ten times the favor, ten times the anointing, ten times the power is released.

A PRAYER FOR TODAY

Father, thank You that You have commanded a blessing upon us as we dwell together in unity. Thank You that we can join our faiths together and overcome the obstacles we face. We believe that we have the ten-times power to accomplish the big things You have in store for us in Jesus' Name. Amen.

Strength under Control

TODAY'S SCRIPTURE

*"Blessed are the meek, for they
will inherit the earth."*

Matthew 5:5 NIV

When we hear the word *meek*, many times we think of someone who is weak, who can't stand up for themselves, and everyone runs over them. That's not meek at all. Meekness is not weakness. It's strength under control, like a wild stallion that has been tamed. The horse is still as strong and powerful as before he was tamed, but now that strength is under control. You can ride him, but don't be fooled. He has just learned how to control his power.

When you're a meek person, you don't go around trying to straighten out your critics, even if it's your spouse. People may be talking about you, but you don't let it bother you because you keep your strength under control. It's not about how you can prove yourselves. If you try to prove yourselves to a critic, all you're doing is sinking to their level. Don't fall into that trap. You are eagles. You can rise above it. You may have the power to straighten out your critic. You may feel like giving your spouse a piece of your mind. Your emotions may tell you, "Pay them back. Get even." Instead, listen to what the apostle Paul told Timothy: "Be calm and cool and steady." He was saying, "Don't give away your power. Keep your strength under control."

A PRAYER FOR TODAY

*Father, we praise and bless You that Jesus is meek and humble
of heart. Thank You for the blessing of meekness and great inner
strength. We choose to be people of self-control. We declare
that we will be calm and cool and steady and not give our
power and peace away in Jesus' Name. Amen.*

We Declare

we are grateful for Who God is in
our lives and for what He's done.
We will not take for granted
the people, the opportunities,
and the favor He has blessed
us with. We will look at what is
right and not what is wrong.
We will thank Him for what we
have and not complain about
what we don't have. We will
see each day as a gift from God.
Our hearts will overflow with
praise and gratitude for
all of His goodness.

Be Restorers

TODAY'S SCRIPTURE

*"...the Samaritan soothed his wounds with olive oil
and wine and bandaged them. Then he put the man
on his own donkey and took him to an inn,
where he took care of him."*

Luke 10:34 NLT

Jesus told the story of the Good Samaritan who saw a man on the side of the road beaten and left for dead. He put him on his donkey and took him to a place where he could recover. He even walked so the injured man could ride.

You're never more like God than when you help hurting people. One of our assignments in life is to help wipe away the tears. Are you sensitive to each other's needs? To your family and friends? Your neighbors? Your coworkers? Many times behind the smile is a person who's hurting, alone, and in turmoil. When someone is struggling, reach out. Be healers. Be restorers.

Your job is not to judge. Your job is not to figure out if someone deserves something, or to decide who is right or wrong. Your job is to lift the fallen, to restore the broken, and to heal the hurting. There is healing in your hands and voices. You are containers filled with God. Right now you are full of encouragement, mercy, restoration, and healing. Everywhere you go you should dispense the goodness of God. The most important thing: the two of you can become someone's miracle.

A PRAYER FOR TODAY

*Father, we praise and worship You with all our hearts. Thank You
for calling us to lift the fallen, to restore the broken, and to help
the hurting. Help us to see others through Your eyes and to
become dispensers of Your goodness. Show us how to connect
with others and be healers in Jesus' Name. Amen.*

Slow to Speak

TODAY'S SCRIPTURE

My dear brothers and sisters, take note of this:
Everyone should be quick to listen, slow to speak
and slow to become angry.

James 1:19 NIV

n any relationship you have, you can't say everything you feel. If your spouse says or does something that makes you feel annoyed, instead of popping off and saying things you'll regret later, you need to take a deep breath and pause for thirty seconds. Think about what you're going to say. Don't speak out of your emotions and let your tongue run wild. Some things are better left unsaid. You don't have to win every argument, or comment on every situation, or set each other straight. Even when you know they're wrong, ask yourself, "Is this worth starting World War III over?"

You've probably heard it said that the reason we have two ears and one mouth is because we're supposed to listen twice as much as we speak. Do you know how many headaches you could save yourselves if you would just zip it up and not say things you're going to regret later? In the heat of the battle it's easy to make hurtful comments. It takes seconds to say it, but years later the pain may still be felt. We can and should apologize, but it doesn't make the pain go away. It's much better to be slow to speak, to think about what you're going to say, and never damage your relationship.

A PRAYER FOR TODAY

Father, we thank You for Your goodness and love and
faithfulness in our lives. We know that our words are powerful
and that we must be disciplined to not speak out of our
emotions. We choose to be slow to speak and slow to
become angry in Jesus' Name. Amen.

Say So

TODAY'S SCRIPTURE

Let the redeemed of the LORD *say so, whom He has redeemed from the hand of the enemy.*

Psalm 107:2 NKJV

Words have creative power. When you speak something out, you give life to what you're saying. For instance, it's important to believe that you're blessed. But when you say, "We are blessed," that's when blessings come looking for you. The Scripture says, "Let the redeemed of the Lord *say so.*" It doesn't say think so, or believe so, or hope so. If you're going to go to the next level, you have to *say so.* If you're going to accomplish a dream, overcome an obstacle, or break an addiction, you have to start declaring it. It has to come out of your mouths. That's how you give life to your faith.

When God created the worlds, He didn't just think or believe them into being. Nothing happened until He spoke. He said, "Let there be light," and light came. His words, not His thoughts, set it into motion. It's the same principle today. You can have faith in your hearts and never see anything change. What's the problem? Nothing happens until you speak. Instead of just believing you're going to get out of debt, *say so.* Declare every day, "We're coming out of debt. God's favor surrounds us like a shield." When you speak, good breaks, promotion, and ideas will track you down.

A PRAYER FOR TODAY

Father, we praise You that You are our Creator. Thank You that when You created the worlds, You didn't just think or believe them into being; You spoke them into being. We believe that we are to speak out words that are true to the faith in our hearts, and that when we say so, You will act in Jesus' Name. Amen.

Live in Freedom

TODAY'S SCRIPTURE

Where the Spirit of the Lord is, there is freedom.
2 Corinthians 3:17 NIV

n any relationship, and especially in your marriage, if you're always thinking about something negative that happened yesterday, last month, last year, there's no freedom there. This *is* a new day. Quit living in what *was* and come over into what *is*. Right now the Spirit of the Lord has freedom, new beginnings, joy, peace, and restoration for you. Living in regrets of what you should have done or what could have been doesn't bring freedom. Being offended and frustrated over what didn't work out will only keep you apart. It's time to drop it and move forward. You may be a product of your past, but you don't have to be a prisoner of your past. God knew every hurt, every loss, and every mistake you would go through. The good news is that for every setback He's already arranged a comeback; for every disappointment, a new beginning; for every failure, restoration; for all the ashes, He has beauty.

As a couple, you have to put your feet down and say, "That's it. We're leaving what *was* and we're coming over into what *is*. We're done carrying negative baggage. We're going to live our lives free and receive God's mercy. It's new every morning. We're going to keep moving forward, knowing that our best days are still ahead."

A PRAYER FOR TODAY

Father, thank You that Your Spirit is working in our lives and bringing us into freedom. Thank You that we can make a clear break with the past and enter into the new beginning and the joy You have for us. We declare that we are leaving behind what was and coming over into what is in Jesus' Name. Amen.

Strengthen Each Other

TODAY'S SCRIPTURE

*David was greatly distressed...But David encouraged
and strengthened himself in the Lord his God.*

1 Samuel 30:6 AMPC

Thirteen years after David was anointed to be the next king of Israel, he was still living as a fugitive from King Saul. One day he and his six hundred men came home from a battle and found their city had been attacked and burned. Their possessions had been taken and their families taken captive. It was the worst defeat of David's life. This was his darkest hour. The Scripture says he and his men wept until they could not weep anymore. He was tempted to think, *God, this is the final straw. I've been doing the right thing year after year. I'm done.*

But David made a decision: "I am not allowing this weariness to stay. I am strong in the Lord. I am anointed." You can talk yourself and each other into defeat or into victory. When you speak the right way, strength comes, courage comes, vision comes, healing comes.

Don't let battle fatigue keep you as a couple from your dreams. When it's the most difficult and you face the greatest temptation to give up, the victory is near. The Scripture says, "Let the weak say, 'I am strong.'" Turn the discouragement around and say, "Yes, this is tough, but we are strong in the Lord." Encourage and strengthen each other in the Lord.

A PRAYER FOR TODAY

*Father, thank You that the power of Your life in us is greater
than the greatest force that can ever come against us. Thank You
that we can put the fatigue behind us and stir up our faith in You.
We believe that no weapon that is formed against us will
prosper in Jesus' Name. Amen.*

Be Young and Strong

TODAY'S SCRIPTURE

He fills my life with good things.
My youth is renewed like the eagle's!

Psalm 103:5 NLT

The reason some people aren't young and strong in their spirit, vibrant and passionate about life, is that there's no room for God to fill them with good things. All the space is taken up with negatives. Worry will make you weak. Living stressed out will make you old, give you wrinkles, and take your passion. Being bitter, angry, and resentful will shorten your lives.

The same can be said for your relationship. Is God trying to fill your relationship with good things, but there's no room? Instead of hanging on to anger after an argument, say, "God, I forgive them. I let it go." You didn't just forgive; you made room for God to fill you with good things. That's when He'll give you beauty for ashes, joy for mourning. You're in a tough time, the bills have piled up, and you could be upset and worried. Instead, say, "God, we trust You. We know that You're fighting our battles." You just made room for God to fill you with abundance. You'll have peace in the midst of the storm. Empty out discouragement, and He'll fill you with joy. If you make room, God promises He'll not only fill you with good things, but He'll keep your relationship young and strong.

A PRAYER FOR TODAY

Father, thank You for the promise that You fill our relationship with good things. We choose to empty out the worry so You can fill us with peace, to empty out the discouragement so You can fill us with joy. We declare that You will keep our relationship young and strong in Jesus' Name. Amen.

Prisoners of Hope

TODAY'S SCRIPTURE

"Return to the stronghold, you prisoners of hope.
Even today I declare that I will restore double to you."
Zechariah 9:12 NKJV

Joseph was sold into slavery by his brothers, then he was falsely accused and put in prison. He could have gotten bitter with his family. Joseph had many opportunities to pull up his anchor of hope in God, but he kept it down. Through all the trouble, his attitude was, *God, You have the final say. People don't determine my destiny. Bad breaks can't keep me from my purpose. All the forces of darkness cannot stop Your plan for my life.* Because he was anchored to hope, he was vindicated, promoted, and put in charge of the nation of Egypt.

To be a "prisoner of hope" means that you can't get away from it. You're held by it. You should be discouraged, but in spite of all that's come against you as a couple, as with Joseph you still believe you're going to see your dreams come to pass. You know that if God is for you, none will dare be against you. One of you may have what seems to be an incurable sickness. You both could be stressed out, but you know nothing can snatch either of you out of God's hand. Your hope is in the God Who breathed life into you. He's the God Who took Joseph from the pit to the palace. Keep your hope in the Lord.

A PRAYER FOR TODAY

Father, thank You that we are prisoners of hope and that
You've promised to restore back double for anything we've lost.
Thank You that You alone determine our destiny and nothing
can stop Your plan for our lives. We believe Your Word
is true in Jesus' Name. Amen.

Created in His Image

TODAY'S SCRIPTURE

So God created mankind in his own image,
in the image of God he created them;
male and female he created them.

Genesis 1:27 NIV

When God created you in His image, He put a part of Himself in both of you. You could say that you have the DNA of Almighty God. You are destined to do great things, destined to leave your mark on this generation. Now here's the key. He is not just the Creator of the universe, the all-powerful God. He is your Heavenly Father. You have His DNA. Imagine what you can do.

But too many times we don't realize who we are. We focus on our weaknesses, what we don't have, the mistakes we've made, and the family we come from. We end up settling for mediocrity when we were created for greatness. If you're going to break out of average, you need to remind yourselves, "We have the DNA of the Most High God. Greatness is in our genes. We come from a bloodline of champions."

When you realize who you are, you won't go around intimidated and insecure, thinking, *We're lacking. We're not that talented. We come from the wrong families.* No, you come from the right family. Your Father created it all. When you know who you are, you'll start thinking like winners, talking like winners, and carrying yourselves like you are winners.

A PRAYER FOR TODAY

Father, we praise You that You created us in Your image and
have made us Your children. Thank You that because You are
our Heavenly Father, we have a destiny to do great things.
We declare that we will not settle for mediocrity or ever say
we've reached our limit in Jesus' Name. Amen.

OUR
BEST
LIFE
TOGETHER

We Declare

a legacy of faith over
our lives. We declare that
we will store up blessings
for future generations.
Our lives are marked by
excellence and integrity.
Because we are making
right choices and
taking steps of faith,
others will want to follow us.
God's abundance is
surrounding our lives today.

Steadfast and Immovable

TODAY'S SCRIPTURE

Be steadfast, immovable, always abounding
in the work of the Lord.

1 Corinthians 15:58 NKJV

The apostle Paul's statement is a powerful choice we need to make as a couple. "We're not going to be moved by our circumstances. We're not going to let what others say to us or even what we say to each other at times to steal our joy. We are not going to live worried about our finances. We're going to do our best and trust God to do what we can't do. We're not going to live in guilt and frustration over a mistake we made, because we know God's mercy is bigger than that mistake."

As long as you're allowing circumstances to determine whether or not you're going to be happy, your life together is going to be like a rollercoaster ride. God is saying, "Be steadfast, be immovable. Go down deeper in your faith." Rather than try to use your faith to control your circumstances, use your faith to control yourselves in the midst of those circumstances. When you stay in peace, that's a place of power and the key to a good relationship. You don't get upset by a setback or live discouraged because your plans don't work out, because you know God has something better in store. You have made the decision: we have the grace from God to handle anything that comes our way.

A PRAYER FOR TODAY

Father, we worship You because You are worthy to be praised.
Thank You for Your peace and joy as we put our trust in You.
Help us to be steadfast and consistent, unmoved by the ups and
downs of life. We believe You have given us the grace to handle
anything that comes our way in Jesus' Name. Amen.

Promotion

TODAY'S SCRIPTURE

*"People look at the outward appearance,
but the LORD looks at the heart."*

1 Samuel 16:7 NIV

Sometimes we're being our best as a couple, honoring God, but it doesn't seem like it's making a difference. We're not making much progress or getting good breaks. It's easy to get discouraged and think God must have forgotten about us.

In the Scripture, David had the job of taking care of his father's sheep. What he was doing was insignificant in his family's eyes, and they discounted him. They looked on the outside, but David had a heart after God. He didn't slack off because nobody was watching or cared. He just kept being his best where he was. And on the day the prophet Samuel showed up to anoint one of David's father's sons as the next king, it was David who was anointed over his seven brothers.

Just because people leave you out doesn't mean God leaves you out. People may overlook you or judge you by your height, your talent, your skin color. God looks on the inside. He sees your faithfulness, your dedication, your integrity. The good news is that promotion doesn't come from people; it comes from the Lord. If you keep being faithful, honoring God, He'll take you from the background to the foreground. People may try to push you down, but God will lift you up. People don't determine your destiny; God does.

A PRAYER FOR TODAY

Father, we praise You that You are not limited to seeing us as other people see us. Thank You that You see our hearts, and You know our faithfulness and our dedication to You. We believe that promotion comes from You and that You are propelling us toward our destiny in Jesus' Name. Amen.

Better Is Coming

TODAY'S SCRIPTURE

Better is the end of a thing than the beginning of it.

Ecclesiastes 7:8 AMPC

You may have had a rough start in your relationship, but you don't have to have a rough finish. "Better is the end." Maybe you've both had a lot of disappointments, had your hearts broken, and dreams that didn't work out. Don't dwell on what happened yesterday. God is saying, "Something better is coming." You may be going through a rough spot today, but don't stay focused on it; better is coming. Now don't cancel out the better by dwelling on the negative, the regrets, the failures. If your mind is always in yesterday, you're going to move in that direction. You can't go forward looking backward.

You could easily go through life not trusting each other, bitter and resentful. But everything you've gone through deposited something on the inside. You're not defined by your past; you're prepared by your past. You're stronger, more experienced, and have greater confidence. If the past hadn't happened, you wouldn't be prepared for the "better" that is coming your way. You may have made some mistakes, but you can't do anything about what happened yesterday. Living with guilt and condemnation is not going to make anything better. It's time to drop it. You'll not only feel a weight lift off you, but you'll step into the "better" things God has in store.

A PRAYER FOR TODAY

Father, thank You for our pasts, the successes and victories as well as the mistakes and failures. Thank You that the past has prepared us for today and for better things You have in store for us. We believe breakthroughs are coming, new opportunities are coming, and healings are coming in Jesus' Name. Amen.

Keep Strife Out

TODAY'S SCRIPTURE

"A home filled with strife and division destroys itself."

Mark 3:25 TLB

One of the biggest challenges you may face as a couple is getting along with each other. We have different personalities, different temperaments, and come from different backgrounds. When we don't agree with each other, or one of us is not doing what the other likes, it's easy to get in conflict—to argue, to try to straighten each other out, to prove our point. Before long we're at odds, mad at each other, and living offended. What's happened? We've allowed strife in. Strife is a negative force that brings division, but peace promotes unity. You can feel the tension, the stress, the disharmony.

If we realized the destructive force that strife is, we would be more careful to not allow it into our relationship. When we let our guard down and say things that are disrespectful, hurtful, or demeaning, we're not just damaging our relationship, we're inviting the destructive spirit of strife into our marriage. That's why the Scripture says, "Give no place to the enemy." Every couple will have an occasional argument and say wrong words, but it's dangerous to allow strife to become a part of who we are as a couple. When we're constantly fighting, arguing, saying hurtful things, being disrespectful, and our home is filled with tension, that's a sign that we're headed down the wrong path.

A PRAYER FOR TODAY

Father, thank You that You brought us together to love each other and to bless each other through our words and actions. We recognize the destructive power of strife and give no place for it in our relationship. We believe that Your peace will rule in and through our lives in Jesus' Name. Amen.

Crowned by Almighty God

TODAY'S SCRIPTURE

*"And have made us kings and priests to our God;
and we shall reign on the earth."*

Revelation 5:10 NKJV

The Scripture speaks about how God has made us to be kings and priests to Him. You need to start seeing each other as a king and a queen. Start carrying yourselves as royalty. Not in arrogance, thinking that you're better than others, but in humility be proud of who God made you to be. You are not better than anyone else, but you are not less than anyone else. Understand, your Father in heaven put a crown of honor on your heads. Now start thinking as royalty, talking as royalty, walking as royalty, and treating each other as royalty.

If the two of you start seeing yourselves as the king and queen God made you to be, you would never be intimidated again. You don't have to be the most talented, the most educated, or the most successful to feel good about yourselves. Because you come from a long line of royalty, you can do like royalty. Just be at ease, be kind, and be confident, knowing that you are one of a kind. You may not think you are the most beautiful woman in the world, but be confident. You're the queen. You may not be the most successful man, but stand tall. You're the king. You are crowned not by people but by Almighty God.

A PRAYER FOR TODAY

*Father, we lift our eyes to You and celebrate who You have made
us. We believe You have crowned us with favor to be royalty.
Thank You that You see us as royalty even when we've failed.
We declare by faith that we are becoming more and more
like who You say we are in Jesus' Name. Amen.*

Self-sufficient in Christ's Sufficiency

TODAY'S SCRIPTURE

*I can do all things...through Him who strengthens
and empowers me [to fulfill His purpose—
I am self-sufficient in Christ's sufficiency...]*
Philippians 4:13 AMP

If you're always depending on others for your approval and self-worth, counting on somebody else to make you happy, you'll become needy and a burden. Your friends and your spouse are dealing with enough issues without having to work on yours. They're not responsible for your happiness. If you're basing your value on how people treat you or what they give you, when they don't measure up to what you expect, you're going to feel devalued. But when you go to God for your approval and value, nobody can take that away. You are a child of the Most High God, and He has already approved you. That's where you get your value.

The apostle Paul said he was "self-sufficient in Christ's sufficiency." When we know that the God Who created the universe lives in us, that He's equipped and empowered us, and that He approves us, we don't have to have other people's approval. If you're not getting what you expect from each other, let that be okay. You can affirm and approve yourself. You are self-sufficient in Christ's sufficiency. You can feel good about who you are, knowing that God handpicked you, He breathed life into you, and He put seeds of greatness on the inside.

A PRAYER FOR TODAY

*Father, we love You and give You all the praise and glory.
We know that it is only in You that we find our value and worth,
and that it's impossible to get it from each other or other people.
We declare ourselves as sufficient in Christ's sufficiency and that
we don't need others' approval in Jesus' Name. Amen.*

The Best Pathways

TODAY'S SCRIPTURE

The Lord says, "I will guide you along
the best pathway for your life. I will
advise you and watch over you."

Psalm 32:8 NLT

God has the wisdom, the guidance, and the direction we need for our lives together, but it doesn't happen automatically. Every morning we have to go to Him and say, "God, make the path clear and show us what to do and give us the words to speak." This is a daily act of surrender. It takes humility to say, "God, You know what's best for us. We can't do this on our own. Open the right doors, close the wrong doors. Show us the best path."

The Scripture says that when we acknowledge God in all our ways, He will direct our path. Too often we make our plans without consulting God, and then we ask Him to bless them. We wonder why it's a struggle. The right way is to ask God first. "God, is this what You want us to do? Should we start this remodel project, should we take this trip, should we make this purchase, should we accept the job in another state?" If you feel peace about it, go forward. If not, hold off. God knows what's best for you. If you take time to acknowledge God and ask Him to keep you on the right path, not only will your day go better, but God will keep you from making major mistakes.

A PRAYER FOR TODAY

Father, we love and praise You that You are the all-knowing God
Who has promised to guide us along the best paths for our lives.
We gladly surrender our lives and plans to You and ask You to
direct us together. We ask You to open the right doors and
close the wrong ones in Jesus' Name. Amen.

No Excuses

TODAY'S SCRIPTURE

"But they all alike began to make excuses."
Luke 14:18 ESV

t's easy to come up with reasons for why we can't be happy, why we can't accomplish a dream, why we can't overcome a problem in our relationship. Excuses give us permission to stay where we are and settle for less than God's best as a couple. As long as you're holding on to something that happened in the past, or blaming how you behave on something your spouse does that bothers you, you'll be stuck where you are. We're asking you to throw out the excuses. You have to say, "I refuse to live with a chip on my shoulder, upset, and offended." If you get rid of the excuses, God will be your vindicator. He'll pay you back for the hurt.

This is your opportunity to step up to a new level. Now have the attitude, *Our relationship is a gift from God, and we're going to enjoy it in spite of whatever is in the past. No excuses to live unhappy or settle for mediocrity. We're pursuing our goals and overcoming obstacles that have held us back. We are children of the Most High God, crowned with favor. No excuses to give up on our dreams. We will become all God created us to be— our best together.*

A PRAYER FOR TODAY

Father, we love You and praise Your holy Name. We let go of all our excuses and refuse to settle for less than Your best for us as a couple. Thank You that our relationship is a gift from You and we're going to enjoy it. We declare that we will become all You created us to be in Jesus' Name. Amen.

OUR BEST LIFE TOGETHER

We Declare

that God has a great
plan for our lives.
He is directing our steps.
And even though we may
not always understand how,
we know our situation is
not a surprise to God.
He will work out every
detail to our advantage.
In His perfect timing,
everything will turn
out right.

Chosen

TODAY'S SCRIPTURE

*The LORD your God has chosen you out of all
the peoples on the face of the earth to be
his people, his treasured possession.*

Deuteronomy 7:6 NIV

n the Scripture, there was a prostitute named Rahab, who had made a lot of poor choices in life and wore the labels "failure, outcast, worthless, no future." One day Joshua and the Israelites were about to attack the city of Jericho where Rahab lived, and of all the people God could have used to protect the Israelite spies sent into the city, He chose Rahab. Risking her own life, she hid them from the king. When the city was conquered, Rahab and her family were the only ones saved. What's interesting is that Rahab later married a Jewish man, and their great-great-grandson was named David. This means that Rahab, a former prostitute, is in the family line of Jesus Christ.

People constantly put labels on us, telling us what we can and cannot become, what we do or don't have. Many times these labels are not in agreement with what God says about us. You may have made mistakes, but you need to remove the wrong labels. Quit thinking about what people have said about the two of you. "They'll never amount to much." "They're not very talented or smart." Don't believe the lies. God says you have been "fearfully and wonderfully made." He has amazing things planned for your future.

A PRAYER FOR TODAY

*Father, we praise You that You never give up on anyone,
including us. Thank You for Your amazing grace that made
Rahab one of Your treasured possessions and placed her in the
family of Your Son. We believe that You have chosen us to be
Your treasured possessions as well in Jesus' Name. Amen.*

Learn to Be Content

TODAY'S SCRIPTURE

I have learned in whatever state I am, to be content:
I know how to be abased, and I know how to abound.

Philippians 4:11–12 NKJV

t's good to have dreams and goals. We should be stretching our faith. But while we're waiting for promises to come to pass, we shouldn't be discontent where we are. Being unhappy, frustrated, and wondering if something is ever going to change is not going to make it happen any sooner. When we're discontent, we're dishonoring God. We're so focused on what we want that we're taking for granted what we have. The right attitude is, *God, we're believing for this, but we're happy with what we have.*

The apostle Paul said he had to *learn* to be content. It's a choice we have to make. Being content doesn't mean that we don't want change, that we give up on our dreams, or that we settle where we are. It means we're not frustrated. We're trusting God's timing. We know He is working behind the scenes, and at the right time He will get us to where we're supposed to be.

Some situations will not change until we change, such as when we're frustrated, thinking, *Why is it taking so long?* If God has us there, we must need it. He is going to use it to do a work in us. When we're content, we're growing and developing character.

A PRAYER FOR TODAY

Father, thank You that no matter what our circumstances
are that we don't have to live stressed and frustrated and
discontentedly. Thank You that You have a purpose in
where we are and what we are doing. Help us to learn
to be content and enjoy today, knowing You
are faithful in Jesus' Name. Amen.

Sing to the Promise

TODAY'S SCRIPTURE

Then Israel sang this song: "Spring up,
O well! All of you sing to it."

Numbers 21:17 NKJV

All of us have things we're believing for as couples—dreams we want to accomplish, problems we're hoping will turn around. We know God has put a promise in our hearts, but we don't see how it can happen. This is how the Israelites felt in Numbers 21. They were in the hot barren desert and desperate for water when they came to a place where there was an old dry well. God told Moses to gather the people around and He would give them water. But there was something the Israelites had to do.

The Scripture says that when it looked impossible, instead of complaining, they began to sing, "Spring up, O well!" They were making a declaration of faith. They *all* sang *to* the well. That was the key. It didn't make sense in the natural, but they started singing this phrase over and over, and suddenly water began to shoot up out of that well.

There are promises God has put in you. Your circumstances may say, "It's not going to happen." You have to do as they did and sing to the promise together. Your praise, your thanksgiving, and your declaration of faith are what causes healing, abundance, and breakthroughs to spring up. Sometimes we're waiting on God, but God's waiting on us. Why don't you start calling forth those promises He's put in your hearts?

A PRAYER FOR TODAY

Father, we thank You for the promises You have put in our hearts
for healing, abundance, and breakthroughs. Teach us what it means
to sing to our promises together. We give You thanks and declare
that they are springing up even now in Jesus' Name. Amen.

What Are You Expecting?

TODAY'S SCRIPTURE

"Open your mouth wide, and I will
fill it with good things."

Psalm 81:10 NLT

J esus said, "According to your faith it will be done to you." He was saying in effect, "If the two of you have a cup, I'll fill your cup with blessings. If you have a barrel, I'll fill your barrel. But if you have a barn, I'll fill your barn."

The question is, do you have your mouths opened wide? What are you expecting as a couple? If you take the limits off God and expect His far-and-beyond favor, He won't disappoint you. When you have your mouths opened wide, you're not just believing you will make the mortgage payments; you're believing you will pay off your house and live totally debt free. You're not just praying that God will keep your child out of trouble; you're praying He makes your child mighty in the land and uses him to do great things. That's barn level.

God promises that if you open your mouths wide, He will fill them. But it all starts with your capacity to receive. You can't go around thinking thoughts of mediocrity and expect to excel. You can't think thoughts of lack and expect to have abundance. The two don't go together. Take the limitations off God. Throw away that cup or barrel and come over to the barn-sized level. God is a God of abundance.

A PRAYER FOR TODAY

Father, we praise You that You are the God of abundance.
We believe that You want to do something new and amazing in
our lives. We are making room for Your far-and-beyond favor,
and we declare that we have positioned our empty containers
before You to fill in Jesus' Name. Amen.

Being Transformed

TODAY'S SCRIPTURE

*But we all, with unveiled face, beholding as in a mirror
the glory of the Lord, are being transformed into
the same image from glory to glory...*

2 Corinthians 3:18 NKJV

Too many couples are so focused on what they're not doing right and mistakes they've made in the past, that they are unhappy with who they are now. If you feel guilty, condemned, and upset that you're not further along, that's going to hold you back from growing in your relationship. Quit taking inventory of all your faults. You may have a lot wrong with you, but you have a lot right with you.

The key is to learn to accept yourselves while you're in the process of "being transformed...from glory to glory." You may not realize it, but you're in a phase of glory right now. Learn to enjoy the glory that you're in while God is changing you and taking you to the next level of glory. You have to start accepting yourselves right where you are as a couple, faults and all. You're not a finished product. God is the Potter, and you are the clay. He's still working on you. It's time you say, "God, we know that only You can give us the grace to change. We're going to do our best, but in the meantime we're going to accept ourselves and enjoy the glory that we're in."

A PRAYER FOR TODAY

*Father, You are the Potter, and we are the clay. Thank You for
the countless things You have made happen for our good
and for the promise that You are taking us from glory to glory.
We believe that You are working right now by Your grace to
lift us to another level of glory in Jesus' Name. Amen.*

Pure Joy

TODAY'S SCRIPTURE

*Consider it pure joy, my brothers and sisters,
whenever you face trials of many kinds...*

James 1:2 NIV

When dark clouds are over your heads and you feel as though life is depressing and gloomy, remember that right above those dark clouds the sun is shining and will break through once again. In the meantime, keep your joy. We all face disappointments, unfair situations, tests, trials, and temptation. But know this: right past the test or difficulty is promotion and increase.

Human nature tends to turn negative in difficult times. But the Scripture tells us to be joyful and glad-hearted in the middle of tough times, because when you lose your joy, you lose your strength. You need your strength more than ever in the difficult times, and your strength is dependent on your joy. When you're facing a financial crisis, dealing with an illness, going through an issue in your relationship, or raising a child, you need your strength together. If you go through those challenges feeling negative, bitter, and discouraged, you will not have the vitality to stand strong and fight the good fight of faith.

You can keep your joy by knowing that on the other side of each test is promotion. On the other side of every setback is opportunity. The difficulties you face are not there to defeat you. They are there to increase you.

A PRAYER FOR TODAY

Father, we praise You that Your joy is our strength. No matter what circumstances we face, we choose to consider it pure joy. We trust that You are always with us, You are for us, and You are working behind the scenes to lead us into victory in every area of our lives in Jesus' Name. Amen.

Stop Comparing

TODAY'S SCRIPTURE

Do you not know that in a race all the runners run,
but only one gets the prize? Run in such a way
as to get the prize.

1 Corinthians 9:24 NIV

There is an underlying pressure in our society to be number one. If we're not the best, the leaders, the fastest, the most talented, the most beautiful, or the most successful, we're taught to not feel good about ourselves. We have to work harder and run faster. If another couple moves into a new house, instead of being happy for them, we're intimidated into thinking, *That's making us look bad. We have to keep up.* If a friend gets a big promotion, we feel as though we're falling behind.

If we're not careful, there will always be another couple or something making us feel we're not up to par or far enough along. As long as you compare your situation to others, you will never feel good about yourselves, because there will always be another couple who are more successful. You have to realize you're not running their race. You're running your race. You have a specific assignment. God has given you exactly what you need for the race that's been designed for you. Another couple may seem to outrun you and outperform you. That's okay. You're not competing with them. They have what they need for their assignment. You have what you need for your assignment.

A PRAYER FOR TODAY

Father, thank You that You have given us specific assignments
in life and gifted us with exactly what we need for the race that
we've been designed to run. We believe that we don't have to
outperform or outproduce anyone, because our assignments
and race are unique to us in Jesus' Name. Amen.

Dare to Ask Big

TODAY'S SCRIPTURE

Jesus stopped and called [the blind men].
"What do you want me to do for you?"

Matthew 20:32 NIV

t seemed like a strange question. It's obvious what the blind men needed. Why did Jesus ask them? Because He wanted to see what they were believing. They could've said, "Jesus, we just need some cash for some food." If they had asked from a limited mentality, it would have kept them in defeat. Instead, they asked big. They said, "Lord, we want to see." When Jesus heard their request, He touched their eyes, and instantly they could see.

God is asking us the same question: "What do you want Me to do for you?" Now, how you answer is going to have a great impact on what God does. Don't say, "God, our family is so dysfunctional, we just want to survive." No, dare to ask big. "God, we want to see our whole family serve You." Ask for your dreams. Ask even for things that seem impossible.

God can make things happen that you could never make happen. He's already lined up the right people, the breaks you need, doors to open that you could never open. Are you asking big? Or are you letting your circumstances talk you out of it? If you go through life praying "barely getting by" prayers as a couple, you'll miss the fullness of your destiny.

A PRAYER FOR TODAY

Father, thank You that just as You restored the sight of the blind men, You can do the impossible in our lives. Thank You that You welcome us to bring the desires of our hearts to You. Help us to be bold and dare to ask You for the big things only You can make happen in Jesus' Name. Amen.

OUR
BEST
LIFE
TOGETHER

We Declare

God's dream for our
lives is coming to pass.
It will not be stopped by
people, disappointments,
or adversities. God has
already lined up solutions
to every problem we
will ever face. The right
people and the right breaks
are in our future. We will
fulfill our destiny.

Peace Stealers

TODAY'S SCRIPTURE

Let us therefore make every effort to enter that rest
[of God, to know and experience it for ourselves]...

Hebrews 4:11 AMP

As couples, we all deal with challenges and interact with people, but we're supposed to do this from a place of peace. "The rest of God" is a place where we know God is in control, we know He's fighting our battles for us. But life is full of peace stealers. There will always be people and circumstances trying to pull you out of peace. If you're going to live in peace, you have to put some boundaries up and be careful about what you feed your inner person.

If you watch the news twenty-four hours a day, you will live worried, fearful, and on edge. Recognize that's a peace stealer. Put on some good news. Feed your inner person encouraging things that build you up and cause you to be positive, hopeful, and inspired.

If you get on social media and you're constantly comparing yourselves to others, you'll never feel good about who you are. That's a peace stealer. Put up a boundary and say, "We're not going to live in somebody else's world, obsessed with what they're doing, where they're going, what they're wearing. We're going to run our own race." Successful people are too busy running their race to look around to see what everybody else is doing.

A PRAYER FOR TODAY

Father, thank You that we can make it our top priority to renew
our thoughts in Your Word, to feed on Your Word, and to be
built up with Your truth. Show us where we need to put up
boundaries from anything that steals our peace. Keep us from
comparing ourselves to others in Jesus' Name. Amen.

Well Able

TODAY'S SCRIPTURE

What shall we say about such wonderful things as these?
If God is for us, who can ever be against us?

Romans 8:31 NLT

God has placed seeds of greatness in you as a couple, so beware of adopting the negative attitudes of people that will rob you of them. Remember, ten of the twelve Hebrew spies sent by Moses into the Promised Land came back and said, "Moses, there are giants in there. *We were in our own sight* as grasshoppers. We'll never defeat them" (see Num. 13). The mental image they had of themselves was as grasshoppers. The battle was lost before it started.

Joshua and Caleb had a totally different report. "Our God is much bigger than any giants. Because of Him, *we are well able.* Let's go in at once and possess the land." They saw themselves as God's men, led and empowered by God.

What a tremendous truth! The two of you are "well able" people. Not because you're so powerful, but because our God is so powerful. He wants you to be a "can do" couple, who are ready, willing, and "well able" to do what He commands. You must learn how to cast down negative thoughts and begin to see yourselves as God sees you. You must reprogram your mind with God's Word and start seeing yourselves as winning. Keep going; keep growing. God has much more in store for you!

A PRAYER FOR TODAY

Father, we praise You for Your goodness in our lives.
We choose to tune out the negative voices of the world, and we
choose to trust You even if no one else around us will. Help us to
have spirits of faith and courage. We declare that we are
"well able" to be victorious in Jesus' Name. Amen.

Supersized

TODAY'S SCRIPTURE

*Now to him who is able to do exceedingly abundantly
above all that we ask or think, according to the
power that is at work within us.*

Ephesians 3:20 NKJV

n a fast-food restaurant, a supersized meal means you'll get
bigger portions than expected. That's what God is going to do
for you as a couple. He's going to take you further than you're
expecting, open doors that you could never have opened, and
give you more influence than you ever thought possible. Whatever
you're believing for, God is going to make it bigger, better, more
rewarding than the two of you have ever imagined.

Your dream may be to get out of debt, but God is going to
supersize it. He's going to bless you in such a way that you not
only can pay off your house, but you'll have an abundance where
you can help other people pay off their debts. Your prayer may be
for your son to get back on course. But when God supersizes it,
He's not only going to get him back on the right course, He's going
to use him to help others in the same situation.

What you're dreaming about may seem big, and you have to
stretch to believe that it will happen, but what you're believing for
is just the starting point. God is going to exceed your expectations.
He has a supersized life in front of you.

A PRAYER FOR TODAY

*Father, thank You for loving us and having such a wonderful
plan for our lives. Help us to see the great things You have for us
and how You will supersize our dreams. We believe and declare
that You are doing exceedingly abundantly above all
that we ask or think in Jesus' Name. Amen.*

Stepping-stones

TODAY'S SCRIPTURE

For he "has put everything under his feet."
1 Corinthians 15:27 NIV

How we see our difficulties very often will determine whether or not we get out of them. When we face challenges and things come against us, it's easy to get overwhelmed and start thinking, *This is never going to work out. We'll just have to learn to live with it.* That kind of thinking not only pushes you down, but it stops God from working. It's going to attract fear, worry, and doubt. Many people settle for mediocrity. You have to change your perspective. If you're going to live in victory, you have to see every sickness, every obstacle, and every temptation as being under your feet. It's already defeated. It's just a matter of time before you walk it out.

If you see life challenges as being too big, that's going to cause you to feel weak, discouraged, and intimidated. You have to shake off the lies that are telling you, "It's too big. It's been this way too long. It's never going to change." All those challenges are under your feet. This is a new day. God is saying, "Every enemy, every sickness, every obstacle; it's not going to defeat you. It's going to promote you." It was meant to be a stumbling block to keep you down. God is going to use it as a stepping-stone to take you higher. Keep the right perspective. It's under your feet.

A PRAYER FOR TODAY

Father, thank You that You have put all things—every sickness, every obstacle, and every temptation—under our feet. Thank You that we don't have to just learn to live with it or put up with it. We declare that all of these challenges are under our feet in Jesus' Name. Amen.

Acceleration

TODAY'S SCRIPTURE

*"Things are going to happen so fast your head
will swim...You won't be able to keep up...
and everywhere you look, blessings!"*

Amos 9:13 MSG

Many times in the natural it looks as though it's going to take years to accomplish our dreams or turn around problems. But God doesn't always follow a natural timeline. He gives you breaks that propel you forward and opens doors that thrust you years ahead. In your finances it looks like it's going to take years to get out of debt. No, get ready, acceleration is coming. God knows how to open the windows of heaven. One good break can put you into overflow. You're going to look up and think, *This should have taken me another ten years to pay off.* What was that? The God of acceleration, making things happen that you couldn't make happen.

This is what the prophet Amos said. Things are going to happen so fast—breakthroughs, promotions, healing—that your heads will swim. Yes, there are times where we have to be patient, seasons of waiting, being faithful, passing the tests, but there are also seasons where God will do things so fast that your heads will spin. God works where there's faith, where there's expectancy. Take the limits off God. Dare to say, "God, we're asking You to make our heads swim and amaze us with Your goodness. Accelerate Your blessings in our lives."

A PRAYER FOR TODAY

*Father, thank You that You are accelerating Your plan in our
lives and that You can take us further faster than we could ever
imagine because we honor You. We take off all the limits and
believe that You have wonderful things in store for us. We ask
You to make our heads swim in Jesus' Name. Amen.*

Make Your Words Sweet

TODAY'S SCRIPTURE

*"And I tell you this, you must give an account on
judgment day for every idle word you speak."*

Matthew 12:36 NLT

Husband, make sure you're treating your wife with respect and honor. If you're saying hurtful, demeaning things, putting her down, you're actually putting yourself down. You're not just hurting her, you're hurting you. The Scripture says that your prayers won't be answered if you're not treating your wife right. You won't reach your dreams or accomplish your goals.

Jesus said that we will give account for every "idle word" we speak, which means negative, discouraging, condescending, hurtful words. You've heard the saying to make your words sweet, for one day you're going to have to eat them. When we come to the end of life, God is going to ask, "Did you love the wife I gave you? Did you help her to grow, to become more confident?" If your wife is not better than when you first met, you need to step it up a notch. Check up on what you're saying. Are you speaking blessings over her? Every time you tell her, "You're beautiful," you're causing her to come up higher. She shines a little brighter. Every time you say, "I love you. I'm so glad your mine," not only is your marriage getting stronger, but she's getting stronger. When you encourage her in her dreams and speak life into her destiny, you are blessing her future.

A PRAYER FOR TODAY

*Father, our desire is to live lives that please You in every way,
and especially our words. Teach us how to love and honor and
bless each other with our words. May the words we speak reflect
Your thoughts and Your heart for us in Jesus' Name. Amen.*

Step-by-Step

TODAY'S SCRIPTURE

Your word is a lamp for my feet,
a light on my path.

Psalm 119:105 NIV

When we type an address into our navigation system, "Route Overview" gives us the details of our trip—where we're going, how long it's going to take, and every turn to make. We can relax, knowing all the details.

God has a route overview for your lives as a couple. He knows your final destination and the best way to get you there, but God doesn't show you the details. The Scripture says His Word is a lamp to our feet. A lamp implies you have enough light to see the path in front of you. He's not giving you the light that shows your life road for the next fifty years. He leads you one step at a time. If you trust Him and take that step into the unknown, not knowing how it's going to work out, He'll show you another step. Step-by-step, He'll lead you into your destiny.

Our question is, will you be bold and take the next step that God gives you with the light you have? The unknown is where miracles happen, where you discover abilities you never knew you had, and where you'll accomplish more than you ever dreamed. If you have the courage to do what you know He's asking you to do, He has the provision, the favor, and all that you need to go to the next level.

A PRAYER FOR TODAY

Father, thank You that what lies ahead and is unknown to us is well known to You. We choose to rely on Your strength and Your Word that guides us step-by-step. We trust that You will go before us and take us to the next level in Jesus' Name. Amen.

Be People Builders

TODAY'S SCRIPTURE

Your love has given me great joy and encouragement,
because you, brother, have refreshed the
hearts of the Lord's people.

Philemon 1:7 NIV

Do you know how many people have never been told: "You are a winner"? There are most likely people in your lives right now—maybe your own family members—who are starving for your approval. They are craving for you to speak blessing and encouragement over their lives. You don't know what it will mean when you let them know that you are proud of them and you think they will do great things. Everyone needs to be valued, appreciated, and encouraged.

What kind of seeds are you planting in each other, in your child, in a friend? Are you believing in anyone? Are you taking an interest to see how you can make someone's life better? Listen to their dreams. Find out what God has put in their hearts. Let them know you're behind them. Give them your approval. If you talk with any successful people, they'll tell you somebody spoke faith when they didn't think they could do something.

We don't realize the power we hold. We don't always realize what it means when we tell somebody, "You have what it takes. I'm behind you 100 percent." We should be encouraging them, lifting them when they've fallen, celebrating when they succeed, praying when they're struggling, urging them forward. Be people builders!

A PRAYER FOR TODAY

Father, thank You for Your hand of blessing in our lives. We ask
You to work through us and help us to speak kind words, offer
compliments, give encouragement, and lift up those around us.
Help us to listen and find out what You have put in their hearts
and be people builders in Jesus' Name. Amen.

OUR
BEST
LIFE
TOGETHER

We Declare

unexpected blessings
are coming our way. We will
move forward from barely
making it to having more
than enough. God
will open supernatural
doors for us. He will
speak to the right people
about us. We will see
Ephesians 3:20, exceedingly
abundantly, above-and-
beyond favor and
increase in our lives.

More Than Enough

TODAY'S SCRIPTURE

"You will possess their land; I will give it to
you as an inheritance, a land flowing
with milk and honey."

Leviticus 20:24 NIV

The Israelites had been in slavery for many years. That was the land of barely enough. They were just surviving, barely making it through. One day God brought them out of slavery and took them into the desert, the land of just enough. Their needs were supplied, but nothing extra. But God eventually took them into the Promised Land. That was the land of more than enough. It's called "the land flowing with milk and honey." *Flowing* means it didn't stop. It never ran out. It continued to have an abundance. That's where God is taking you.

You may be in the land of barely enough right now. You don't know how you're going to make it. Don't worry. God clothes the lilies of the field. He is going to take care of you. You may be in the land of just enough. Your needs are supplied. You're grateful, but there's nothing extra. God is saying, "I didn't create you to live in the land of barely enough or just enough." They are not permanent. You are passing through. God has a Promised Land for you. He has a place of abundance, of more than enough, where it's flowing with provision, not just one time, but you'll continue to have plenty.

A PRAYER FOR TODAY

Father, thank You that You are El Shaddai, the God of more
than enough and not the God of barely enough or the God of
just help us make it through. You are the God of abundance.
We believe that You are going to bring us into a life of
overflow in Jesus' Name. Amen.

Renew Your Strength

TODAY'S SCRIPTURE

Those who hope in the LORD will renew their strength.
They will soar on wings like eagles; they will run and
not grow weary, they will walk and not be faint.

Isaiah 40:31 NIV

First Samuel 30 describes the worst defeat that David suffered, and yet how at his darkest hour he stirred up his faith and went out and defeated the enemy. Very soon after that, King Saul was killed in battle and David took the throne he had waited thirteen years to receive. He was closest to his victory when he faced his greatest challenge. The reason David saw the promise fulfilled is not because he never felt weariness and was never tempted to quit. It was that he didn't allow that weariness to stay.

The two of you may be facing battle fatigue today. You've been dealing with a challenge in your health, your finances, or your relationship for many years. When you feel that weariness, look up and know that you don't have to overcome it on your own. What causes your strength to be renewed is when you live with the hope that God is working in your lives. When you come to Him, you get your thoughts going in the right direction, and He gives you rest. As with David, God is filling you with fresh vision, with courage, with energy. Together, you will soar like eagles.

A PRAYER FOR TODAY

Father, thank You for the promise that You will renew our
strength. We ask You to breathe new life into our spirits and
cause us to soar like eagles. When weariness comes knocking,
help us to keep the door shut. We believe that we will run
and not be weary in Jesus' Name. Amen.

Full of Joy

TODAY'S SCRIPTURE

A relaxed attitude lengthens a man's life;
jealousy rots it away.

Proverbs 14:30 TLB

After one of our services, there was a lady standing in the lobby who was celebrating her hundredth birthday. She was beautiful, had almost no wrinkles, was full of joy, and her mind was sharp. When asked what her secret was, she said, "I don't worry. I let things go. I laugh a lot, and I enjoy the people in my life." In one hundred years, you know she's had trouble, had people hurt her, and made mistakes, but she didn't hold on to them. She kept emptying the negative out, knowing that God is in control and will do what He promised. He filled her with good things, and she's stayed young and strong.

No matter what age you are, you can be young at heart, full of faith and energy and creativity. Your spirit never ages. The same is true of your relationship. It doesn't have to get old and stale. You can stay young in spirit together. The way that happens is to get in a habit of emptying out any offenses between you. Empty out the worry and anxiety. If you made a mistake, empty out the guilt. If you didn't do your best, empty out the regret. If you get good at emptying out the negative in your relationship, you'll be strong, vibrant, full of faith, and full of joy together.

A PRAYER FOR TODAY

Father, we love and honor You. Thank You that our relationship never needs to get old and stale and that we can stay young in spirit together. We choose to empty out the worry and mistakes and offenses and let negative things go. Fill us with joy to overflowing in Jesus' Name. Amen.

Perfect Peace

TODAY'S SCRIPTURE

You will keep in perfect peace all who trust in you,
all whose thoughts are fixed on you!

Isaiah 26:3 NLT

David says in Psalm 20, "Some trust in chariots and some in horses, but we trust in the name of the Lord our God." Today he would say, "Some trust in their money and some in their jobs, but our trust is in Jehovah Jireh, the Lord our Provider." When you meditate on Him, you'll be at total rest. You know God is in control, and He can give you total victory. But it all depends on what's going on in your thought lives. You can meditate on problems or on the promises. What you allow to play in your minds will determine what kind of lives you live together.

God said there is a way not only to have peace but to have perfect peace. How? Keep your thoughts fixed on Him. Pay attention to what is playing in your minds. When you dwell on negative thoughts, you're not going to have peace. You have to change what you're dwelling on. All through the day, go around thinking, *God has us in the palms of His hands. All things work together for our good. Many are the afflictions of the righteous, but the Lord delivers us out of them all.* When you meditate on that, you'll have greater peace, joy, and strength.

A PRAYER FOR TODAY

Father, we praise You that You are Jehovah Jireh, the Lord our Provider. Thank You that we can put our trust in You completely and fix our minds on You. We declare that You give us perfect peace and we will rest in You in all the circumstances of our lives in Jesus' Name. Amen.

The Hand of God

TODAY'S SCRIPTURE

Praise the LORD, my soul, and forget not all his benefits—
who forgives all your sins and heals all your diseases,
who...crowns you with love and compassion.

Psalm 103:2-4 NIV

When you look back over your lives, think of some of the things you've faced that at the time you didn't think you could make it through. The obstacle was so large, the betrayal by your friend hurt you so badly, the medical report was so negative. You didn't see a way, but God turned it around. He gave you strength when you didn't think you could go on. He promoted you, gave you that good break, and now you're further along than you ever imagined. That wasn't a coincidence. It was the hand of God.

Those challenges not only prepared you for your future, they've also given you a history with God. When you're in a tough time, instead of being discouraged and negative, you can go back and remember how God brought you out of trouble. When you remember how God has protected you, faith will rise in your hearts. Instead of thinking, *We'll never get out of this problem*, you'll say with confidence, "God made a way for us in the past. He's going to make a way in the future." When you come through the next challenge, that victory will be the fuel you use that gets you to the next level of glory.

A PRAYER FOR TODAY

Father, we thank You for Your past goodness, protection,
provisions, and favor in our lives. You have done amazing things
for us. We believe that no matter what we face today that You
made a way in the past and You will make a way for us
now in Jesus' Name. Amen.

Redeem the Time

TODAY'S SCRIPTURE

Therefore see that you walk carefully [living life with honor, purpose, and courage...], not as the unwise, but as wise...making the very most of your time.

Ephesians 5:15-16 AMP

Time is more valuable than money. You can make more money, but you can't make more time. To make the most of your time means, don't waste it. Don't live this day unfocused, undisciplined, and unmotivated. Use your time wisely. This day is a gift. Are you living it to the full? With purpose and passion? Pursuing your dreams? Or are you distracted? Indifferent? Just doing whatever comes along? Are you in a job you don't like? Hanging out with people who are pulling you down? That's wasting the time.

The first step in investing your time wisely is to set short-term and long-term goals. What do you want to accomplish together this week? Where do you want to be as a couple five years from now? Do you have a plan? Are you taking steps to get there? Life is flying by. You don't get a do over.

Paul said in effect that if you're going to reach your highest potential, you have to be "on purpose" people. You know where you're going. You're focused, making the most of each opportunity. You have to be disciplined to stay focused on what's best for the two of you.

A PRAYER FOR TODAY

Father, thank You that You are calling us to invest our time and to run our lives with purpose and passion. Help us to reevaluate what we are doing, to refocus our lives and relationships, and to get rid of anything that's distracting us from Your plan for our lives in Jesus' Name. Amen.

Forget the Past

TODAY'S SCRIPTURE

I am still not all I should be, but I am bringing all my energies to bear on this one thing: Forgetting the past and looking forward to what lies ahead.

Philippians 3:13 TLB

For all the amazing things the apostle Paul did, he said in effect, "What's more important is letting go of what lies behind." He knew that if he carried negative baggage from the past, it would keep him from his destiny. Paul had been through a lot of adversity. Many opponents tried to discredit him and his ministry with false accusations. Some of the churches he founded hurt him, and some believers turned against him. If he hadn't learned this principle of letting go of the past, he would have become bitter and discouraged.

Sometimes we spend more energy holding on to the negative past than we do letting it go. How do you drop it? Don't rehearse negative things that have happened between the two of you. Make a decision that you're not going to talk about it another time. The reason some couples never see "what lies ahead" is that they're always opening up old wounds. If you're going to get free, you need to bury it. Put it away once and for all. Focus all your energy on moving forward, having dropped the offenses, the guilt, the self-pity, and the hurts.

A PRAYER FOR TODAY

Father, thank You for the freedom that comes as we drop the negative baggage from the past. We are not all we should be yet, but we are focusing our energy on forgetting the past and moving forward in our relationship. Help us to become experts at letting go and looking forward in Jesus' Name. Amen.

Remember Your Dream

TODAY'S SCRIPTURE

Delight yourself also in the Lord, and He will give you the desires and secret petitions of your heart.

Psalm 37:4 AMPC

We all have dreams we're believing for. Deep down we feel them so strongly, but we hit some setbacks. Our dreams can become buried under discouragement, past mistakes, rejection, failure, and negative voices. It's easy to settle for mediocrity when we have all this potential buried on the inside. Your dream may be buried, but the good news is that it's still alive. It's not too late to see it come to pass. The key to reaching your destiny is to remember your dream. Remember what God promised you. Remember what He whispered to you in the middle of the night.

What has God put in your hearts? What did you used to be excited about? Why do you think it's too late, it's too big, it's not possible? Get your passion back. You haven't missed your opportunity or had too many bad breaks. You're not lacking, and you didn't get shortchanged.

If you start believing again, stir your faith up, God is going to resurrect what you thought was dead. You may have tried and failed, but dreams that you've given up on are going to suddenly come back to life. Problems that looked permanent are going to suddenly turn around. God has the final say. He hasn't changed His mind.

A PRAYER FOR TODAY

Father, we praise You for the dreams and desires that You have put in our hearts. Thank You that we can stir our faith and know that You can resurrect what we have thought was dead. We declare that it is never too late to see our dreams come to pass in Jesus' Name. Amen.

OUR
BEST
LIFE
TOGETHER

We Declare

that God will accelerate His plan for our lives as we put our trust in Him. We will accomplish our dreams faster than we thought possible. It will not take years to overcome an obstacle, to get out of debt, or to meet the right people. God is doing things faster than before. He will give us victory sooner than we think. He has blessings that will thrust us years ahead.

Something New

*"I am about to do something new. See, I have
already begun! Do you not see it? I will make
a pathway through the wilderness..."*

Isaiah 43:19 NLT

You can't go through life thinking that you've reached your limits as a couple. "Well, we'll never be able to afford a nicer house." "Our daughter got off course, and it doesn't look as though she'll ever get back." Thinking like that is going to stop God's best. Quit declaring defeat over your relationship. What God has destined for your lives will come to pass. It may not happen all at once, but that's just a test of your faith. You always face the greatest opposition when you're close to your victory. The enemy wouldn't be fighting you so hard if he didn't know something amazing was in front of you. You have to dig your heels in and say, "God is about to do something new. His plans for us are for good, and any moment things could change in our favor." When you live with that expectancy, that's what allows God to do great things.

You don't know what new thing could happen today. The loan could go through this week. Your son could break that addiction this month. There's something new from God that's already begun. Do you see it? God doesn't do things halfway. He's the author and the finisher. Get up every morning and thank Him that He's about to do something new.

A PRAYER FOR TODAY

*Father, thank You that You are the God Who is always doing
something new and Whose plans are always good. We believe
that even now You are working in ways we don't yet see.
We declare You are the author and finisher of our
faith in Jesus' Name. Amen.*

Be Willing to Change

TODAY'S SCRIPTURE

You husbands must give honor to your wives.
Treat your wife with understanding as you live
together...as you should so your prayers
will not be hindered.

1 Peter 3:7 NLT

We know a couple who had been doing everything they could to have a baby for many years with no success. One day the husband, who is a minister, was very discouraged and thought, *God, it's not fair. I'm helping people, doing what You've asked me to do. Why can't we have a baby?* He sensed God say to him, "Son, you're not going to have a baby until you start treating your wife better." He was a good man who loved the Lord, but he knew he'd become disrespectful, argumentative, and wasn't putting any effort into their relationship.

The good news is that he was willing to change. Maybe like him, you've drifted down a similar path. You know you're not being your best in this area. God's not here to condemn us and make us feel bad about ourselves, but He will convict us and challenge us to come up higher. We have to do as this man did and say, "Okay, I'm willing to change. I can do better in this area." If God is speaking to your heart about this, ask Him, "Lord, how can I change? What am I doing that is keeping us from the fullness of Your blessing?"

A PRAYER FOR TODAY

Father, thank You for challenging us to come up higher and to
be our best for each other. Show us if there is anything that we're
doing that is keeping us from the fullness of Your blessing.
We want to change, and we believe You have the power
to change us in Jesus' Name. Amen.

Send Out New Invitations

TODAY'S SCRIPTURE

...my tongue is the pen of a skillful writer.

Psalm 45:1 NIV

All through the day, whether we realize it or not, the power of "We are" is at work in our lives. We make a financial mistake and out of our mouth tumbles, "We are never going to get out of debt." We look in the mirror, shake our heads, and say, "We're always worn out." Many times we wield the power of "We are" against ourselves. We don't realize how it's affecting our future.

Here's the principle. *Whatever follows the "We are" will always come looking for you.* When you say, "We are so unlucky," bad breaks come looking for you. "We're so broke." Struggle comes looking for you. It's as though you're handing it an invitation, opening the door, and giving it permission to be in your lives.

The good news is that you get to choose what follows the "We are." When you go through the day saying, "We are blessed," blessings come looking for you. "We are talented." Talent comes looking for you. You're inviting that into your lives.

You need to send out some new invitations. Use your words to invite good things into your lives. "We are blessed. We are strong. We are talented. We are wise. We are prosperous." When you talk like that, Almighty God says, "Go find that person." Health, strength, and abundance start heading your way.

A PRAYER FOR TODAY

Father, we commit our words to You. Thank You that our words have creative power and that we can use our words to become who we want to be. We choose to invite good things into our lives with spoken words that are true to Your Word in Jesus' Name. Amen.

Just Pebbles

TODAY'S SCRIPTURE

*My people will live in peaceful dwelling places,
in secure homes, in undisturbed places of rest.*

Isaiah 32:18 NIV

When you throw a rock out into a lake that is calm as glass on the surface, it sends ripples across the whole lake. It looks like it causes a big disturbance. But the truth is that one foot beneath the surface, the water didn't move. Nothing on the surface affects the water down deep. It stays calm and peaceful.

If the pebbles that get thrown into your relationship are stealing your joy, you need to go down deeper in faith together. "But the promotion at work fell through, and we were counting on it." That's a pebble. "Our friends offended us." Another pebble. "Our loan was denied." Just a pebble rippling the surface. If you put your trust in your job, it may not last. If you put your trust in people, they'll let you down sometimes. If you put your trust in money, things can change overnight. Yes, those things affect the outside and look like big disturbances, but when you get beneath the surface, you know God is still on the throne and that He will pay you back for the unfair things. Then even though on the surface it's all disturbed, down deep where you choose to live, you'll feel a peace, you'll be at rest, and so will your home.

A PRAYER FOR TODAY

*Father, we love and praise You for being the God of all peace.
We want to draw closer to You and live deeper in You. We refuse
to allow circumstances in our lives or what others say and
do to steal our joy. We declare that we will walk in peace
and be at rest in Jesus' Name. Amen.*

The Garment of Praise

TODAY'S SCRIPTURE

"To give them...the garment of praise for the spirit of heaviness; that they may be called trees of righteousness, the planting of the LORD..."

Isaiah 61:3 NKJV

When you feel that heaviness and discouragement is trying to overtake you as a couple, the first thing to do is take off the old coat of heaviness and put on a new coat of praise. When you put on the garment of praise, that spirit of heaviness has to go. Sometimes you won't feel like being grateful. That's why God says to offer up the sacrifice of praise. God knew it would not always be easy. You will have to dig your heels in and say, "God, we're tired and discouraged. But we know You are good and You are good all the time, so we choose to give You praise."

When you offer up that sacrifice of praise, supernatural things begin to happen. Scripture tells us the story of the apostle Paul and his companion Silas being unjustly beaten and imprisoned for sharing their faith, yet singing praises to God at midnight in their jail cell. Sure enough, their sacrifice of praise led to a miraculous deliverance. God has victories in your future that will amaze the two of you. You may be in a tough time right now, but remember this: God will show up and show out in unusual ways. He has something great in store for you.

A PRAYER FOR TODAY

Father, we come to You and take off heaviness and discouragement and choose to put on the garment of praise. Thank You that You are here with us now, inhabiting our praises and driving out the enemy. We declare we will see the victory You have for us in Jesus' Name. Amen.

Be a Barrier Breaker

TODAY'S SCRIPTURE

Don't become so well-adjusted to your culture that you fit into it without even thinking. Instead, fix your attention on God. You'll be changed from the inside out.

Romans 12:2 MSG

So often we let our environment—how we were raised, people's expectations of us—set the limits for our lives. We adapt to what's around us. It's easy to just fit in and be like everybody else, but God didn't create you to be average. He created you to go beyond the norm, to leave your mark on this generation. He put seeds of greatness in you both.

Perhaps you were raised in an environment where people have addictions, low self-esteem, depression, and poverty. Your mind might have been conditioned to think, *This is who we are. We'll always struggle with these problems.* But that's not who you are. That might have been the norm, but the good news is that you're barrier breakers. You have the power, the ability, the anointing, and the favor to break out and go to a new level.

Nothing will change until you make up your mind that you are going to break out of the box of mediocrity. There's so much potential in you. You have to put your foot down and say, "We refuse to be mediocre because people around us are negative and have low expectations. We are barrier breakers. We're setting a new standard."

A PRAYER FOR TODAY

Father, thank You that we can get our thinking in line with Your Word and retrain our thoughts to break through the barriers that have held us back. We declare that we are breaking out of the box of mediocrity and tapping into our seeds of greatness in Jesus' Name. Amen.

Love Is Honest

TODAY'S SCRIPTURE

The goal of this command is love, which comes from a pure heart and a good conscience and a sincere faith.

1 Timothy 1:5 NIV

t's easy to go through life wearing masks, acting one way for our boss, one way for our friends, and another way for our spouse. Because we're not secure in who we are, we feel a need to impress, to prove something to people, so we pretend, even with each other. We're all for having an attitude of faith, not being controlled by your circumstances, but in order to get well, you have to get real. It's time to take off that mask and be honest. When you get down to the real you, that's when God can turn things around.

It's easy to hide behind personal masks. Oftentimes it's the mask of pride. "We don't have any issues. We don't need any help." You may wear masks when you're around others. "We're so happy together. Everything is great." But God will not bless who you pretend to be. God blesses people who are real, people who are honest enough to say, "God, we argue all the time at home. We need Your help, so we're taking off the masks. We need to talk with a counselor." When you're honest, you open the door for God to come in and change things. But as long as you're pretending, not dealing with the real issues, it's not going to improve.

A PRAYER FOR TODAY

Father, we praise You that You are the God Who sees. Thank You that You bless us when we are real and honest and stop pretending in our relationship and with others. We choose to take off the masks and deal with where we are really at together in Jesus' Name. Amen.

Finishing Grace

TODAY'S SCRIPTURE

*...looking unto Jesus, the author and finisher
of our faith, who for the joy that was set
before Him endured the cross...*

Hebrews 12:2 NKJV

Starting is easy—a diet, school, a family. Finishing is what can be difficult. Any two people can get married, but it takes commitment to stick with it. Any couple can have a dream, but it takes determination, perseverance, and made-up minds to see it come to pass. Too many people start off well. They have big dreams. But along the way they have some setbacks, get discouraged, and think, *It's never going to work out.*

You may be up against challenges right now as a couple. You are moving forward, making progress, but it's hard. Keep reminding yourselves that God has not only given you the grace to start; He has given you the grace to finish. He helped you to get started, and He is going to help you to finish. He is the author and the finisher of your faith. He didn't bring you this far to leave you. The Scripture says, "God began a good work in you, and He will continue to perform it until it is complete." One translation says, "He will bring you to a flourishing finish"—not a defeated finish, where you barely make it and are beat up and broke. You are coming to a flourishing finish, a finish more rewarding than you ever imagined.

A PRAYER FOR TODAY

*Father, we praise You that Jesus is the author and finisher of our
faith and that we can follow in His footsteps. Thank You that
You have given us not just the grace to start our race but to
finish it. We believe that You will bring us to a flourishing
finish in Jesus' Name. Amen.*

OUR
BEST
LIFE
TOGETHER

We Declare

Ephesians 3:20 over our lives.
God will do exceedingly
abundantly above all that
we ask or think. Because we
honor Him, His blessings will
chase us down and overtake
us. We will be in the right place
at the right time. People will
go out of their way to be good
to us. We are surrounded
by God's favor.

Shame Be Gone

TODAY'S SCRIPTURE

Then the LORD said to Joshua, "Today I have rolled away the reproach of Egypt from you."

Joshua 5:9 NIV

A *reproach* means "shame, blame, disgrace." For over four hundred years the Israelites had been beaten down in Egyptian slavery and allowed the emotional abuse to steal their sense of value. They felt inferior, insecure, as though they had no worth. Abuse victims often start to feel as though they deserve what's happening to them and internalize the shame. As they were about to enter the Promised Land, God had to roll away their sense of shame, feeling unworthy, not valuable.

In the same way, you both may have brought a heavy load of guilt and shame into your relationship due to past mistakes, failures, even things that weren't your fault. Before you can reach your highest potential and your best life together, you have to get rid of the shame. Whatever your Egypt is, God is saying, "This day, I am rolling away the reproach, the shame, the guilt." Now it's up to you to accept it. The moment you asked God to forgive you, He forgave you and doesn't remember it anymore. You have to let it all go. When those thoughts come saying, "Shame on you," you have to answer right back, "Shame off me. God's mercy is bigger than my mistake. I've been forgiven and restored. God doesn't remember it, so I'm not going to remember it."

A PRAYER FOR TODAY

Father, thank You that Your mercies are new every morning and that You roll back the reproach of guilt and shame over our pasts. Thank You that the moment we ask You to forgive us, You also forget it. We believe we are forgiven and declare shame off us in Jesus' Name. Amen.

Continual Joy

TODAY'S SCRIPTURE

"Indeed, the water I give them will become in them
a spring of water welling up to eternal life."

John 4:14 NIV

We all face difficulties at work and home. If we're not careful, we'll let the pressures of life weigh us down and start to complain and become negative. But we were created to enjoy life. While we can't control what happens on the outside, we can control what happens on the inside. Happiness for many people is based on their circumstances. "It's the weekend, so I'm happy." But joy is not dependent on what's happening around you; joy is deep down within you, a calm delight. You're at peace, you're content. When you know God's in control, you're tapping into the joy on the inside.

In John 4, Jesus told the woman at the well that there is a spring of joy in you that's supposed to bubble up and continually flow, but we have to tap into that joy. Ephesians 5:18 says, "Be ever filled with the Spirit." Notice that it says "be ever filled." On a regular basis we have to keep filling ourselves up. How do we do it? The next verses say, "Speaking to yourselves in songs, making melody in your heart to the Lord, giving thanks always." The way to have continual joy is to always keep a song of praise in your heart for what's right all through the day.

A PRAYER FOR TODAY

Father, thank You that the joy of the Lord is our strength.
We come to You with hearts full of praise and have so much
to be grateful for because of Your goodness. We declare
that there is a spring of joy inside us that is welling up
and overflowing in Jesus' Name. Amen.

Celebrate Partial Victories

TODAY'S SCRIPTURE

*When the builders completed the foundation of
the Temple, the priests...blew their trumpets; and...
crashed their cymbals to praise the Lord...
singing this song: "He is good..."*

Ezra 3:10-11 TLB

The Israelites had a dream to rebuild the temple. It was a huge task. People came from all over to help. After much work, all they had completed was the foundation, yet they had a huge party. They didn't have any walls up or the roof. They could have been frustrated at how far they had to go, but instead they celebrated the small victory.

We all have things in our lives that are incomplete. The dream hasn't come to pass, a problem hasn't turned around. We've made some progress, we've seen signs of God's favor, but it's still unfinished. The mistake we make too often is to wait for the total victory to celebrate. "As soon we're totally out of debt, we'll be grateful." But the key to seeing it come to fulfillment is to celebrate partial victories along the way. When you pay off one credit card, celebrate the partial victory. Your child may not be on course yet, but he was respectful this morning. Thank God for it. Don't let the completion of what you're believing for hold your thanksgiving hostage. When you celebrate your partial victories, it gives you the strength to keep moving forward. If you pass the test of being grateful for the small things, He'll release big things in your lives—more favor, more healing, more strength.

A PRAYER FOR TODAY

*Father, praise You for Your faithfulness in our lives. We thank
You for the partial victories that You have given us, and we know
that You are working even now to bring them to completion.
We declare that we will continue to be grateful and see every
promise fulfilled in Jesus' Name. Amen.*

Miracles Out of Mistakes

TODAY'S SCRIPTURE

"As for Ishmael, I...will make him a great nation."
Genesis 17:20 NLT

Abraham and Sarah had God's promise of a son, but in their impatience took matters into their own hands, and Abraham had baby Ishmael with Hagar, Sarah's maid. Ishmael was a mistake, bringing extreme dysfunction to their home. Yet God spoke to Abraham that even though it was a mess, He would make Ishmael a great nation. And amazingly, it was descendants of Ishmael who came along at the right moment and kept Joseph, Abraham's great grandson, from dying in the pit when his brothers betrayed him (see Gen. 37). The mistake of Abraham became the miracle of Joseph, who helped save the rest of their family. That's how amazing God is. He knows how to bring good even when we fail.

We all have times when we blew it, got involved in things we shouldn't have, and made a mess. We think, *Too bad for us. This is what we deserve.* The accuser constantly whispers, "You're shameful failures. God's never going help you." Don't believe those lies. God has mercy for every mistake. If the two of you will stay in faith, He won't just bring you through it, He'll take the mess you made, clean it up, and bring you out better. God works all things for your good. He not only can correct a complicated situation, but years later He can use it to somehow bless your descendants!

A PRAYER FOR TODAY

Father, we praise You for designing a perfect plan for our lives. Thank You that You take even our worst mistakes and messes and find a way to somehow bring good out of them. We believe that You will turn everything around for our good in Jesus' Name. Amen.

Built on the Rock

TODAY'S SCRIPTURE

"He makes His sun rise on the evil and on the good,
and sends rain on the just and on the unjust."

Matthew 5:45 NKJV

Just because we have faith doesn't exempt us from difficulties. Jesus told a parable about a person who built his house on a rock. He honored God. Another person built his house on the sand. He didn't honor God. The same storm came to both people. The wind blew and the rain fell on both houses. The difference is that when you honor God, after the storm is done, you will still be standing. The enemy may hit you with his best shot, but you'll come through the storm stronger, increased, and better than you were before.

Colossians 3 says, "God has given us the power to endure whatever comes our way with a good attitude." Maybe at the office you're not being treated fairly. It doesn't take any faith to go to work negative and complaining. If you want to pass the test, go to work with a positive attitude and do more than you're required. At home, if you want to pass the test, you have to be good to your spouse even when they're not being good to you. You have to do the right thing when the wrong thing is happening. Every time you do the right thing, a blessing will follow. There will always be a reward.

A PRAYER FOR TODAY

Father, we praise You for Your grace in our lives. Thank You
for giving us the strength to handle anything that comes our way.
We choose to take hold of Your power and have a positive
attitude to do the right thing when the wrong thing is
happening in Jesus' Name. Amen.

Created to Give

TODAY'S SCRIPTURE

*"Whoever wants to become great among you must
be your servant...just as the Son of Man did not
come to be served, but to serve, and to give
his life as a ransom for many."*

Matthew 20:26-28 NIV

Jesus said, "If you want to be great in the kingdom, there's a simple key: serve other people." He was talking about a lifestyle in which you're always looking for ways to serve. When you live a "serve others" lifestyle, you help each other and friends, volunteer in your community, and take care of loved ones. It becomes a part of who you are. You develop an attitude of giving to everyone you meet. That's when you'll experience a greater happiness and fulfillment as a couple. You live not to receive, but to give.

God has put people in your lives on purpose so you can be a blessing to them. Don't look for them to pay you back. They may not even thank you, but let us assure you that when you serve others, there is applause in heaven. God sees your sacrifices, and He's the One Who matters. He sees your acts of kindness. He sees you volunteer at the hospital. He sees you show up each week to serve in the church nursery. He sees you helping your neighbor. When you serve others, God says you'll be great in the kingdom.

A PRAYER FOR TODAY

*Father, we praise You that Jesus came to serve and gave His
life for us. Thank You that You created us to serve others,
to be truly fulfilled together by living to give and not to receive.
What is our assignment today? Help us to see the people
You want us to serve in Jesus' Name. Amen.*

Overcoming Love

TODAY'S SCRIPTURE

Do not be overcome by evil,
but overcome evil with good.

Romans 12:21 NKJV

f you argue long enough with each other, you're going to say things you regret later. A ten-minute argument can set your relationship back ten years. You have to learn to walk away. You're not going to accomplish anything positive in a heated, disrespectful, contentious situation. The Scripture says that you "overcome evil with good." You don't overcome disrespect with more disrespect, or overcome insult with insult, or overcome shouting with more shouting. You do it by staying respectful. Scripture says, "Avoiding a fight is a mark of honor." You be the first to walk away.

When David was a teenager, his oldest brother, Eliab, spoke to him in the most condescending, disrespectful, and accusatory way in front of others (see 1 Sam. 17:28). Rest assured that David felt like telling his brother off. His emotions said, "Let him have it." He had his speech all lined up. But he kept his mouth closed and walked away. No wonder David took the throne. No wonder God entrusted him to do great things. David had the character to back up the anointing on his life. God can give you a great anointing, and He can have a big future in store, but if you don't develop your character, you won't step into all that He has. Taming the tongue is a major part of reaching our destiny.

A PRAYER FOR TODAY

Father, we love You and give You all the praise and glory.
Thank You for giving us the grace to overcome evil with good
by the help of the Holy Spirit. We believe that You will
help us tame our tongues and walk together in peace
and love in Jesus' Name. Amen.

Worry Is a Thief

TODAY'S SCRIPTURE

...casting all your care upon Him,
for He cares for you.

1 Peter 5:7 NKJV

Worry is a thief. It will rob you of your joy, your energy, and your sleep at night. You don't make good decisions as a couple when you're worried. You weren't created to be constantly trying to figure out what to do, worried and stressed out. You weren't designed to carry that load. You have to turn your cares over to God. Here's the key: when you rest on purpose, God goes to work; but when you work, God rests. If you try to carry it yourselves, God says, "Okay, you're on your own." But when you come back to a place of peace and say, "God, we trust You. We're going to be still and know that You are God," that's when God goes to work.

David had all kinds of opposition, enemies coming against him. He could have lived upset and worried, but he understood this principle: "The Lord is my shepherd...He leads me to restful waters." David was saying, "The way I protect my peace on a regular basis is to go down to the still waters. I empty out all the worry, all the anxiety, all the fear." He let his mind rest. We're talking about in your spirit. It can be chaotic all around you—traffic, people, problems, drama—but on the inside, you're at rest, there's a calmness.

A PRAYER FOR TODAY

Father, we know that although we can't make things happen
on our own, You can and will on our behalf. We come to the
restful waters and cast our cares upon You. We declare that
we are resting in You alone in Jesus' Name. Amen.

OUR
BEST
LIFE
TOGETHER

We Declare

we are special and
extraordinary. We are not
average! We have been
custom-made. We are one
of a kind. Of all the things
God created, what He is the
most proud of is us. We are
His masterpieces, His most
prized possessions. We will
keep our heads held high,
knowing we are children of
the Most High God, made
in His very image.

Suddenly

TODAY'S SCRIPTURE

*...the immeasurable (limitless, surpassing) riches of His
free grace (His unmerited favor) in [His] kindness and
goodness of heart toward us in Christ Jesus.*

Ephesians 2:7 AMPC

Some years ago a man stopped by the church and brought a large donation to the ministry. He said he had received an inheritance from a family member he had never met before. In fact, he didn't even really know that they were related, but this man unexpectedly left him a gift that thrust his family to a whole new level.

The apostle Paul said that we would see "the unlimited, immeasurable, surpassing greatness of God's favor." That's favor as we've never seen it before. That's how the word *explosion* is defined. It means, "sudden, widespread increase." That's what God wants to do for us. *Suddenly*. You won't expect it. It's out of the ordinary, and it's not small. It's so amazing you know it had to be the hand of God.

You may think your situation is permanent. You don't see how you could ever rise any higher and accomplish your dreams as a couple. All the calculations are telling you that you'll never get out of debt, but God is saying, "You need to get ready. You haven't seen My explosive blessings. You haven't seen the surpassing greatness of My favor. I will bless you beyond your normal incomes. I have blessings that will catapult you years ahead. I have increase that goes beyond your calculations."

A PRAYER FOR TODAY

*Father, thank You for Your unlimited favor and supply of
everything we need in this life. We open our hearts to You and
ask You to increase our capacity to receive. We choose to take
the limits off because we know all things are possible
to You in Jesus' Name. Amen.*

Divine Empowerment

TODAY'S SCRIPTURE

"...how God anointed Jesus of Nazareth with the Holy Spirit and power, and how he went around doing good and healing all."

Acts 10:38 NIV

We don't have to go through life doing everything on our own, trying to accomplish our dreams and overcome challenges only in our own abilities, strengths, intellects, and hard work. God has placed His anointing on us. The anointing is a divine empowerment. It enables you to do what you could not do on your own, to accomplish dreams even though you don't have the talent, and to overcome obstacles that looked insurmountable.

You can own the most expensive car, but if you don't put gasoline in it, you're not going anywhere. In a similar way, you've been made in the image of Almighty God. You are full of incredible potential. The fuel you need to release your greatness is the anointing on your lives. The anointing is only activated where there is faith. When you start declaring, "We are anointed, equipped, empowered, and well able," you're stirring up your anointing. That's when you'll see breakthroughs. Situations will suddenly change in your favor.

God has already equipped and empowered you for every situation. When you are speaking words of victory, "We can do all things through Christ. We are strong in the Lord," you're putting fuel in your car. That's when you'll go places that you couldn't go on your own.

A PRAYER FOR TODAY

Father, we thank You that You have placed Your anointing on us to enable us to do what we cannot do on our own. We declare we are anointed, equipped, and more than conquerors in Jesus' Name. Amen.

Always in Blossom

TODAY'S SCRIPTURE

*"Do you really believe I can do this?" They said,
"Why, yes, Master!" He touched their eyes and said,
"Become what you believe." It happened. They saw.*

Matthew 9:28-29 MSG

Jesus said to two blind men whom He healed, "Become what you believe." If you believe you're going to get laid off, don't be surprised if you do. You're going to become what you believe. We're asking you to get rid of the negative thoughts and believe what God says about you. Believe that you are blessed, strong, healthy, talented, creative, and well able.

The writer of Psalm 1 said, "If you will meditate on God's Word day and night, you will be like a tree planted by the water. Your leaf will not wither, but you will bear fruit in every season without fail." Notice that it is in *every* season of your lives. That means even if the economy goes down, you'll be thriving. When others have fear, you'll have peace.

One Bible translation says that when you meditate on God's Word, "You're a tree...always in blossom." That's God's dream for your lives—that you're always in peace and always excited about your future even when you face adversities. In those difficult times, because you have your thoughts fixed on Him, deep down you will know that God is fighting your battles, and you're not only going to come out, you're going to come out better off than you were before.

A PRAYER FOR TODAY

*Father, thank You that Your plan for every season of our lives
is that we always be in blossom, that we're always bearing
fresh fruit. Thank You for giving us Your Word to meditate
upon. We declare that we are going to become what
we believe in Jesus' Name. Amen.*

The Power You Give It

TODAY'S SCRIPTURE

"Don't seek vengeance. Don't bear a grudge; but love your neighbor as yourself, for I am Jehovah."

Leviticus 19:18 TLB

n the Scripture, Joseph was sold into slavery by his own brothers, then falsely accused and put in prison for thirteen years. He could have used excuse after excuse to be bitter and angry. But he had a "no excuses" mentality. He kept shaking off the discouragement and overlooking the offenses. And in the end he came out vindicated, promoted, and in a place of influence and respect.

You might have been through some bad breaks as a couple. People may have said things about you and done things to you that hurt and offended. Don't waste your time looking back, reliving what they did—those are distractions. The only power those have over you is the power that you give them. Let it go, and God will fight your battles. God will be your vindicator.

Life is too short for you to waste another day being upset, offended, in self-pity. You might have been through a rough time, but you don't have to have a rough finish. God wants to pay you back for the unfair things that have happened. It's not always easy to get over it and move forward, but here's the key: the pain of letting it go is less than the pain of holding on and missing your destiny.

A PRAYER FOR TODAY

Father, we praise You that You are the God Who fights our battles and vindicates us. Thank You for Your love and grace that are upon us. Right now, we let go of all the hurts and offenses and wounds of the past. We declare that they have no power over us in Jesus' Name. Amen.

Hope On in Faith

TODAY'S SCRIPTURE

[For Abraham, human reason for] hope being gone,
hoped in faith that he should become the
father of many nations...

Romans 4:18 AMPC

When God gave Abraham a promise that he and his wife, Sarah, were going to have their "very own son" (see Gen. 15), she was around seventy-five years old. Abraham could have thought, *I must have heard God wrong. No one has a baby at Sarah's age.* But Scripture says that when all human reason for hope was gone, Abraham hoped on in faith, knowing that God is a supernatural God. Fifteen years later, Sarah gave birth to a son. The promise was fulfilled. There had been many times when they were tempted to think, *This can never happen.* If they had pulled up their anchor of hope in God, they would have drifted into doubt, discouragement, and never seen the promise come to pass.

Sometimes there's no logical reason to have hope. There may be many reasons your situation will never work out. But as a couple you have to, against all hope, hope on in faith as Abraham did. Get your hopes up. Just because you've had some bad breaks and God's promise hasn't happened yet, doesn't mean it's not going to happen. If what you're experiencing isn't going to work for your good, God wouldn't allow it. Shake off the disappointment. What God promised you, He's still going to bring to pass!

A PRAYER FOR TODAY

Father, thank You that because You are supernatural, we can
hope on in faith even when we can find no other reason for hope.
We trust that what we're experiencing is going to work for
our good. Thank You that what You promised us is going
to come to pass in Jesus' Name. Amen.

Transform Your Thinking

TODAY'S SCRIPTURE

*...be made new in the attitude of your minds;
and to put on the new self, created to be like
God in true righteousness and holiness.*

Ephesians 4:23-24 NIV

Your life together as a couple will follow your thoughts. If your thoughts have been running in a negative pattern for month after month, year after year, it's as though they've been digging a deep riverbed, and the negativity can flow in only one direction. With every pessimistic thought, the riverbed is a bit deeper and the current stronger.

Fortunately, we can dig a new river, one going in a positive direction. When you start to dwell on God's Word and see the best in situations, one thought at a time, you are redirecting the flow of that river. It may not look like much at first, but as you continue to reject negative thoughts and redirect the flow, as you choose faith instead of fear, expecting good things and taking control of your thought lives, that negative stream will dwindle and the positive river will flow with faith-filled thoughts of victory.

Keep in mind, though, that river of negativity wasn't formed overnight, nor will it be redirected without some conscious, strenuous effort on your part. God will help you. Start expecting good things. Stay full of faith, full of joy, full of hope. If you will transform your thinking, God will transform your lives.

A PRAYER FOR TODAY

*Father, thank You that it is possible for us to enter into the flow
of positive, faith-filled thoughts of victory. We choose to start
seeing the best in situations. We believe that as we dwell on
Your Word that our minds will be renewed and our lives
will be transformed in Jesus' Name. Amen.*

Set Times

TODAY'S SCRIPTURE

And so after waiting patiently,
Abraham received what was promised.

Hebrews 6:15 NIV

n life we're always waiting for something—for a dream to come to pass, for a problem to turn around. When it's not happening as fast as we'd like, it's easy to get frustrated. But you have to realize that the moment you prayed, God established a set time to bring the promise to pass for your healing, your promotion, and your breakthrough. It may be tomorrow, next week, or five years from now.

When you understand that the time has already been scheduled by the Creator of the universe, it takes all the pressure off. You'll relax and enjoy your lives, knowing that the promise has already been set. Maybe you have been praying together about a situation for a long time and don't see anything happening. But if God allowed you to see into the future, and you saw that on February 12 at 2:33 in the afternoon your prayer would be answered, you wouldn't be discouraged. You would be excited because you know the big day is coming.

Here's where it takes faith. God promises that there are set times in our future, but He doesn't tell us when they will be. Are you willing to wait with a good attitude, knowing that they're on the way? God has a set time. Don't let negative thoughts talk you out of it.

A PRAYER FOR TODAY

Father, we come to You today with open and humble hearts.
Thank You that You have established set times to bring
Your promises to pass in our lives. We believe that we
will receive them in Jesus' Name. Amen.

Take the Limits Off

TODAY'S SCRIPTURE

*You do not have because you do not ask. You ask
and do not receive, because you ask amiss,
that you may spend it on your pleasures.*

James 4:2–3 NKJV

The Scripture says, "You ask and do not receive, because you ask amiss." That word *amiss* in the original language means "sick, weak, miserable." When we ask to just get by, to endure, to barely make it, that's a weak prayer. That's asking amiss. God is saying, "I created the whole universe. Don't come to Me with a weak prayer, asking Me to help you live in mediocrity. Ask big, knowing that I'm the God of more than enough." He's saying, "Ask Me to show out in your lives. Ask Me to heal you from that disease. Ask Me to accelerate your goals."

When you ask big, God calls that a healthy prayer. Ask to be the difference makers in your family. Ask to set a new standard. When you say, "God, we need more space for our family, and we don't have the funds for a bigger house, but we want to thank You that opportunity is headed our way, that blessings are chasing us down," that's your faith being released. That's what allows God to do great things.

Take the limits off God. Ask big. This is the time for God to show out in your lives, to accelerate His goodness, to propel you into your destiny together.

A PRAYER FOR TODAY

*Father, thank You that You want to do great things in our lives
so that You will be glorified. Help us to pray healthy prayers
together, prayers that release Your favor and open new doors
of opportunities. We declare that we are taking the limits
off You in Jesus' Name. Amen.*

We Declare

that God is bringing about
new seasons of growth.
We will not get stagnant
and hold on to the old.
We will be open to change,
knowing that God has
something better in
front of us. New doors
of opportunity,
new relationships,
and new levels of favor
are in our future.

Let Go of Yesterday's Baggage

TODAY'S SCRIPTURE

*"Oh, what joy for those whose disobedience is forgiven,
whose sins are put out of sight."*

Romans 4:7 NLT

We all make mistakes, and some are very painful. Maybe you need to bury mistakes you made. You've lived feeling guilty, condemned, and down on yourselves long enough. Have a funeral and put it behind you. No more talking about it. No more letting the accuser make you feel unworthy, saying, "You don't deserve to be blessed. You're a failure." When the defeat, the mistake, the hurt comes back up on the movie screen of your mind, change the channel. Have the attitude, *I'm not living in regret and rehearsing failures. I'm moving forward.*

Pay attention to what you're dwelling on all day. Listen to what you're saying. You only have so much emotional energy each day. When you spend that time and energy on negative things, rehearsing your failures, discouragements, and being down on yourselves, that's energy you should be using to move forward. Don't relive that loss in your mind another time. Don't tell another person about the mistake you made. You had a funeral and buried it. The difference between couples who are positive, happy, and expecting good things and those who are negative, discouraged, and bitter is simply that the second group holds on to the baggage while the first group has learned the principle to drop it, to let it go.

A PRAYER FOR TODAY

*Father, thank You that You've given us the power to stop the
negative things from our pasts that replay in our minds. We refuse
to continue to live in regret and to be down on ourselves.
We declare that we are dropping the baggage and moving
forward together in Jesus' Name. Amen.*

Be Glad-Hearted

TODAY'S SCRIPTURE

*Be happy [in your faith] and rejoice and be
glad-hearted continually (always).*

1 Thessalonians 5:16 AMPC

We've found that most of the time we have what we need to be happy. We just don't always have the right perspective. For instance, you may not be happy with the job you have right now. But if you lost that job and went months without any income, you probably would be very happy to win it back. You see? You had what you needed to be happy. You just didn't realize it.

There was a couple who complained for years that their house was too small and too far out in the country. But when the economy went down, they came very close to losing that house. Just before the bank foreclosed on it, they were able to refinance it. Today they think that house is the greatest thing in the world. What happened? They changed their perspective.

Wives complain about their husbands, and husbands complain about their wives: "[He or she] is just too much of this" or "not enough of that." But if their spouse was suddenly gone, and they were lonely month after month, they may be very happy just to get their spouse back.

Keep your lives in the right perspective. The two of you have something right now to be happy about: your health, your jobs, your families, or an opportunity. Appreciate the gift of today.

A PRAYER FOR TODAY

*Father, we come to You with hearts full of praise because You
are worthy Almighty God! Thank You for the gift of today and
all that You've given us to enjoy. Help us to keep the right
perspective on our lives and to maintain an attitude of
glad-heartedness in Jesus' Name. Amen.*

Agree to Disagree

TODAY'S SCRIPTURE

If you are angry, don't sin by nursing your grudge.
Don't let the sun go down with you still angry—
get over it quickly.

Ephesians 4:26 TLB

At one time or another, after one of us have hurt or offended the other, we have all faced the temptation to disconnect by giving the offender the silent treatment. We have learned that silence is not the best way to handle a disagreement. Trying to pull back is one of the most common relationship mistakes that couples make.

The Scripture says it's not good to go to sleep mad and frustrated, because you'll wake up with that same anger and frustration. We may not have the resolution to a disagreement by the time the evening comes, but we have decided that sometimes we just have to agree to disagree. One of the most freeing experiences is to recognize that you are two different people who see things differently, and you can still love each other and stay connected. Just because you have a disagreement does not mean there are not plenty of other areas on which you agree. It just means you have a difference of opinion. Having the same heart and the same goal is what maintains a good connection. There will be times when we do not agree on every decision or subject, but we should always believe in each other, support each other, and move forward through life together—connected.

A PRAYER FOR TODAY

Father, thank You that You brought us together to love and honor and cherish. Help us to see that we can agree to disagree about different matters and still love each other. We refuse to give each other the silent treatment and declare we will stay connected in Jesus' Name. Amen.

The God of Jacob

Then he said, "I am the God of your father, the God of Abraham, the God of Isaac and the God of Jacob."

Exodus 3:6 NIV

t's easy to understand that God is the God of Abraham, the father of our faith. We can understand how He is the God of Isaac, who was extremely obedient, even willing to be sacrificed. But when it says He is the God of Jacob, that doesn't make a lot of sense. Jacob went around deceiving people. He stole his brother's birthright. Jacob was known for making poor choices. What was God saying? "I'm not just the God of perfect people who never make a mistake. I'm the God of people who have failed and blown it."

It's interesting that later in Jacob's life, when he got his life straightened out, God changed his name from Jacob to Israel. That was to signify his new beginning. God could have been known as "the God of Abraham, Isaac, and *Israel*." That was Jacob's new redeemed name. But God on purpose left it as "the God of Abraham, Isaac, and Jacob" to forever settle it that "I'm the God of imperfect people."

You may have made mistakes, but be encouraged. He is still your God. You may have lost your tempers and said things to each other that you regret. Don't beat yourselves up. He is the God of Jacob. He is your God, too.

A PRAYER FOR TODAY

Father, we praise You for being the God of imperfect people. Thank You that You cleanse us and restore us when we fail. We believe that we are forgiven, that Your mercy and forgiveness cover our mistakes, and that we will become all You've created us to be in Jesus' Name. Amen.

Your Legacy

TODAY'S SCRIPTURE

*I am reminded of your sincere faith, which first lived in
your grandmother Lois and in your mother Eunice and,
I am persuaded, now lives in you also.*

2 Timothy 1:5 NIV

When you hear the word *legacy*, you probably think of what you will leave behind or how you will be remembered as a couple when you're gone, but there is something even more significant. The Scripture talks about how we can store up mercy for our children and future generations by living a life of excellence and integrity.

You are where you are because somebody prayed. Somebody served. And now God is honoring them by releasing His goodness in your lives. None of us got to where we are on our own. The apostle Paul was saying, "Timothy, what I see in you started because you had a praying grandmother who stored up mercy that was passed down to your mother, and now I can see it in you."

Your challenge is to live in such a way as to cause others to win. With every right decision you make and every temptation you resist, you are winning for your children. Every time you help someone in need, every time you serve and give, you are storing up mercy. It may be for your children, for your grandchildren, or even a hundred years from now for somebody in your family line who will experience God's goodness because of the lives you've lived.

A PRAYER FOR TODAY

*Father, we praise You that we can leave a legacy of faith and
mercy for our children and future generations. Thank You that
with every decision we make, every temptation we resist, and
every time we serve, we are storing up mercy. Help us
fulfill our destiny in Jesus' Name. Amen.*

Everything You Need

TODAY'S SCRIPTURE

*But to do this, you will need the strong belt of truth
and the breastplate of God's approval.*

Ephesians 6:14 TLB

Sometimes the reason people don't give you what you think you need in a relationship is because they didn't see it modeled growing up. If they didn't see family members giving love and encouragement and expressing their feelings, they don't have it to give. If you're trying to get it from them, you're going to be frustrated. Why don't you let them off the hook and go to God for what they can't give. Here's the key: God has everything you need. When you learn the principle to not rely on people, but to rely on Him for your approval, value, and encouragement, you won't live stressed out because somebody is not giving you what you expect.

You are responsible for your own well-being. You can't rely on your spouse, your parents, or your friends to give you that. They may be good people, but they cannot give you everything you need. Only God can. If you only look to them, when they fall short, you're going to be resentful and bitter. The truth is, it's not their fault. Maybe they could do better in some areas, but when you rely on God, you're not dependent on them. God didn't base the plan for your life upon other people. The right attitude is, *Nobody owes me anything. God alone has everything I need.*

A PRAYER FOR TODAY

Father, we praise You for approving and loving us. Thank You that You made us to be just as we are. Thank You that we don't have to live for the approval of others. We declare that we find everything we need in You alone in Jesus' Name. Amen.

Pure in Heart

TODAY'S SCRIPTURE

"Blessed are the pure in heart, for they will see God."

Matthew 5:8 NIV

When Jesus said "pure in heart," the word *pure* in the original language is where we get our word *catharsis* from, which means "cleansing, releasing, purifying." After a surgery, the doctor may put in what's called a catheter, which is from the same root word. It's a tube that drains out the impurities in the body—the infection, the toxins, the waste. The doctor knows that these contaminates will come naturally. He's not alarmed unless they're not released, when the body holds on to what should be flushed out.

When God says, "Blessed are the pure in heart," He's saying that you're going to be blessed when you get in a habit of emptying out all the things that will infect you and your relationship. Bitterness, guilt, worry, doubt, and self-pity are impurities that will come, but you have to flush them out. They can't hurt you if they just pass through. It's when you hold on to them that it's going to contaminate your spirit and cause problems in your relationship. You weren't created to carry around worry about your children, guilt about a past mistake, bitterness about a disappointment—those will poison you. The good news is that when you let go of the guilt, the blame, the regret, the jealousy, it's just a matter of time before God will fill your lives and relationship with good things.

A PRAYER FOR TODAY

Father, we love You for Your continued faithfulness if our lives.
Thank You that we can release any worries, any doubts,
any guilt and bitterness and flush them out of our relationship.
Help us to forgive whatever needs forgiving and let go of
the past in Jesus' Name. Amen.

Defining Moments

TODAY'S SCRIPTURE

God is faithful, and he will not let you be tempted
beyond your ability, but with the temptation
he will also provide the way of escape.

1 Corinthians 10:13 ESV

One evening King David walked around on the roof of the palace and saw a beautiful young lady taking a bath. Whenever we face temptation, God will always have a moment of grace, a time where you have the strength and the ability to resist and walk away. But that moment of grace doesn't last hour after hour. Right at the start, you have to be disciplined and do the right thing. David let his guard down and one compromise led to another.

We all make hundreds of routine decisions each day, but there are certain defining moments that not only affect us, but they affect our children and future generations. When you're in a situation where you're tempted to compromise, to get upset, to be bitter, you have to dig down deep, be disciplined, and not go by what you feel. When you're in the heat of the moment, and every voice tells you, "Just do it. Just say it. It doesn't matter. It's not going to hurt anything," don't believe those lies. Every temptation starts with a thought. When those tempting thoughts come, get them out of your mind. That's the battlefield. If you let it stay, it's going to draw you in and lead you to compromise. It's going to affect your destiny.

A PRAYER FOR TODAY

Father, thank You that You promise a way of escape to any
temptation we face. Help us to guard our minds and hearts and
to be strong to resist temptation and compromise. We choose
to take captive every thought that is contrary to Your
Word in Jesus' Name. Amen.

We Declare

that we will use our words
to bless people. We will
speak favor and victory
over each other and
our family, friends,
and loved ones. We will
help call out their seeds of
greatness by telling them
"we're proud of you, we
love you, you are amazing,
you are talented, you are
beautiful, you will do
great things in life."

A Destiny Frame

TODAY'S SCRIPTURE

By faith we understand that the worlds were framed by the word of God...

Hebrews 11:3 NKJV

When the Scripture says "the worlds were framed by the word of God," it's not just talking about the physical *worlds*. The word in the original language is *eons*, meaning, "ages" or "times." It's saying that God has a frame around your times. He has put a boundary around your lives. Nothing can penetrate your frame that God doesn't allow. Trouble, sickness, accidents—they can't just randomly happen. The frame is set.

You don't have to worry about your future. There's a frame around your health and finances set by the Creator of the universe. Not only can nothing get in without God's permission, but even better news, you can't get out. It's a destiny frame. God won't let you get so far off course that you can't still fulfill your purpose. You may come right up to the edge and be about to do something to get you in trouble, but you'll bump into the frame. God will push you right back.

God has the right people not only lined up for you, but for your children, for your grandchildren. They've been framed. They may get off course and run with the wrong crowd, but sooner or later they'll bump into the frame again and again, until they finally say, "I'm tired of fighting. God, have Your way in my life."

A PRAYER FOR TODAY

Father, we praise You that when You framed the worlds by Your word, You also framed our lives with a boundary that nothing can penetrate that You don't allow, and that You even have a way of keeping us in it. We believe that nothing just randomly happens to us in Jesus' Name. Amen.

Daily Bread

TODAY'S SCRIPTURE

"I will rain down bread from heaven for you.
The people are to go out each day and
gather enough for that day."

Exodus 16:4 NIV

When the Israelites were in the desert headed toward the Promised Land, God gave them manna to eat each morning. It was something like bread that formed on the ground and spoiled if you tried to keep it overnight. The principle was that every morning you had to go out and get a fresh supply.

That same principle is found in the Lord's Prayer. Jesus taught us to pray, "Give us this day our daily bread." He didn't say our weekly bread. Every morning you need to go to God for fresh wisdom and direction. The word *manna* in Hebrew is translated, "What is it?" When we go to God each day for that fresh manna, the right attitude is, *God, what is it that You want us to do, what is the right path?* We're saying, "God, show us the path, show us how to overcome this challenge, show us how to accomplish our dreams. Give us Your ideas, Your wisdom, Your direction."

Are you getting your daily manna? Are you getting your brand-new assignment each morning, asking God, "What is it?" It's available. It has your name on it. Remember, you can't live off yesterday's manna. Take time each day to ask God to lead you down the right paths for your lives.

A PRAYER FOR TODAY

Father, thank You that we can come to You for our daily bread,
for wisdom and direction for our lives. Thank You for the
new assignments and fresh ideas You give. Show us the right
paths for our lives and replenish our supply of grace to
overcome every challenge in Jesus' Name. Amen.

Use What You Have

TODAY'S SCRIPTURE

*Finding a fresh jawbone of a donkey, he grabbed
it and struck down a thousand men.*

Judges 15:15 NIV

You may feel you don't have the talents or the education you'd like to have, but as long as you think you're lacking as a couple, it will keep you from God's best. Take your faith one step further and believe you are equipped and empowered, that you have the talent, the resources, the personalities, everything you need to fulfill your destiny. Here's the key: you have exactly what you need. If you will use what God has given you, He will get you to where you're supposed to be. It's not necessarily the amount of talent, education, or money. What makes the difference is that with God's anointing on your lives, you'll go further than others with exceptional talent.

You can have an extraordinary problem, but with the favor of God, He can provide an ordinary solution and make you victorious. When Samson was surrounded by a huge army, he had no weapons. All he could find was the jawbone of a donkey. But Samson realized that the ordinary jawbone was part of his destiny, and it became extraordinary when God breathed on it.

You don't have to be the strongest couple to overcome your obstacles or have great talent in order to do something great. When you honor God with your lives, He knows how to take something ordinary and make it extraordinary.

A PRAYER FOR TODAY

*Father, we praise You that You made us just the way we are
and empowered us with the talents, resources, and personalities
You wanted us to have. We believe that we have exactly what
we need to fulfill our destiny and You will multiply it
as well in Jesus' Name. Amen.*

You Are Approved

TODAY'S SCRIPTURE

[Abraham] was accepted and approved through his faith...assuring us that God will accept us in the same way.

Romans 4:23-24 TLB

Something powerful happens to us as couples when we have the boldness to say, "God, we know You approve of us because of our faith, so we approve of ourselves. We are happy with who we are." Voices will scream, "You're hypocrites! You have issues." Just answer back, "We're not approved because we're perfect. We're approved because we are children of the Most High God. God's still working on us."

Too often we get our performance mixed up with our identity. You ask somebody, "Who are you?" and they answer, "I'm a nurse." But that's what they do, not who they are. You are the children of God. That's where your value comes from—your *who*, not your *do*. You may do some wrong things, but that is not who you are. Nothing that you do changes your value, because your value comes from your Creator. So feel good about who you are as a couple. When you're positive toward yourselves, you're in agreement with God. If you make a mistake, the moment you ask God to forgive you, He not only forgives you but He forgets it. Quit listening to all the accusing voices telling you what you're not. Your performance wasn't perfect, but your hearts are turned to Him. That's what matters to God.

A PRAYER FOR TODAY

Father, we praise You that You are our God. Thank You that You accept and approve of us because of our faith and not because of our performance. We declare that we feel good about who we are and ask You to help us to become our best together in Jesus' Name. Amen.

A Harvest of Peace

TODAY'S SCRIPTURE

For wherever there is...contention (rivalry and selfish ambition), there will also be confusion (unrest, disharmony, rebellion).

James 3:16 AMPC

A lot of times we think, *When she changes, I'll change. When he starts treating me better, I'll be nice.* But here's the key: God will reward you in a greater way if you put your ego down and take the first step. Pride will tell you, "When they're acting wrong, don't treat them right. They don't deserve it." But you're not doing it for them; you're doing it unto God. You're not saying, "I approve of how you treat me." You're saying, "God, I'm going to be a peacemaker, even though I don't like this. I know that You will make it up to me."

Human nature says, "You want to be sarcastic, argumentative, hard to get along with? Okay, you've met your match!" All that's going to do is make matters worse. God brought your spouse into your life on purpose. It was all a part of His plan. We all have weaknesses and shortcomings that get on each other's nerves. Learn to rise above the strife and be the difference maker. When you honor your spouse by treating them with respect even when they don't deserve it, that's what causes them to rise higher. If you make the first move, that seed you're sowing will be what God uses to bring you a harvest of peace.

A PRAYER FOR TODAY

Father, thank You that You made us to be difference makers by the way we love and respect each other. Help us to remember that You brought us together as a part of Your plan to glorify Your Name. We look forward to the harvest of peace You are bringing us in Jesus' Name. Amen.

Hold Them Up

TODAY'S SCRIPTURE

When Moses' hands grew tired...
Aaron and Hur held his hands up...so that
his hands remained steady till sunset.

Exodus 17:12 NIV

One time Moses was on the top of a big hill watching a battle that was taking place. As long as he held his rod up in the air, the Israelites were winning. But whenever he put his hands down, the Amalekites started to win. Finally, Moses was too tired and would have needed miraculous strength to continue. Aaron and Hur got on each side of Moses and held his hands in the air. Because they became the miracle, the Israelites won the victory.

There are people God puts in our paths who need us to hold up their hands. They're not going to win by themselves. They need your encouragement, your rescuing hug, to know that you care. They're praying for a miracle. Become the miracle.

We don't always see how powerful we really are. God has put healing in you. Your hugs can cause people to get better. Your kind words can put people back on their feet. The Scripture says, "A gentle tongue brings healing." A phone call, giving someone a ride, taking them out to dinner, encouraging them in their dreams— there are miracles in both of you waiting to happen. Some people just need to know that you believe in them. That may seem simple to you, but to the other person it can be life-giving.

A PRAYER FOR TODAY

Father, thank You that You bring people across our paths so
we can be the answer to their prayers and become their miracle.
Help us to encourage others to follow their dreams, to speak
a kind word, and to lift them up when they're hurting
in Jesus' Name. Amen.

Sealed Lips

TODAY'S SCRIPTURE

Whoever wants to embrace life and see the day
fill up with good, here's what you do:
Say nothing evil or hurtful…

1 Peter 3:10 MSG

Our mouth gets us into more trouble than just about anything else. You can't go around saying hurtful things, pushing people down, and expect to step into the fullness of what God has for you. Many times it's not big things that are keeping us from God's best as a couple; it's not some big sin or big mistake. It's small things. The apostle Peter said that if you want to enjoy life and see good things, say nothing evil or hurtful. How much higher would we go if we didn't have to have the last word when we disagree, not have to be right, but just quietly keep honoring God, being respectful, staying on the high road?

David faced a lot of opposition in his life. He had plenty of opportunities to get upset, lose his cool, and tell people off. But rather than pray for the defeat of his enemies, he prayed, "God, I know I'm going to be tempted to say things I shouldn't, to complain, to argue, to be disrespectful. So I'm asking You in advance to help me zip it up." That's a great prayer. Every morning when we wake up we should pray, "God, help us to know when to keep our lips sealed."

A PRAYER FOR TODAY

Father, we come to You with thanksgiving in our hearts.
Thank You that we can embrace life and see our days filled with
good by taking control of what we say. We ask You to help us
to keep our lips sealed when we're tempted to complain
and argue in Jesus' Name. Amen.

Keep in Balance

TODAY'S SCRIPTURE

Then he lay down under the bush and fell asleep.
All at once an angel touched him and said,
"Get up and eat."

1 Kings 19:5 NIV

The prophet Elijah had seen God raise a child from the dead, prayed and it did not rain for over three years, and even called down fire from heaven. Yet a threat upon his life overcame Elijah with fear and he fled into the wilderness where he finally lay down to sleep and wanted his life to end. Why was Elijah depressed, discouraged, and not wanting to go on? He was exhausted and needed some sleep. Elijah didn't need a miracle; he just needed some rest and a good meal. The angel didn't say, "Be free of the depression." He said, "Get up and eat." He was saying, "Take care of yourself. Get back in balance."

Too often we're fatigued, discouraged, losing our passion, because we're not taking care of ourselves. We're three-part beings—spiritual, physical, and emotional. We have to take care of all three parts. Living balanced is the key. You can't drink ten cups of coffee a day, eat sugar and junk food, not get proper sleep, and expect to have any energy and feel good. Perhaps the best thing we can do for each other is to change our diet, send each other to bed early when we're tired, and pray for each other.

A PRAYER FOR TODAY

Father, thank You that is not Your will for us to push ourselves
so hard that we have nothing left to give to each other. We ask
You to give us wisdom as to how to live our lives in balance.
Help us to make any changes we should make with our
diet and sleep times in Jesus' Name. Amen.

We Declare

that we have sound minds
filled with good thoughts,
not thoughts of defeat.
By faith, we are well able.
We are anointed. We
are equipped. We are
empowered. Our thoughts
are guided by God's Word
every day. No obstacle can
defeat us, because our
minds are programmed
for victory.

Ignore It

TODAY'S SCRIPTURE

Overhearing but ignoring what they said,
Jesus said to the ruler of the synagogue,…
only keep on believing.

Mark 5:36 AMPC

When you receive negative reports that are true, don't deny them and act as though they don't exist, but also don't dwell on them. Don't let them consume you to where that's all you think and talk about as a couple. Learn to put things in perspective.

In today's Scripture, while Jesus was on His way to pray for a very sick girl, people from her house came and said, "Tell Jesus it's too late. She's already dead." Jesus overheard the negative report, but He ignored it. He didn't meditate on it. He didn't get discouraged, turn around, and go back home. He also didn't deny that the girl was dead. But He knew people don't have the final say. God has the final say. Sometimes in order to stay in faith you have to do as Jesus did and ignore a negative report. You have to ignore what somebody said about you and what your own thoughts are telling you.

There will be times when it feels as though every voice is telling you, "You can't do it. It's not going to work out." It may be the voices of the people around you or just your own thoughts trying to discourage you. You have to choose to ignore it, and choose to believe a better report.

A PRAYER FOR TODAY

Father, we praise You that no matter what happens in our lives,
You have the final say. Thank You that we can stay in faith
and choose to not dwell on negative reports. We believe that
as we get our thoughts in agreement with Your Word that
we shall overcome in Jesus' Name. Amen.

Bloom Where You're Planted

TODAY'S SCRIPTURE

Our lives are a Christ-like fragrance rising up to God.

2 Corinthians 2:15 NLT

Through an opening in the woods, as far as one could see, there were acres of dead, dried-up, brown, ugly weeds. And blooming right in the middle of the weeds, there was one beautiful flower, so bright, so colorful, so refreshing. That's what God wants us to do as couples. Just bloom where we're planted.

Too many people are negative and discouraged because they don't like their jobs, their coworkers, or where they live. If they have to work late, it sours their day. They are always fighting against something. They are always looking for a different house in a new neighborhood.

If you live and work in the midst of weeds, that doesn't have to stop you from blooming. But you'll have to learn that God is more interested in changing you than He is in changing your circumstances. As long as you're sour at work, discouraged because the two of you can't seem to agree on something, upset because the business isn't growing, that attitude will keep you right where you are. If you want to see change, you cannot wait until everything becomes better before you decide to have a good attitude. The two of you have to be the best you can be right where you are. When you bloom where you're planted, you're sowing a seed for God to do something new.

A PRAYER FOR TODAY

Father, we praise You that our hopes are rooted in You. Even when we don't understand our circumstances, we know You are working things out for our good. Help us to bloom where we're planted and to be the best we can be at all times as a testimony to You in Jesus' Name. Amen.

The Voice of Faith

TODAY'S SCRIPTURE

A man has joy by the answer of his mouth, and a word spoken in due season, how good it is!

Proverbs 15:23 NKJV

n your lives, there are always two voices competing for your attention—the voice of faith and the voice of defeat. You'll hear one voice piping in, "You can't possibly raise that amount of money." You'll be tempted to worry, to be negative, to complain. But if you listen carefully, you'll hear the voice of faith saying, "God has a way. Favor is coming. Breakthroughs are coming." One voice will point out that you don't have what it takes. The other voice is clear and matter-of-fact: "You are well able. You can do all things through Christ."

Now, here's the beauty. The two of you get to choose which voice comes to life. The way you do it is by what you speak. When you verbalize that thought, you're giving it the right to come to pass. If you say, "We'll never overcome this problem," you are choosing the wrong voice. You have to get in agreement with God. The other voice may seem louder, but you take away all its power by choosing the voice of faith. You have to dig your heels in and say, "We're not giving life to any more defeat. No more speaking mediocrity, fear, or doubt. We're choosing the voice of faith. We're strong, healthy, and blessed. We are victors and not victims."

A PRAYER FOR TODAY

Father, thank You for Your loving-kindness. We humbly submit our thoughts and our words to You. Show us when we speak words of doubt, discouragement, and negativity so we can change. Help us to give our faith a voice by speaking Your Word daily in Jesus' Name. Amen.

Running Over

TODAY'S SCRIPTURE

*"Give, and it will be given to you. A good measure,
pressed down, shaken together and running over,
will be poured into your lap."*

Luke 6:38 NIV

n the book of Acts, when Peter and John walked by a crippled man at the temple, he looked up expecting to receive a gift of money. Peter said, "I can give you something better. In the name of Jesus rise and walk." Peter took him by the hand, and as he did, the man's legs were completely healed. The man only expected a few coins, but God did something extraordinary.

Like this man, you may be expecting the ordinary. You're going through the routine of life, being your best with what you have as a couple. Where you are looks like that's the way it will always be. But God is saying, "I'm about to exceed your expectations and thrust you to a new level. Good breaks are about to find you." You didn't ask for it. You weren't expecting it. It's just the goodness of God.

The Scripture talks about how as we give, we'll be blessed in good measure, pressed down, shaken together, and running over. You're about to come into those running-over blessings—with resources, creativity, strength, health, and joy. God is a running-over God. He's not a get-by God. He's a more-than-enough God. He has ways to bless you that you've never thought of or expected. Just dare to believe.

A PRAYER FOR TODAY

*Father, we praise You for being the God of infinite grace
Who always exceeds our expectations. Thank You that as
we give freely of ourselves, You will bless us to the point
of overflowing. We dare to believe that You are the
more-than-enough God in Jesus' Name. Amen.*

Not Knowing

TODAY'S SCRIPTURE

*By faith Abraham, when called to go to a place he
would later receive as his inheritance, obeyed and went,
even though he did not know where he was going.*

Hebrews 11:8 NIV

God told Abraham to pack up his household and head
out to a land that God was going to give him. The only
problem was that God didn't give him *any* details. It's
easy to imagine all the questions Sarah asked, concluding with, "Are you sure that God told you this?"

God doesn't give you a blueprint for your whole life together. If
you had all the details of what He wants you to do and how it will
work out, you wouldn't need any faith. He's going to send you out,
not knowing everything. To step into the unknown takes boldness.
It's not always going to make sense. Other people may try to talk
you out of it. Your own thoughts will ask you, *What if it doesn't
work out?*

The psalmist said, "The steps of a good person are ordered by
the Lord." If you take that step, not knowing all the details but
trusting that God knows what He's doing, then each step of the
way there will be provision, favor, and protection. Yes, it's uncomfortable not knowing the details; and, yes, you have to stretch, to
pray, and to trust. But every step you'll not only have God's blessing; you'll also be growing and getting stronger together.

A PRAYER FOR TODAY

*Father, thank You that You have a blueprint for our life
together and that we need not fear the unknown. We ask
You to make clear the next step we should take, and we
declare that we will take it in Jesus' Name. Amen.*

His Masterpieces

TODAY'S SCRIPTURE

*For we are God's masterpiece. He has created
us anew in Christ Jesus, so we can do the
good things he planned for us long ago.*

Ephesians 2:10 NLT

Psychologists say our self-worth is often based upon what we believe the most important people in our lives think of us—a parent, a spouse, a friend, or a mentor. The problem is that sooner or later people say something that cuts like a knife and brings heartache and pain, or they show by their actions that we're not really that important. If we're receiving our value and worth only from those who hurt us, we'll likely feel inferior, insecure, and less and less valuable over time.

The key to gaining a true sense of value is to let your Heavenly Father be the most important person in your lives. If you will learn to listen to what He says about you, you'll feel accepted, approved, redeemed, forgiven, confident, and secure. You will feel extremely valuable, and that's exactly the way God wants you to be.

The apostle Paul says, "You are God's masterpiece." You've been custom-made, one of a kind. You're not average or ordinary. God created you in His very own image. He looks right at you and says, "There's My masterpiece. That's My son. That's My daughter. That's what brings the most joy to My heart." And that is exactly how we should view and treat each other.

A PRAYER FOR TODAY

*Father, we praise You that because You have made us, there can be
nothing ordinary about us. Thank You that we are Your children
and created in Your image. We believe and declare that we are
Your masterpieces, designed by You on purpose just the
way we are in Jesus' Name. Amen.*

All Is Well

TODAY'S SCRIPTURE

Let your roots grow down into [the Lord]
and draw up nourishment from him.

Colossians 2:7 TLB

Second Kings 4 records the story of a mother whose little boy was suddenly taken ill and tragically died in her arms. Yet even when it looked unbearable, she knew that unexpected trouble wasn't a surprise to God. She remained steadfast and immovable in her faith and immediately set out to get her friend the prophet Elisha. Twice in the middle of this calamity she was asked if her child was well, and she answered, "All is well." Despite how she felt and what the circumstances looked like, she knew that God could make a way where she didn't see a way. Elisha went and prayed for the little boy, and he miraculously came back to life.

We all face unexpected challenges as couples—the loss of a loved one, a personal failure, a sudden layoff, a sickness. It's easy to get overwhelmed. But rather than complain and talk about how unfair it was, go deeper and instead have a report of faith, "All is well. God's in control." Then because you have deep roots, even when you may have panicked in the past, you'll feel the peace from God that passes understanding. You'll have the strength to endure what should have taken you out. You aren't rooted in your circumstances; you are rooted in the Most High God. Because He never changes, you can be immovable.

A PRAYER FOR TODAY

Father, thank You for Your love and goodness in our lives.
Thank You that You see every unexpected and uncertain
circumstance we will ever face together. We declare that our
peace and strength are in You and that our roots are
firmly set in You in Jesus' Name. Amen.

We Will Say

TODAY'S SCRIPTURE

*I will say of the LORD, "He is my refuge and my fortress,
my God, in whom I trust."*

Psalm 91:2 NIV

The psalmist says, "I will say of the Lord," and in the next verse he adds, "He will deliver me." Notice the connection: *I will say* and *He will do*. It doesn't say, "I believe He is my refuge." The psalmist spoke it out: "The Lord is my refuge." Notice what happened. God became his refuge and strength. God was saying in effect, "If you're bold enough to speak it, I'm bold enough to do it."

When we were trying to acquire the Compaq Center, we prayed about it together, believed that it would happen, and then we took the most important step and declared that it was ours. It became a part of our everyday conversation. "When we renovate it…When we have the grand opening…" We declared it, and God did it.

What are the two of you saying of the Lord? Are you declaring victory over your lives, over your family, over your careers? Nothing happens until you speak. You need to make some declarations of faith. Whatever God has put in your hearts, declare that it will come to pass. When you say of the Lord, "You're our healer, our way maker, our restorer, our vindicator, our health, our peace, our victory," God will show up and do more than you can ask or think of.

A PRAYER FOR TODAY

*Father, praise You for Your supernatural strength in our lives.
Thank You for Your Word that is refreshing water to our souls.
You are our refuge and strength. We choose to have an
attitude of faith and expectancy and to agree to say what
You say about us in Jesus' Name. Amen.*

OUR
BEST
LIFE
TOGETHER

We Declare

that we will live as healers.
We are sensitive to the
needs of those around us.
We will lift the fallen,
restore the broken, and
encourage the discouraged.
We are full of compassion
and kindness. We won't
just look for a miracle;
we will become someone's
miracle by showing
God's love and mercy
everywhere we go.

Your Mountain

TODAY'S SCRIPTURE

*"Now therefore, give me this mountain of which
the LORD spoke in that day…"*

Joshua 14:12 NKJV

When Caleb was eighty-five years old, forty years after the negative report of the other ten spies had kept him and the Israelites out of the Promised Land, he wasn't sitting around feeling sorry for himself and saying, "The others kept me out. I was so close to my destiny." No, he went back to the same mountain where three giants still lived, the place that the others refused to go in, and he said, "God, give me this mountain." There were many other mountains with less opposition, but Caleb said, "I'm not going to settle for mediocrity. That mountain is the dream that's been burning in me for all these years." Forty years after the dream was given, he conquered the mountain that God promised him.

Have the two of you allowed any dreams to get buried in you? At one time you thought you could do something great, but you had some bad breaks. You have a good excuse to settle; nobody would blame you if you did. But God sent us to light a fire inside you. That dream is still alive. God is saying to you what He said to Caleb, "Go back and try again. This is your time. Your destiny is calling out to you. Stir up your gifts, and go after what I put in your hearts."

A PRAYER FOR TODAY

*Father, thank You that whether Your promise is fulfilled in
our lives today or years from now, You will bring it to pass in
Your perfect time. Thank You that we too can declare that
every giant, every obstacle that stands in the way, will be
conquered in Jesus' Name. Amen.*

Serving Others

TODAY'S SCRIPTURE

*Jesus said, "The food that keeps me going is
that I do the will of the One who sent me,
finishing the work he started."*

John 4:34 MSG

Part of the reason God brought you together is to make
the lives of others better. Someone needs what you
have—your love, your smiles, your encouragements,
and your gifts.

When you serve others, you'll feel a satisfaction, peace, a
joy, a strength, and a fulfillment together that only God can give.
The Scripture tells a story about the disciples' surprise when they
found Jesus sitting beside a well, totally refreshed. When they had
left him, he was tired and hungry after traveling a long way to
Samaria. But in the meantime He had met a woman and given her
life a new beginning. Jesus explained the secret to His strength: "I
get fed by doing what God wants Me to do. My strength, peace,
joy, and satisfaction come when I serve others."

When you do the will of your Father, you feel energized, stronger, and refreshed. You may volunteer in your community or get up
early on Sunday and serve in the children's ministry. You'd think
you would leave tired, but when you help others, you get replen-
ished. Strength, joy, energy, peace, and healing come to those who
serve. God reenergizes and refreshes you so that at the end of the
day you aren't down, you are up. God pays you back.

A PRAYER FOR TODAY

*Father, we praise You that You brought us together to help
make the lives of others better. Thank You that we have something
that someone else needs and that we can follow Jesus' example
of a servant attitude. We declare that our food is to do Your
will in Jesus' Name. Amen.*

Remember Well

TODAY'S SCRIPTURE

*But do not be afraid of [the stronger nations];
remember well what the Lord your God
did to Pharaoh and to all Egypt.*

Deuteronomy 7:18 NIV

The Israelites had just come out of slavery and were up against huge armies. They had no military training or weapons and were just trying to survive in the desert. Headed toward the Promised Land, they didn't know how they could possibly overcome their enemies. But God was saying to them, "When it looks impossible, the way to stay encouraged is to remember what I've done in the past."

As with the Israelites, we have seen with our own eyes those times when God made a way. When you face tough times as a couple and your dream looks impossible, just remember. Go back and replay your victories. Relive the times when you thought you were stuck, but God opened a door. Remember how He put you at the right place at the right time and you met each other and fell in love. Remember how He spared your lives from that accident. If you're going to overcome obstacles, if you're going to reach your best life together, you have to learn to remember. When you're constantly thinking about God's goodness, how He's protected, vindicated, and promoted you, not only will faith rise in your hearts, but it's that attitude of expectancy that allows God to do great things.

A PRAYER FOR TODAY

Father, thank You for the history we have with You and for the mercies You have shown out in our lives. Thank You that we can remember the victories You've given us and the times when You made a way. We believe that You will continue to do great things in Jesus' Name. Amen.

Leave It Behind

TODAY'S SCRIPTURE

If you have anything against anyone, forgive him
and let it drop (leave it, let it go).

Mark 11:25 AMPC

Jesus was talking about what we should do when somebody does us wrong. Notice the principle of forgiveness:
drop the matter, leave it, and let it go. It's true for every
relationship you have, and especially for your marriage.
It's easy to get upset and be offended, but try a different approach:
drop it, leave it, and let it go. Don't spend another day being angry
or bitter. You're not hurting the other person; you're poisoning
yourselves.

The reason that Jesus says to leave it is that you may drop it at
first, but tomorrow when you think about what was said or done,
you'll want to pick up the hurt again. Some people keep picking up
the same offense for years. It's not a bag they carry anymore; it's a
part of who they are. You have to leave it.

What was done might not have been fair or kind, but God is a
God of justice. He'll make your wrongs right. When you leave it,
you're saying, "God, we trust You to be our vindicator and make
it right. We're leaving that offense with You." Your relationship is
too important to go through the day weighted down by offenses,
bitterness, guilt, and anger. Make the decision to not only drop it
but to leave it.

A PRAYER FOR TODAY

Father, thank You that we can forgive and release each other
from past offenses and hurts. Thank You that we can let go of
whatever it is, knowing You will make things right. Thank You
that we can drop the weights that hold us down and leave
them in Your hands in Jesus' Name. Amen.

Who's Your Father?

TODAY'S SCRIPTURE

See what great love the Father has lavished on us, that we should be called children of God! And that is what we are!

1 John 3:1 NIV

When you gave your lives to Christ, the Scripture says you were born into a new family. Now imagine that somehow we could take a sample DNA from your Heavenly Father, then a sample DNA from you, and run all the tests. The good news is that it would come back a perfect match. You are God's children!

Given your royal DNA, don't you dare go around thinking that you're average. *We could never accomplish our dreams or get out of debt.* Are you kidding? Your Father created worlds. There's nothing too much for you. You can overcome that sickness, build and support that orphanage, and take your family to a new level. Why? Because of Who your Father is.

Now when negative thoughts intrude, just go back and check your spiritual birth certificate. Remind yourselves of who you are, and just reply out loud, "Let's verify what's in our DNA from God's Word. Are we supposed to live average, lonely, and struggling? No, it says, 'God's favor surrounds us like a shield.' It declares, 'No weapon formed against us will prosper.' It says, 'We will lend and not borrow. Goodness and mercy are following us. Good breaks are chasing us down.'" That's what's in your DNA. Keep reminding yourselves of who you are.

A PRAYER FOR TODAY

Father, we praise You for the great love You have lavished upon us, that we should be called Your children and have royalty in our blood. Help us to remember who we are. We declare that there is nothing too much for us because You are our Father in Jesus' Name. Amen.

Connected

TODAY'S SCRIPTURE

How beautiful you are, my darling!...
How handsome you are, my beloved!

Song of Solomon 1:15–16 NIV

Your relationship is precious, a treasure from heaven, and you should handle it carefully, always looking for ways to build bridges to each other's hearts. The apostle Paul prayed that our love would abound and grow in knowledge and depth of insight, and that applies especially to our love as a couple. That tells us that we cannot put our love on autopilot. If we assume our spouse will "know" that we love them, our relationship will not grow or be as fruitful as it is intended to be. That's why it's so important to make every effort to keep strong connections.

Several years ago when we assumed leadership at the ministry, our lives became fuller and more complicated. Oftentimes, we found ourselves moving in different directions, so we had to make an extra effort to connect with each other. We decided to acknowledge each other every time we pass. Sometimes we high-five, sometimes it's a quick "I love you" or a kiss on the lips. Leaving sweet notes around the house is another easy way to keep connections. It's not so important *how* we connect, but it is important *that* we connect.

It takes time and effort to maintain the connections in your relationship. Take the time to regularly put everything else on hold for moments while you connect with loving words and touches. Keep your connection strong and you'll keep your hearts moving in the same direction.

A PRAYER FOR TODAY

Father, help us to be sensitive to each other and show
us how to stay connected. We declare that we will
take the time to keep our relationship strong
in Jesus' Name. Amen.

How Big God Is

TODAY'S SCRIPTURE

Death and life are in the power of the tongue,
and those who love it and indulge it will eat its fruit
and bear the consequences of their words.

Proverbs 18:21 AMP

Our words have tremendous power and are like seeds. By speaking them aloud, they are planted in our subconscious minds, take root, grow, and produce fruit of the same kind. Whether we speak positive or negative words, we will reap exactly what we sow in our relationship. We can't speak words of defeat and failure to each other and expect to live in victory.

You create an environment for either good or evil with your words, and you live in the world you've created. If you're always murmuring, complaining, and talking about how badly life is treating you, you're going to live in a pretty miserable world. However, God wants us to use our words to *change* our negative situations.

The Scripture clearly tells us to speak to our mountains (see Matt. 21:21). Maybe your mountain is a sickness, or trouble in your relationship, or a floundering business. Whatever your mountain is, you must do more than pray about it; you must speak to that obstacle. The Scripture says, "Let the weak say, 'I am strong.'" Start calling yourselves healed, happy, whole, blessed, and prosperous. God is a miracle-working God. Stop talking to God about how big your mountains are, and start talking to your mountains about how big your God is!

A PRAYER FOR TODAY

Father, thank You for the tremendous power that You give our words to change our lives. We choose to speak words of life to each other and over ourselves and our future. We declare that You are greater than any mountain we face in Jesus' Name. Amen.

Be Imitators of Christ

TODAY'S SCRIPTURE

*Therefore become imitators of God [copy Him
and follow His example], as well-beloved
children [imitate their father].*

Ephesians 5:1 AMP

The Scripture tells us to be imitators of Christ. His life should be our example as individuals and as a couple. If we're going to be like Jesus, this means that we're going to have some people come against us, people who talk and try to make us look bad. We're going to be misunderstood and criticized. We're going to have a Garden of Gethsemane where we feel alone and abandoned. This is why many couples get bitter and sour. They let excuses hold them back, such as, "Look what happened to us. These people did us wrong."

It's interesting that when Judas came to betray Jesus, even though Jesus already knew it, He said to Judas, "Friend, what are you here for?" Jesus still called him "friend." His attitude was, *I won't let what you're about to do to steal My joy. My Father has the final say. In the end I'm going to come out wearing the victor's crown.* When we go through these times that seem unfair, if we'll do like Jesus and not get bitter, but trust God to work it out for our good, it won't get the best of us. At some point we too will be wearing the victor's crown and move into a new level of our destiny together.

A PRAYER FOR TODAY

*Father, we love You for calling us to become imitators of Jesus.
When we go through unfair things, we thank You that we can copy
His example and trust that You will work it out for our good.
We believe that we will come out of it wearing the victor's
crown in Jesus' Name. Amen.*

We Declare

we will put actions behind
our faith. We will not be
passive or indifferent.
We will demonstrate our
faith by taking bold steps
to move toward what God
has put in our hearts.
Our faith will not be hidden;
it will be seen. We know
that when God sees our
faith He will show up and
do amazing things.

A Hundredfold Harvest

TODAY'S SCRIPTURE

When Isaac planted his crops that year, he harvested
a hundred times more grain than he planted,
for the LORD blessed him.

Genesis 26:12 NLT

During a great famine in the land, Isaac was about to move to Egypt, but God said, "No, stay where you are among the Philistines. I'm blessing you right here." So Isaac obeyed God's command and planted his fields. The Philistines ridiculed him for planting grain during the famine. But Isaac, whose name means "laughter," stayed in peace. Several months later, his critics were amazed to see his hundredfold harvest, but Isaac knew God had blessed him.

At some point, you may be dealing with critics, backbiters, those who are jealous and who say you'll never succeed, but you don't have to leave in order to be blessed as a couple. God wants to bless you right where you are. Part of His vindication is promoting you so the opposition can see it. Your attitude should be: *They may be laughing now, but this challenge is preparing the way for God to promote us!*

Let us assure you that God will make sure they see you promoted, honored, and accomplished. Let God right your wrongs. If you let Him do the avenging, you will always come out better. He will use it to thrust you forward. God is faithful. In the end, you will have the last laugh. He will bring justice into your lives.

A PRAYER FOR TODAY

Father, thank You for giving us Your promises to meditate upon
and for the promise to bless us right where we are. We believe
that You will multiply us even in the midst of famine. We receive
Your peace and rest knowing that You will bring justice
into our lives in Jesus' Name. Amen.

Wonderfully Made

TODAY'S SCRIPTURE

I praise you because I am fearfully and wonderfully made; your works are wonderful, I know that full well.

Psalm 139:14 NIV

When God created you both, He went to great lengths to make you exactly as He wanted. You didn't accidentally get your personality, your height, your looks, or your gifts. God designed you on purpose to be the way you are. You have what you need to fulfill your destiny. If you needed to be different in any way, God would have made you that way. You have to be confident in who God made you to be. When He created you, He stepped back and stamped His "Made by Almighty God" approval on you.

How many of us are bold enough to say as David did, "I am amazing. I am fearfully and wonderfully made." Those thoughts never enter into most people's minds. They're too busy putting themselves down, focusing on their flaws, comparing themselves to others they think are better. Your Creator says, "You're amazing. You're My most prized possessions. You're masterpieces." Now it's up to you to get in agreement with God.

The recording that should be playing in your minds all day long is, "We are valuable. We are masterpieces. We are children of the Most High God." Could it be this is what's holding you back? Your recordings are negative. Don't be against yourselves. Change your recording. Start seeing yourselves as the masterpieces God created you to be.

A PRAYER FOR TODAY

Father, thank You that we didn't accidentally get our personalities, our looks, or our gifts. Thank You that we are Your masterpieces, and that's what You have declared about us. We boldly declare that we are fearfully and wonderfully made in Jesus' Name. Amen.

Burst into Song

TODAY'S SCRIPTURE

*"Sing, barren woman, you who never bore
a child; burst into song, shout for joy,
you who were never in labor."*

Isaiah 54:1 NIV

Too often we think, *When we see God's promise, we'll
sing and thank Him.* But that's backward; you have to
sing first. Notice that Isaiah wasn't writing this Scripture
to women who had been blessed with a promised child.
It's a promise written to people who are waiting for the promise,
believing for the healing, hoping for the child to come home. What
are you supposed to do when you're barren? Complain and get
discouraged? No, Isaiah said, "Sing! Burst into song."

Here's the key: praise is the birth position. The Scripture says,
"God inhabits the praises of His people." Thanking God is what
causes the promise to come to pass. When you start singing, we
can imagine God saying to the angels, "What's that sound I'm
hearing? Most people would be complaining, but they're thanking
Me that the answer is on the way. They're singing about the victory
before they've seen the victory. Angels, go to work and bring that
dream to pass." When you kick into praise and say, "Lord, thank
You for Your goodness in our lives, for Your favor, for new levels,
for new opportunities," that's getting into the birth position. If
you'll live with an attitude of praise, you'll give birth to everything
God has put in your hearts.

A PRAYER FOR TODAY

*Father, You alone are worthy of our praise, and we come to
You with hearts full of praise. Thank You that You inhabit our
praise, that You are here with us now and in all the circumstances
of our lives. We choose to live with an attitude of praise
and honor in Jesus' Name. Amen.*

Embrace the Change

TODAY'S SCRIPTURE

"Woe...to him who quarrels with his Maker...
Shall the clay say to the potter, 'What are you doing?'"

Isaiah 45:9 AMP

Sometimes God will stir us out of comfortable situations and push us into situations that force us to stretch our faith and enter into a new season as a couple. It may be uncomfortable, but God loves you too much to let you get stagnant. You may be in a perfectly fine situation for years, but just as He opened that door, all of a sudden He closes it. Nothing happens by accident. God is directing each of your steps. That means if a friend does you wrong, if you go through a setback, if you lose someone, or if your workplace changes, you can either embrace that change and God will use it to take you higher, or you can resist it and end up becoming stagnant and settling for mediocrity. Stay open for change. It may be negative on the surface, but remember that God would not allow it if He didn't have a purpose for it.

It's easy to become negative or bitter: "God, why is this happening? We thought we had Your favor." But a much better approach is to just stay open and know that God is still in control. If you will embrace that change, the winds that you thought would defeat you will actually push you to your divine destiny.

A PRAYER FOR TODAY

Father, we love You for being our Maker. You are the Potter and we are glad to be the clay. Thank You that You are behind the changes in our lives, and You are working them in our behalf. We choose to put our trust in You alone and to embrace the changes in Jesus' Name. Amen.

Blessed Indeed

TODAY'S SCRIPTURE

Jabez cried out to the God of Israel, "Oh, that you would bless me and enlarge my territory!"

1 Chronicles 4:10 NIV

The name *Jabez* literally means "pain, sorrow, suffering." Every time someone said, "Hello, Jabez," they were saying, "Hello, sorrow. Hello, pain." They were prophesying defeat and failure. You can imagine how he could have let that make him feel inferior and insecure. But despite what people labeled him, despite the expectancy that he would live depressed and defeated, he had the boldness to ask big, that God would bless him and enlarge his territories. He was saying, "God, let me see abundance. Let me see more of Your favor." And God blessed him indeed.

Like Jabez, you may have plenty of reasons to settle where you are—what you didn't get, what people said, how impossible it looks. The odds may be against you as a couple, but the good news is that God is for you. He knows how to make up for what you didn't get. He can thrust you further than you ever imagined, but you have to pray bold prayers. Ask in spite of what the circumstances look like and what people are telling you. Ask in spite of what the enemy keeps whispering in your ears. If you're going to beat the odds, stand out in the crowd, and reach your best life together, you have to learn this principle of asking big.

A PRAYER FOR TODAY

Father, thank You that when the odds are against us, You are for us. Thank You that nothing and no one is more powerful than You and that we can dare to pray bold prayers. We believe that You are blessing us as You did Jabez and enlarging our territory in Jesus' Name. Amen.

When the Pressure Is On

*"I will not speak with you much longer,
for the ruler of the world (Satan) is coming."*

John 14:30 AMP

Toward the end of Jesus' life, He knew He was coming into His most difficult season. He knew He would be betrayed, arrested, and crucified on the cross. He realized that He was going to be under incredible pressure, so He told His disciples, "I've already made up My mind that I'm not going to be talking much more with you." He was saying, "I'm going to watch My words carefully. I'm not going to complain when I'm betrayed, or argue with the soldiers, or be disrespectful to My accusers."

When you face situations where it's stressful for you as a couple, pressured situations where you know you're going to be tempted to say things you shouldn't, you need to make up your mind ahead of time that you're going to watch your words carefully. If Jesus, the Son of God, Who has all power, said, "I'm not going to talk much in this pressured situation," how much more should we be careful about what we say in pressured times? You need to make up your minds, "We're not going to say everything we feel. We're going to be extra careful. We're going to keep our cool and not open the door to strife, arguing, and contention." All through the day, say, "Lord, thank You for keeping our lips sealed."

A PRAYER FOR TODAY

*Father, thank You that Your hand of protection is upon our
lives and that You are watching over us. We choose to watch
our words carefully when stress and pressure come against us.
We believe that You will help us to keep the door to strife
shut, helping us to know when to keep our lips
sealed in Jesus' Name. Amen.*

Always Give Thanks

TODAY'S SCRIPTURE

*Be thankful in all circumstances, for this is God's will
for you who belong to Christ Jesus.*

1 Thessalonians 5:18 NLT

David spent years in the lonely shepherds' fields taking care of his father's sheep. What's interesting is that he had already been anointed to be the next king of Israel. David could have thought, *God, You promised me great things. What am I doing stuck out here?* But David knew that God was in control, so he just kept being his best, going to work with a good attitude, grateful for where he was. Because he was content in the shepherds' fields, he made it to the throne. He passed that test.

You have to train your mind to see the good, to be grateful for what you have. Life will go so much better if you will be content in each season. Content when you have a lot, and content when you don't. Content whether your children are in diapers or whether they're in college. Content whether you're in maintenance or management.

You have the grace you need to enjoy each season. If your dreams are not coming to pass, that's a test. Will you choose to enjoy that season and not just endure it, thinking, *God, when is this ever going to change?* Maybe it's going to change when you change. You have to be satisfied with where God has you right now.

A PRAYER FOR TODAY

*Father, we come to You with thanksgiving for all the circumstances
in our lives. Help us to keep the right perspective on what is
going on, to always see the good, and to be grateful for what
we have now. We choose to enjoy the season we are in and
not just endure it in Jesus' Name. Amen.*

Pregnant with Possibility

TODAY'S SCRIPTURE

...being confident of this, that he who began a good work in you will carry it on to completion until the day of Christ Jesus.

Philippians 1:6 NIV

Psalm 7 says the ungodly "are pregnant with trouble." The good news is that that's not you. You are the righteous. You're not pregnant with trouble, with bad breaks, sickness, or lack. You are pregnant with favor, with talent, with victory. All through the day keep saying, "Lord, we thank You that we're pregnant with Your promises, that we will give birth to everything You've put in us." It may not look in the natural as though anything is changing, but you choose to believe that conception has occurred. In God's perfect timing, you're going to give birth to the promises.

Your family may be struggling with dysfunction in your home. Don't live worried. You are pregnant with restoration, with the breakthrough. Maybe business is slow, but you can feel something kicking on the inside, something saying, "You are the head and not the tail. Whatever you touch will prosper and succeed." Realize that you are pregnant with possibility. Quit telling yourselves that you can never get ahead, that you don't have enough of this, enough of that. You are pregnant with success, with ideas, with your destiny. You're going to give birth to what God has put in you. What God started, He will finish.

A PRAYER FOR TODAY

Father, thank You for all the potential You have placed within the two of us, all the gifts, talents, and ideas. Thank You that the seed has taken root in our lives and is growing. We declare that in Your perfect timing we will give birth to what You have put in us in Jesus' Name. Amen.

OUR
BEST
LIFE
TOGETHER

We Declare

breakthroughs are coming
in our lives, sudden bursts of
God's goodness. Not a trickle.
Not a stream. But a flood
of God's power. A flood of
healing. A flood of wisdom.
A flood of favor. We are
a breakthrough people,
and we choose to live
breakthrough minded.
We are expecting God to
overwhelm us with His
goodness and amaze
us with His favor.

Space for the Good Things

TODAY'S SCRIPTURE

*"The accuser of our brethren, who accused them before
our God day and night, has been cast down."*

Revelation 12:10 NKJV

The enemy is called "the accuser of the brethren." He'll
remind you of everything you've ever done wrong. It's
easy to live in regrets, thinking, *We should have raised our
children better. We should have saved more for retirement
and been more disciplined in going to church.* Don't go through
life looking in your rearview mirror, being down on yourselves.
You can't do anything about the past, but you can do something
about your future. The moment you asked God to forgive you, He
forgave you. Why don't you forgive yourselves and empty out all
the guilt? Turn off the accusing voices that try to deceive you into
living with condemnation.

If you are giving *any* space to guilt, to regret, to being down on
yourselves, it's too much. You need that space for the good things
God has for you as a couple—His grace, mercy, and favor. None
of us deserve to be blessed. This is what mercy is all about. Your
sins have already been paid for and forgiven. You don't have to
pay God back. When you fall, get back up. When the accuser says,
"Look at the two of you. You blew it again!" just answer, "We're
not perfect, but we are forgiven and we're moving forward."
Don't let guilt poison your future together.

A PRAYER FOR TODAY

*Father, thank You that there is no condemnation for those who
are in Christ Jesus, and that includes us. Thank You that the
enemy has no power over our lives. We declare that we're
not perfect, but we are forgiven, and we're moving forward
in victory in Jesus' Name. Amen.*

Keep the Door Shut

TODAY'S SCRIPTURE

*"Any kingdom divided by civil war is doomed. A town
or family splintered by feuding will fall apart."*

Matthew 12:25 NLT

Many years ago, our family went for a bike ride. Things
hadn't gone my way that day, and I was aggravated
by some little thing Victoria had done that I chose to
magnify and let sour me. I knew it was wrong, but the
flesh likes to have its way. I remember thinking, *She aggravated me.
I'm miserable, and I'm going to make her miserable.* I opened the
door to the enemy.

We were riding on a paved bike trail and supposedly having
fun, but I was wrecking it by the tension I created. Then suddenly
another biker came down the trail full speed, and when our son,
Jonathan, looked up at him, he drove his bike right into the man's
path. They had a huge head-on collision. Jonathan went flying
off his bike, the man tumbling over in the grass. I ran over as fast
as I could, thinking Jonathan must have broken his arm or leg.
Thankfully all he and the man had were scrapes and bruises. As
we walked back to the car, I felt an inner impression saying, "Joel,
this could have all been avoided if you had kept the strife out."
The Scripture says that where there's strife, there's going to be
unnecessary trouble. Don't be stubborn as I was. Don't open the
door to trouble.

A PRAYER FOR TODAY

*Father, we have no excuses for those times when we blow it
in our relationship. Thank You that there is always forgiveness
and restoration through the shed blood of Jesus. We believe
that You have the power to help us shut any doors that
bring us trouble in Jesus' Name. Amen.*

A New Song

TODAY'S SCRIPTURE

He lifted me out of the pit of despair...
He has given me a new song to sing,
a hymn of praise to our God.

Psalm 40:2-3 NLT

The apostle Paul said, "Do all things without complaining." It's easy to complain. There's always some reason to complain about your boss, about the traffic, about each other. We create much of our own unhappiness by how we respond to negative things, how we approach life. Here's the key: when you complain, you remain; but when you praise, you'll be raised. When you have this new song in your heart, you'll see more of His favor. When you develop a habit of always thinking about God's goodness, seeing the best, singing a hymn of praise, you'll have joy despite what's happening around you.

David didn't say that God gave him a song of "I can't believe this happened. You should see the hardships I've endured and the people who have done me wrong." No, it was a song of praise and thanksgiving in his heart. You might have been through some difficulties together, but you have to start making a new melody in your heart. Start thanking God that new doors are opening and that your best days are still ahead. If you get your song back, you'll start feeling the joy bubbling up, you'll get your passion back, and see your dreams start coming to life.

A PRAYER FOR TODAY

Father, we worship You because You are worthy Almighty God.
Thank You that You put a new song in our hearts that lifts us
up no matter what is happening around us. We choose to
shut the door of complaining and declare that our best days
are still ahead in Jesus' Name. Amen.

Different Gifts

TODAY'S SCRIPTURE

We have different gifts, according to the
grace given to each of us.

Romans 12:6 NIV

O ne of the best things we've ever learned is to be comfortable with who God made us to be and the gifts He's given us. You don't have to have a great gift for God to use it in a great way. Did you know that the gift that put David on the throne wasn't his leadership skills, his dynamic personality, or his ability to write and play music? It was his gift to be a sharpshooter with a slingshot. He could have thought, *Big deal. This is not going to get me anywhere.* But it was this seemingly insignificant gift that enabled him to defeat Goliath and eventually put David on the throne.

The gifts that God has given you may seem insignificant compared to other people you know. But there's something God has given you that's unique, something that will cause you to leave your mark on this generation. That slingshot, your gift, may seem ordinary, but it's not so much what you have. It's the anointing that God puts on it. When God breathes on it, you'll defeat a giant twice your size. You'll be promoted beyond your talent. You'll go places where you weren't qualified. You weren't next in line, but suddenly a door opened and the dream comes to pass.

A PRAYER FOR TODAY

Father, we love You and worship You with all our hearts.
Thank You that we can just be the best that we can be with
what we have, and You will take care of the rest. We believe
that as we walk in Your anointing that our gifts and talents
will come out to the full in Jesus' Name. Amen.

The Right People

TODAY'S SCRIPTURE

*Do two people walk hand in hand if they
aren't going to the same place?*

Amos 3:3 MSG

The word *crutch* is used to describe something or some-one we may rely on short-term to help us get through a period of challenge, just until we heal or can get by on our own. The term takes on a bad connotation when used to describe someone whom we've become unnecessarily dependent upon, usually to the detriment of our physical, mental, or emotional progress. One of the hardest things to accept is that God brings some people into our lives for only a season, maybe a mentor, a teacher, or a friend, to help us through a certain stage of life or a difficult time. If God didn't move them away, we would become too dependent. Instead of helping us, they would limit our growth.

Just as God brings people into our lives, He moves some out. You have to recognize when someone's part in your life story is over, whether individually or as a couple. When a person walks away and you think you can't get along without them, that's God saying, "It's time for you to go to a new level." Don't try to per-suade them to stay beyond their usefulness. Let them go. Your destiny is not tied to them.

God will always bring the right people into your lives, but unless you let the wrong people walk away, the right people will never show up.

A PRAYER FOR TODAY

Father, thank You that we can submit every relationship in our lives to You. We trust that You are connecting us to the right people and removing people who are no longer tied to our purpose. Give us wisdom and grace to choose the best relationships in Jesus' Name. Amen.

Come Over into Hope

TODAY'S SCRIPTURE

Hope deferred makes the heart sick,
but a longing fulfilled is a tree of life.
Proverbs 13:12 NIV

f you don't have hope that your problems are going to turn around, hope that your relationship can be renewed every day, that the new house is in your future, that your baby is on the way, then your heart is going to be sick. When you're not hopeful, positive, and expecting God's goodness, something on the inside is wrong. We all go through seasons in life when things aren't exciting. It's easy to have the blahs and lose our enthusiasm. No couple lives on cloud nine with everything perfect and exciting every day. Part of the good fight of faith is to stay hopeful in the dry seasons.

Remember, if you're not anchored to hope, over time you'll become anchored to discouragement, self-pity, and even bitterness. You'll become so focused on who hurt you and what wasn't fair that bitterness poisons your whole lives. We're not making light of what's happened. You may have a good reason to feel that way. We're simply saying that being anchored to those negative things is going to cause you to miss your purpose. It's time to cut that anchor and come over into hope. God created you to be anchored to hope, to go out each day expecting His goodness, believing that the days ahead are better than the days behind.

A PRAYER FOR TODAY

Father, this is a new day for us, and You empower us with
hope to cut any line that anchors us to negativity. Thank You
for the sense of expectancy rising in our hearts that You
have good things in store for us. We're coming over
into hope in Jesus' Name. Amen.

A Second Time

TODAY'S SCRIPTURE

The angel of the LORD came back a second time
and touched him and said, "Get up and eat,
for the journey is too much for you."

1 Kings 19:7 NIV

The prophet Elijah had just gone from one of the greatest victories of his life to running away in defeat at the threats of Queen Jezebel. He was sitting under a tree so depressed that he didn't want to live. He'd just seen a tremendous miracle, but now he was tired of fighting, tired of standing strong. Maybe like Elijah you've been doing the right thing, praying and believing, seeing victories, but now you're tired. You've lost your drive. You may not have given up on life but given up on your dreams. Here's the good news: God will send somebody to breathe new life into the dreams you have together. Maybe we're that somebody for you. You're not reading this by accident. God is saying that the best of your life as a couple is still out in front of you. He has new victories, new friendships, new mountains for you to climb.

God doesn't condemn us or write us off because we weren't strong enough. God sent an angel to feed Elijah once, and then a second time to strengthen him. That is how good God is, and that is what He'll do for you. He's coming a second time with blessings to push you into the fullness of your destiny.

A PRAYER FOR TODAY

Father, we praise You for Your peace that passes understanding.
Thank You for Your promise of coming to us a second time to
renew us with strength and breathe new life into our dreams.
We believe that You are coming again to cause blessings to
chase us down in Jesus' Name. Amen.

From Good to Very Good

TODAY'S SCRIPTURE

And God said, "Let there be light," and there was light.
God saw that the light was good.

Genesis 1:3–4 NIV

On day one of creation, God said, "Let there be light," and light came. There were no planets and the earth was formless and empty, but God said it was "good." If someone had been watching, they would have said, "But it's a mess. Nothing is in order." And He would have responded, "I'm not finished. Wait till you see what it looks like when it's 'very good' at the end of day six."

Sometimes we're hard on ourselves as couples. We focus on the areas where we don't measure up. We all have flaws, weaknesses, and shortcomings, but being down on yourselves only makes you do worse. Dwelling on that is going to hold you back. You need to focus on what you're doing right. Find the good.

If you're complaining about what's not working out, why you're still dealing with your tempers or arguing, you're going to get stuck. Don't wait till it's totally complete, till it's very good, to give God thanks. Find the good along the way; thank Him for the partial. If you don't celebrate the good in day one, in the season that you're in, you won't see day two. If you'll be grateful for the good, God will get you to very good.

A PRAYER FOR TODAY

Father, we praise You that You created the heavens and earth,
and You made us as well. Thank You that You're not finished
working in our lives, and we celebrate the good in our relationship.
We believe that as we give thanks for the good that You will
get us to very good in Jesus' Name. Amen.

OUR
BEST
LIFE
TOGETHER

We Declare

there is an anointing of
ease on our lives. God is going
before us making crooked
places straight. His yoke
is easy and His burden is
light. We will not continually
struggle. What used to be
difficult will not be difficult
anymore. God's favor
and blessing on our lives
are lightening the load
and taking the
pressure off.

Look Down in Triumph

TODAY'S SCRIPTURE

In his unfailing love, my God will stand with me.
He will let me look down in triumph on all my enemies.

Psalm 59:10 NLT

D avid faced all kinds of enemies and looked down on them in triumph. Notice that David did not say "*some* of my enemies." No, "*all* my enemies." You may be facing a sickness or financial difficulty that doesn't look or feel like it's under you. But we walk by faith and not by sight. In the natural, a setback or fear or depression may look huge, but when you talk to these obstacles by faith, you need to look down. They're under your feet.

If God be for you, who dare be against you? Quit telling yourselves, "We'll always struggle in this area. We'll never lose weight. We'll never get out of debt." Change your perspective. You are not weak, defeated, or inferior. You are full of "can do" power. The same Spirit that raised Christ from the dead lives on the inside of both of you. Now start putting things under your feet. Jesus says, "I have given you power to tread over all the power of the enemy" (see Luke 10:19). One translation says "power to trample." If you will see these obstacles as being under your feet, as being already defeated, a new boldness will rise up. Your faith will activate God's power in a new way.

A PRAYER FOR TODAY

Father, we praise You for Your loving-kindness. Thank You that You have given us power to tread on all the power of the enemy and to become mighty overcomers by the power of Your Holy Spirit at work in us. We declare that we will live with a victor's mentality in Jesus' Name. Amen.

When You Just "Know"

TODAY'S SCRIPTURE

*...now we serve...[under obedience to the promptings]
of the Spirit in newness [of life].*

Romans 7:6 AMPC

We know that God says things such as "go into all the world and preach the good news." But He also says, "Slow down on the freeway, forgive your coworker, be good to your neighbor." Pay attention to His promptings. One way you can know God's promptings is when you hear it again and again. It comes up at night, when you're not thinking about it. That's the Holy Spirit trying to get your attention. The more you respond in obedience, the more favor God will release in your lives.

Isaiah 1:19 says, "If you are willing and obedient, you shall eat the best of the land." Learn this principle to just obey, so that when you hear a prompting to be more disciplined in your spending, or perhaps to call a friend who needs an encouraging word, you're obedient. You have that knowing on the inside—*we know we need to eat healthier, to take that class at church together, or to spend more time with the children.* Here's a key: the "we knows" are God talking to you. *We know we need to forgive.* That's not just you deciding to do it. That's God saying to do it. Don't discount it or push it down. That still small voice is going to lead you down the best path.

A PRAYER FOR TODAY

Father, we love You and worship You. Thank You for the ways that You are speaking to us. We ask You to make us sensitive to Your promptings so that we know beyond a shadow of a doubt what You want us to do. We believe that You have the best life in store for us together as we keep believing in Jesus' Name. Amen.

Controllers

TODAY'S SCRIPTURE

The fear of human opinion disables;
trusting in God protects you from that.

Proverbs 29:25 MSG

Some people are peace stealers. They always have a problem, always want your help, and always are in crisis mode. They expect you to come running, to cheer them up, to keep them encouraged. And if you don't, they make you feel guilty. You love them, but you should put up a boundary to keep them from continually dumping their problems on you. You are not responsible for other people's happiness or to keep them fixed.

You have to protect your peace. You have a limited supply of emotional energy each day. If you're taking on all their problems, you're not going to have the emotional energy for each other and for your family. You're not their savior; they already have a Savior. A lot of times instead of helping these people, we're simply enabling their dysfunction.

If you put up some boundaries, your lives will be more peaceful and more effective. When you tell someone, "I can't talk with you now. I'm not going to bail you out again. I don't have time to come over," if they get upset, they really weren't your friend; they were controllers, manipulators. They like you for what you can do for them, not for who you are. You don't need "friends" like that. Make a change, and God will give you true friends.

A PRAYER FOR TODAY

Father, You alone are our Provider. Thank You that You have
called us to love and help others, but not to try to fix them or
make them happy. Help us to protect our own emotional energy.
We declare that we are not responsible for other people's
happiness in Jesus' Name. Amen.

Take Responsibility

TODAY'S SCRIPTURE

And he said to them, "...I know that this
great tempest is because of me."
Jonah 1:12 NKJV

God told the prophet Jonah to go preach to the city of Nineveh, but when he got on a boat headed in the opposite direction, the Lord sent a violent storm to get his attention. You can't pray away the winds when you're the reason for the storm. God loves you too much to let you miss your destiny. Fortunately, when confronted by the sailors, Jonah admitted, "I'm the cause." That's the first step to victory. God ultimately spared Jonah and gave him a second chance to do the right thing.

Our great God has fish ready to come and save us. He'll make a miracle out of your mistake. But as long as you make excuses, the difficulties are going to continue. At some point you have to take responsibility and say, "We've been negative and critical with each other. We've not been disciplined in our spending or in what we're watching. The problem is our own." God's not asking you to never make a mistake, but He is asking you to deal with things that are holding you back, to not let the same areas of compromise keep you down year after year. He wants to grow you up. God has some Ninevehs for you to go to, people for you to impact, new levels of your destiny.

A PRAYER FOR TODAY

Father, we praise You that You love us too much to let us miss
our destiny. Thank You that You give us second chances when
we go the wrong way. We choose to stop making excuses
for our mistakes and to deal with whatever holds us back
from the next level in Jesus' Name. Amen.

Crowned with Favor

TODAY'S SCRIPTURE

You have crowned him with glory and honor.

Psalm 8:5 AMP

n the Scripture, many of God's promises are put in the past tense as though they already happened. God says, "I have blessed you with every spiritual blessing." "I have made you worthy." "I have surrounded you with favor as a shield." Now you must do your part and come into agreement with God. You may not feel blessed today as a couple. A lot of things may be coming against you with your family, with your finances, or with your health. But you have to say, "God, since You say we're blessed, our report is we are blessed."

When you get in agreement with God like that, it allows Him to release the promises that already have your name on them. You have to reprogram your thinking. For instance, God says He has already crowned you with favor. You may not realize it, but there are crowns of God's favor, glory, and honor on your heads right now. If you are to activate that favor, you must get in agreement with God by declaring, "We do have favor." When discouraging thoughts come and try to convince you that nothing good is in store, just as an act of faith you need to reach up and make sure your crowns of favor are on straight. God has already blessed you. He has already given you crowns of favor.

A PRAYER FOR TODAY

*Father, praise You that You have put a crown of glory
and honor on our heads. Thank You for Your abundant
provision of favor. We declare that we do have
Your favor and it is ours as a gift of righteousness
in Jesus' Name. Amen.*

A Spacious Land

TODAY'S SCRIPTURE

*"So I have come down to...bring them up out
of that land into a good and spacious land,
a land flowing with milk and honey."*

Exodus 3:8 NIV

Receive this into your spirits. God is bringing you into a spacious land that's flowing with increase, flowing with good breaks, flowing with opportunities, where you not only have enough for yourselves, but you're running over. Running over with space, with supplies, with opportunities. If you're not in a good and spacious place, don't settle there. That is not your permanent address. God is taking you to a good and a spacious land.

We call this having an abundant mentality. The apostle John prayed "that in every way you may succeed and prosper and be in good health, just as your soul prospers" (see 3 John 2). Prosperity to us is having your health, having peace in your minds, being able to sleep at night, and having good relationships. We can't find a single verse in the Scripture that suggests we are supposed to drag around not having enough, not able to afford what we want, living off the leftovers, in the land of not enough.

Jesus came that we might live an abundant life. It's that we are children of the King. We represent Almighty God here on this earth. We should be examples of His goodness—so blessed, so prosperous, so generous, and so full of joy that other people want what we have.

A PRAYER FOR TODAY

*Father, we praise You for Your goodness. Thank You that You
take pleasure in providing for our prosperity and health and
well-being. Help us to develop an abundant mentality.
We believe that You are bringing us into a life of overflow
and abundance in Jesus' Name. Amen.*

Only Believe

TODAY'S SCRIPTURE

*But overhearing what they said, Jesus said to the ruler
of the synagogue, "Do not fear, only believe."*

Mark 5:36 ESV

O ne of the greatest abilities God has given each of us is our ability to believe. If you believe, you can be successful, overcome mistakes of the past, and fulfill your God-given destiny. The apostle Paul prayed that we would understand the incredible greatness of God's power for those who believe. That means right now the Creator of the universe is just waiting to release healing, restoration, favor, promotion, and abundance. The only catch is that we have to believe.

Notice the phrase "only believe" in today's Scripture. This was Jesus' promise to the father who had just been told his daughter had died. Jesus prayed for the little girl, and she came back to life. You may be facing situations that seem impossible. In the natural you can't see how you could ever be healthy or how your family could ever be restored. But God is saying, "Only believe, and breakthroughs will head your way."

It's not complicated. God didn't say, "If you pray three hours a day together, I'll do it for you." No, He said, "Only believe." If you will just get your minds going in the right direction and believe, you can rise higher. Believe you can overcome the obstacle. Believe your family can be restored. Believe you can do something great and make your mark in this generation.

A PRAYER FOR TODAY

*Father, when You put a promise in our hearts that seems
impossible, help us to respond with "Lord, we believe." We want
to get into agreement with You and see the incredible greatness
of Your power activated. We believe that breakthroughs are
headed our way in Jesus' Name. Amen.*

Your Inner Circle

TODAY'S SCRIPTURE

He did not let anyone follow him except Peter,
James and John the brother of James.

Mark 5:37 NIV

Your destiny as a couple is too great to reach on your own. God has already arranged supporters to speak faith into you, to inspire and challenge you to accomplish your dreams. But some couples never reach their best life together because they never get away from the wrong people. Not everyone can go where God is taking you. Connect with those who understand your destiny, who appreciate your uniqueness, who can call forth your seeds of greatness.

Is your inner circle of friends holding the two of you back? Are those closest to you *with* you but not *for* you? If you find that it takes constant effort to win their support and encouragement, they likely don't understand your destiny. True friends, people who really believe in you, won't be jealous of your gifts or constantly question who you are. They won't try to talk you out of your dreams. Rather, they'll give you ideas, connect you with people they know, and help push you further along. If that doesn't describe those in your inner circle, move them out. You can still be friends from a distance. But it is better to have two good friends who you know are for you 100 percent than to have fifty friends who are only for you 80 percent.

A PRAYER FOR TODAY

Father, thank You for the people You've brought into our lives
who inspire us to become the people You want us to be. Empower
us with boldness to walk away from those who are dragging
us down and holding us back so we can make room for the
right relationships in Jesus' Name. Amen.

OUR
BEST
LIFE
TOGETHER

We Declare

that we are calm and peaceful. We will not let people or circumstances upset us. We will rise above every difficulty, knowing that God has given us the power to remain calm. We choose to live our lives happy, bloom where we are planted, and let God fight our battles.

Have Fun Together

TODAY'S SCRIPTURE

He makes me lie down in green pastures,
he leads me beside quiet waters.

Psalm 23:2 NIV

The Scripture says that our body is the temple of the Holy Spirit and we must take care of it. You can't go against natural laws and expect God to bless you. Constant busyness and fatigue will make you feel flat and your marriage seem stale. It's easy to get up early, stay up late, and always be thinking about business and problems you must solve. That's doing yourselves and the people around you a disservice. Your mind needs a break; your body needs to relax. That's why God required the people in the Old Testament to take a Sabbath. They had to rest.

If you live stressed out and overworked, don't eat right or sleep enough, eventually God will *make* you lie down in green pastures. You'll probably wear yourselves out to a point where you have to rest. You need to take time for recreation and laugh and have fun together. Laughter is like medicine that releases stress and causes you to have more energy. Don't be so busy that you become unaware of each other's needs or those of your family. Listen to what they're saying. Pray with and for each other and with your children. Speak positive and encouraging words over each other, and you will reap a harvest in due season.

A PRAYER FOR TODAY

Father, thank You that You made us to work hard and be
productive, but also to rest and relax, to laugh and have fun
together. Help us to guard our relationship and keep
it healthy in Jesus' Name. Amen.

Speak to the Mountain

TODAY'S SCRIPTURE

"...if anyone says to this mountain, 'Go, throw yourself into the sea,' and does not doubt in their heart but believes...it will be done for them."

Mark 11:23 NIV

When David faced the giant Goliath, he didn't complain and say, "God, why do I always have huge problems?" No, he changed his whole atmosphere through the words that came out of his mouth. Rather than focus on the magnitude of the obstacle before him, David focused on the greatness of God. He spoke directly to the mountain of a man in front of him and said, "You come against me with sword and shield, but I come against you in the name of the Lord God of Israel," and he brought him down! He didn't merely *think* or *pray* these words of faith.

Those are the kinds of words you must learn to speak together in your everyday circumstances, and especially in times of crisis and adversity. There is a miracle in your mouths. If you want to change your world, start by changing your words. When you're facing obstacles in your path, you must boldly say, "Greater is He Who is in us than he who is in the world. No weapon formed against us is going to prosper. God always causes us to triumph." If you learn how to speak the right words and keep the right attitude, God will turn your situations around.

A PRAYER FOR TODAY

Father, we praise for Your presence in our lives. We refuse to be intimidated or to shrink back and think that our problems are too big. We speak to the mountains in our lives and say, "Be moved!" We declare that You are greater than anything that is against us in Jesus' Name. Amen.

Strength in Reserve

TODAY'S SCRIPTURE

"As your days, so shall your strength be."
Deuteronomy 33:25 NKJV

As long as you drive a large SUV with an eight-cylinder engine on flat roads, the engine is quiet. But when you start going up a steep mountain road, you hear those extra two cylinders kick in and actually feel the extra power. It was always available as strength in reserve. The good news is that God has some strength in reserve for you. The psalmist said, "God is a very present help in times of need." When you hit a tough time, you will feel a peace that passes understanding. You're going to feel a force pushing you forward, taking you where you could not go on your own. You should be falling apart, but there is grace for every season.

The Scripture says your strength will always be equivalent to what you need. If you were to get a negative medical report, you're going to have the strength to deal with it. You're not going to fall apart. You may face some challenges where you think, *We don't know how we're going to make it up this.* The reason you think that way is you haven't felt the full force of finishing grace. When it kicks in, you're going to climb mountains that you thought were way too steep and overcome obstacles that looked insurmountable. How could you do this? You tapped into strength in reserve.

A PRAYER FOR TODAY

Father, we love You and praise You for Your strength in difficult times. Thank You that You always have strength in reserve to help us move forward through every season of our lives. We declare that we can do all things through the full force of finishing grace in Jesus' Name. Amen.

Forgive

TODAY'S SCRIPTURE

*Make allowance for each other's faults, and forgive
anyone who offends you. Remember, the Lord
forgave you, so you must forgive others.*

Colossians 3:13 NLT

There was a man in the Scripture named Ahithophel who served as a counselor to King David for over twenty-five years. But when David's son Absalom made an attempt to take over the throne, Ahithophel deserted David and started advising Absalom on how to overthrow his father. Many scholars believe that Ahithophel was the grandfather of Bathsheba, with whom David had an affair and whose husband David had had killed. That would explain the reason why he turned on David—instead of forgiving David, for all those years that poison was simmering on the inside. He smiled on the outside and gave David advice, but on the inside something wasn't right. However, when his counsel to Absalom was thwarted, Ahithophel ended up tragically taking his own life.

What David did was horribly wrong. Ahithophel had a reason to be angry. But when you carry around that negative baggage, you're not hurting the other person, you're contaminating your own lives. When you hold on to unforgiveness, bitterness, and anger, it's actually holding you. That poison will lead you down the wrong path. Don't hold on to negative baggage. Forgive—drop it, leave it, and let it go. When you do, God will heal your hurts and restore your broken pieces. He'll pay you back for the injustice.

A PRAYER FOR TODAY

*Father, thank You that in Your mercy You have forgiven us
and cleansed away our sins. Thank You that we can do the
same with each other and not allow what's past to simmer
on the inside. We believe that You are healing our hurts
and restoring us in Jesus' Name. Amen.*

Inner Fire

TODAY'S SCRIPTURE

"[God, Your] word is in my heart like a fire,
a fire shut up in my bones. I am weary of
holding it in; indeed, I cannot."

Jeremiah 20:9 NIV

God put a promise in Jeremiah that he would be a prophet and speak to the nations. But people and obstacles came against him. He got so deeply discouraged, but just when you thought Jeremiah was going to quit, he said, "God, all the odds are against me. But this promise You put in me is like a burning fire. I can't get away from it." When Jeremiah let the fire burn, his life passion was restored.

You may be at a place where you can easily be discouraged and give up on what God has placed in your hearts. But there is a fire shut up in your bones, a promise that God has spoken over you that will not die. Your thoughts or others may try to convince you it's never going to happen, but deep down you feel a burning, a restlessness, a fire. That's the promise God has put in you. You're going to accomplish more than you thought possible. You're going to see the exceeding greatness of God's power. What He's spoken over your lives will come to pass. If you will be the best that you can be together, right where you are, God will get you to where He wants you to be.

A PRAYER FOR TODAY

Father, thank You for the fire of the promise that is burning
deep inside our lives. Help us to stir up the fire of faith in Your
promises and let it become a flame. We believe that we are
going to see Your power help us accomplish more than
we thought possible in Jesus' Name. Amen.

Shame Removal

TODAY'S SCRIPTURE

"You will forget the shame of your youth and
remember no more the reproach..."

Isaiah 54:4 NIV

n the Scripture, Isaac had a son named Jacob, which means "trickster, deceiver, swindler." He was called that for so long, he became exactly that—a con man. Later in life, Jacob got tired of living that way. One night the angel of the Lord told Jacob, "God has a new name for you. Instead of Jacob, you will be called Israel," which means "prince with God." God took a man who had lived a life of dishonesty and instead of saying, "Jacob, shame on you," He said, "Jacob, shame off you. I've called you to be a prince and to reign in life."

Maybe like Jacob, you have let circumstances, failures, or what people have said put a label on you that says washed up, not valuable, made too many mistakes, poor spouse, bad parent. No, this is what grace is all about. None of us deserve it, but God says, "I'm removing the shame. I know who you are. I'm changing your names to prince, to princess, to highly favored, to redeemed, to forgiven. I'm going to make your lives so rewarding, so blessed, that you won't even think about the shame." When those thoughts of shame and guilt try to relabel you, just remind yourselves, "We are who God says we are. He says we are approved, valuable, redeemed, and masterpieces."

A PRAYER FOR TODAY

Father, we praise You that because of what Jesus has done on the cross, You remove the shame from our lives. Thank You that You have made us into royalty and crowned us as highly favored, redeemed, and forgiven. We believe You have called us to reign in life in Jesus' Name. Amen.

Stay in Peace

TODAY'S SCRIPTURE

"Therefore do not worry about tomorrow,
for tomorrow will worry about itself.
Each day has enough trouble of its own."

Matthew 6:34 NIV

Are you trying to solve problems that haven't happened? "What if I get laid off? What if this pain is something serious?" Jesus said to not worry about tomorrow, for tomorrow will have enough worries of its own. God gives you the grace for today. You don't have grace for tomorrow. Trying to figure out the what-ifs will make you depressed. Sure we should plan ahead and use common sense, but at some point you have to say, "God, You give us grace for every season. Just as You clothe the lilies of the fields, You said You take care of us. So we're going to rest in You." Then the peace that passes all understanding will guard your hearts.

In the book of Hebrews, it talks about entering into the rest of God. That means you have a problem, but you're not losing sleep over it. You know God's still in control. You had a setback in your finances, you lost a client, but you're not upset because you know God will supply all your needs. One of the main ways you show God that you're trusting Him is by staying in peace. You're not up when your circumstances are up, and you're not down when they're down. You're in the rest of God.

A PRAYER FOR TODAY

Father, thank You for the assurance that just as You clothe the lilies of the fields, You will provide us with exactly what we need for every season we are in. We choose to rest, knowing that You are in control. We will not worry because You supply all our needs in Jesus' Name. Amen.

Don't Be Intimidated

TODAY'S SCRIPTURE

And in no way be alarmed or intimidated
[in anything] by your opponents.

Philippians 1:28 AMP

When our children were young, we were at the beach one time when a bumblebee came and frightened our daughter. After we swatted him out of the way, only to have him come right back, we knocked him down to the sand with a towel, but a minute later he was flying by our heads. This time we used a tennis shoe to squash him into the sand. To our amazement he got back up again slowly and buzzed by our heads again. At that point he deserved to live. He won.

No matter how big the enemy looks, that's the way you need to see yourselves. Don't be intimidated by that financial problem or by what somebody said about you. That sickness is no match for you. There is an anointing on your lives that seals you, protects you, enables you, and empowers you. God has infused you with strength. The Scripture calls it "can do" power.

Refuse to give up, refuse to fall into self-pity, refuse to let it overwhelm you. Instead, have this attitude, *We're ready for and equal to anything that comes our way. We have been anointed with "can do" power. We are armed with strength for this battle.* When you have this "We can handle it together" attitude, all the forces of darkness cannot keep you from your destiny.

A PRAYER FOR TODAY

Father, praise You for Your loving-kindness. Thank You that
we have "can do" power for all things. We refuse to give up
or to be overwhelmed or to be intimidated by whatever
is coming against us in Jesus' Name. Amen.

OUR
BEST
LIFE
TOGETHER

We Declare

God's supernatural favor
over our lives. What we
could not make happen
on our own, God will
make happen for us.
Supernatural opportunities,
healing, restoration, and
breakthroughs are coming
our way. We are getting
stronger, healthier, and
wiser. We will discover talent
that we hadn't known we
had, and we will accomplish
our God-given dreams.

Be the Difference Maker

TODAY'S SCRIPTURE

In the first month of the first year of his reign,
[Hezekiah] opened the doors of the temple
of the LORD and repaired them.

2 Chronicles 29:3 NIV

King Hezekiah was raised in a dysfunctional family. His father set up idols for the people to worship, refused to honor God, and closed the temple. The nation went into poverty and was crushed by several armies. Hezekiah grew up in this environment of defeat and compromise. He could have let his mind become conditioned to the negative and turned out like his father. But Hezekiah was a barrier breaker. When he became the king, the first thing he did was to reopen the temple and begin a powerful national restoration of the worship of God.

If you were raised in a negative environment, Hezekiah would tell you, "You don't have to stay there. How you started is not important; how you finish is what matters." Do yourself and your spouse and family a favor and don't pass the negative along to each other or down to the next generation. You can be the difference maker. You can be the one to put your family on a path to honoring God, a path of blessing, favor, and victory. You can recondition your mind and get rid of any strongholds that are keeping you back. Dare to take steps of faith, be barrier breakers and step into a new level of your destiny.

A PRAYER FOR TODAY

Father, we praise You that You are the God of difference makers.
Thank You that You are leading us straight through the barriers
of our past and onto the pathway of blessing and favor.
We will not allow any strongholds to keep us from moving
forward in Jesus' Name. Amen.

It's a Partnership

TODAY'S SCRIPTURE

You must have the same attitude that Christ Jesus had.
Though he was God…he took the humble position
of a slave and was born as a human being.

Philippians 2:5-7 NLT

t's great to serve other people, but don't forget to serve your own family. Husbands should serve their wives. "Honey, I'm going in the kitchen. Can I bring you anything?" "Let me run and fill your car's gas tank so you won't have to do it tomorrow." If we all had this servant's attitude toward our spouses, more marriages could stay together. Some men expect their wives to do everything for them—cook, clean, wash the clothes, keep the house straightened up. That's not a wife; that's a maid! If you want a wife—a friend, a lover, and someone to make your life great—you have to be willing to serve her. Pick up your dirty clothes. Help with the children. Make her feel special. Marriage is not a dictatorship. It's a partnership!

Jesus Christ modeled a servant attitude that overflowed with joy. He had all the power in the world. Yet He pulled out His towel, bowed down, and washed His disciples' feet. He gave us His example of service to others so we would know we're never too important or successful to bow down and serve another person. The more you walk in humility, and the more willing you are to serve others, the higher God can take you.

A PRAYER FOR TODAY

Father, thank You that Jesus modeled a servant attitude that
bowed down and washed others' feet. We humble ourselves
before You and especially ask You to help us serve each
other and our loved ones with overflowing joy
in Jesus' Name. Amen.

Paid in Full

TODAY'S SCRIPTURE

"Forgive us our debts, as we forgive our debtors."
Matthew 6:12 NKJV

When God talks about debts, He's talking about the times when people hurt you and do you wrong. It is a debt because human nature says, "I was wronged. Now I want justice. You have to pay me back." But the mistake many people make is in trying to collect a debt that only God can pay. Your parents can't pay you back for not providing a loving childhood. Your spouse can't pay you back for the pain they caused by something they said or did. Only God can truly pay you back.

If you spend your lives trying to get from others what only God can give, it will ruin relationships. Your attitude should be, *God, You've seen every wrong. I will not be bitter, trying to get people to give me what they don't have. You promised You would settle my cases and pay me back double for every injustice. So I'm letting them off the hook, and I'm leaving it up to You.*

When you see the person who did you wrong, stamp the account PAID IN FULL in your imagination. It's very freeing to say, "They can't pay me back. I'm on God's payroll, and He never misses a payment." God will settle your cases. Forgive so you can be free. Forgive so God can pay you back double.

A PRAYER FOR TODAY

Father, we don't want to let bitterness, anger, or an offense to have control over our lives. We release it all to You. We choose to look to You to heal our hurts and right the wrongs done to us. We declare that no one owes us anything because You have set us free in Jesus' Name. Amen.

A Royal Anointing

TODAY'S SCRIPTURE

Then Samuel took the horn of oil and anointed David...
and the Spirit of the LORD came mightily upon
David from that day forward.

1 Samuel 16:13 AMP

When David was a teenager, the prophet Samuel anointed him to be the next king of Israel. What's interesting is that David worked for years as a shepherd even though he had a king's anointing. The Scripture tells us to "reign in life as a king." You have a king's anointing, a queen's anointing. This means to live an abundant life and to accomplish your God-given dreams. As with David, even though you've been anointed, on the way to your destiny there will be times of testing when you don't see anything happening, when you have to be patient and keep doing the right things. You have to keep believing, *Our time is coming. We may not see how it can happen, but we have a secret weapon. The anointing is on our lives.*

You may think you don't have the skills, the talents, or the experience to accomplish what's in your hearts, but that's okay. The anointing on your lives will make up for what you don't have. It is not just your intellects, talents, expertise, or experiences that determine how high you're going to go. It's the fact that Almighty God is breathing on your lives. The anointing will cause you to accomplish dreams you could never accomplish on your own.

A PRAYER FOR TODAY

Father, thank You that You have given us a royal anointing
that we might reign in life as a king and queen. Thank You that
we are not weak, defeated, or powerless. We declare that
You are breathing on our lives and we are well able to
overcome in Jesus' Name. Amen.

You Have What You Need

TODAY'S SCRIPTURE

*The LORD said to Gideon,
"You have too many men."*

Judges 7:2 NIV

The Midianites had joined forces with two other armies and were about to attack the Israelites. Gideon put out a call to all the warriors, and thirty-two thousand showed up to fight. Gideon was feeling good, but God told him, "You have too many men," and He cut that number down to three hundred! It's easy to imagine Gideon thinking, *God, You only left me one percent of what I thought I needed. This is impossible.* God was saying, "Gideon, you don't need what you think you need. You're depending on people and not on Me." Then He supernaturally helped them defeat this huge army.

God is saying to us that the less we depend on people to meet our needs, the greater the anointing on our lives. It is so easy to think you could accomplish your dreams and overcome obstacles if you just had the support of so-and-so. It's so easy to rely on somebody else, even your spouse, to make the difference, thinking they're the savior. Have a new perspective: *you have what you need.* The most powerful force in the universe is on your side. You and God are a majority. Quit trying to get from other people what only God can give. If you stop relying on others, you're going to overcome obstacles that look insurmountable and accomplish dreams that look impossible.

A PRAYER FOR TODAY

Father, we lift our eyes to You and give You all the praise and glory. Thank You that You have uniquely equipped us with all that we need to accomplish our dreams and overcome obstacles. We declare that we look to You as our only Savior in Jesus' Name. Amen.

Not a Faultfinder

TODAY'S SCRIPTURE

If any of you lacks wisdom, you should ask God,
who gives generously to all without finding fault,
and it will be given to you.

James 1:5 NIV

God is not keeping a record of your faults as a couple. Sometimes we think He's in heaven, waiting to catch us. "I saw that failure. I heard that comment—that was really bad. And they didn't go to church last week. I'll have to withhold My goodness." No, God is not a faultfinder. He doesn't say, "You failed, so you're on your own." God is not waiting for you to perform perfectly and then He's going to show you His goodness. He is full of mercy. He'll show you favor that you don't deserve.

When you have the right image of God, you know that He's for you, that's He's not basing His goodness toward you on your performance. He's looking for hearts that are turned toward Him, upon which He can pour out His favor. Then all the guilt and condemnation won't have a chance. When you have hearts to do what's right, that's what matters to Him. When you say, "God, we love You and can't do this on our own. Help us to become who You created us to be as a couple," He will give you the grace to overcome anything that's holding you back as well as the favor to reach your best life together.

A PRAYER FOR TODAY

Father, we praise You for Your unfailing love for us.
Thank You that You are not a faultfinder but You are full
of mercy. Our hearts are turned toward You. We believe that
You are giving us the grace to become all that You created
us to be together in Jesus' Name. Amen.

New Directions

TODAY'S SCRIPTURE

*"Strike the rock, and water will come out
of it for the people to drink."*

Exodus 17:6 NIV

When the Israelites were desperate for water in the wilderness, God told Moses to *strike* a rock and water flowed out freely. It was a great miracle. At a later time, once again the people needed water, and God told Moses to *speak to* the rock at Kadesh (see Num. 20). The problem was, Moses was on autopilot. He thought, *I've overcome this challenge once. I can do it again.* Moses struck the rock twice, and though water gushed forth, because Moses didn't listen and do it God's way, his actions kept him from going into the Promised Land.

The principle is, yesterday's instructions may not work today. What worked in your marriage in the past may not work today. God wants us to rely on Him, not some past formula. "If we do this and do that, God will bless us." That's not faith. God changes the method so we have to come to Him for newness of life together. Could it be that you're stuck in how it worked in the past, when God wants to do a new thing, in a new way, with new ideas, bringing new talents out of each of you? If you listen to and do what God is saying now, you will see water begin to flow in greater ways.

A PRAYER FOR TODAY

*Father, we praise You for Your love in our lives. Thank You
that we can come to You for newness of life together and to lead
us in victory. Help us to truly rely upon You and follow Your
leading to do new things, with new ideas and new
people in Jesus' Name. Amen.*

Faith God Can See

TODAY'S SCRIPTURE

When Jesus saw their faith, he said to the paralyzed man,
"Son, your sins are forgiven."

Mark 2:5 NIV

When a man who was paralyzed heard that Jesus was speaking in a certain house, he convinced his friends to carry him there. When they arrived, the place was packed and they couldn't get in. What a disappointment! They could have easily given up. But they had a "never say die" attitude and carried him to the roof, lowered him down through an opening, and put him right in front of Jesus. At that moment it says Jesus "saw their faith" and made the man whole.

There were other people in the room who did not get well. What was the difference? This man put action behind his faith. God is looking for people who have a faith He can see. Not just a faith He can hear. Not just a faith that believes, but also a faith that is demonstrated. If you really want to get God's attention, put actions behind what you believe.

You have to have that same "never say die" attitude when it comes to that difficulty you're facing together. Are you doing something out of the ordinary to show God you believe in Him? If you can't get in the door, why not be bold and go through the roof? Like this man, do something to demonstrate your faith.

A PRAYER FOR TODAY

Father, thank You for placing faith in our hearts. We choose to exercise our faith in You. Help us to grow in faith as we read Your Word and stay close to You. We declare that we want our faith to be seen by You when it comes to every difficulty we face in Jesus' Name. Amen.

We Declare

we will live victoriously.
We were created in the
image of God. We have the
DNA of a winner. We are
wearing a crown of favor.
Royal blood flows through
our veins. We are the head,
never the tail; above,
never beneath. We will live
with purpose, passion,
and praise, knowing that
we were destined to
live in victory.

The Appointed Time

TODAY'S SCRIPTURE

For the vision is yet for an appointed time...Though it tarries, wait for it; because it will surely come.

Habakkuk 2:3 NKJV

Sometimes we think, *We're not getting to where we want. Why are we still stuck where we are?* Don't get discouraged. God is in control. Habakkuk did not say "the appointed time might come." Not, "I hope so." God has already set the date on your calendar. One translation says, "It won't be one second late." Sometimes God will take you from A to B to C, and then thrust you all the way down to V. What happened? You hit a set time that pushed you years ahead. Just be the best that you can be together. Keep honoring God with your lives. He has lined up solutions for you down to the very second.

Trust God's timing. What you're praying about and what you're believing for are not going to be one second late. If it hasn't happened yet, it doesn't mean God is mad at you or that it's never going to work out. God has already established the time. You don't have to worry or live frustrated. Stay in peace. Your steps are being directed by the Creator of the universe; not randomly, but down to the most finite, small detail. Whether it's twenty minutes or twenty years, you know that what God promised He will bring to pass.

A PRAYER FOR TODAY

Father, You are worthy to be praised. Thank You that You know what we need and have an appointed time set to get it to us. We choose to stop stressing out over what we don't have, knowing it will be here down to the very second of when we really need it in Jesus' Name. Amen.

Good to All

TODAY'S SCRIPTURE

*Therefore, as we have opportunity, let us do good
to all people, especially to those who belong
to the family of believers.*

Galatians 6:10 NIV

J esus said that people will know true believers by the good fruit we bear, not by how many Scriptures we quote or the Christian bumper stickers on our car. This world does not need to hear another sermon nearly as much as it needs to see us being good to people. People are going to know that we're believers when we're helping other people, meeting needs, and blessing people with our words and actions. We were created to make a difference in the lives of others through our love for them. True love is seen in our actions—giving our time, our money, an encouraging word. When you show love, you are showing God to the world. You're never more like God than when you take time to do something for someone else.

People are watching you as a couple, and one of the best witnesses you can have is simply by being good to people. The Scripture says to be on the lookout for those you can bless. All around you are hurting people who need your love and encouragement. Listen to what they're saying. Be willing to be inconvenienced. Don't miss the miracle of the moment to do good whenever situations cross your paths to bless people.

A PRAYER FOR TODAY

*Father, we praise You for all You have done in our lives. Help us
to be more aware of the people and needs around us. Our desire
is to love others as You have loved us. Use us to be a blessing
and a testimony of Your goodness so that others may
come to know You in Jesus' Name. Amen.*

Move toward Jesus

TODAY'S SCRIPTURE

*For she kept saying, If I only touch His garments,
I shall be restored to health.*

Mark 5:28 AMPC

This lady had been sick for many years, spent all her money on the best doctors, but nothing worked. When she heard Jesus was coming through town, she kept saying to herself, "When I get to Jesus, I know I will be made whole." In the midst of the difficulty, she was prophesying victory. All through the day, over and over, she kept saying, "Healing is on its way. Brighter days are ahead." When she started making her way to Jesus through the thick crowd, she didn't complain, but just kept saying, "This is my time." The more she said it, the closer she got. Finally she reached out and touched the edge of His robe and was instantly healed.

Notice the principle: whatever you're constantly saying, you're moving toward. This works both in the positive and in the negative. If you're always saying, "We never get any good breaks," you're moving toward more disappointment. You may be struggling in your finances, but when you keep declaring, "We are blessed. We are prosperous. We have the favor of God," you're moving toward increase. You're getting closer to seeing that come to pass. If you will change what you're saying, you will change what you're seeing. The Scripture says, "Call the things that are not as if they already were."

A PRAYER FOR TODAY

*Father, thank You that You provide us with everything we need.
Thank You that You've put dreams in our hearts as well, and we
believe that as we speak words of faith that we are moving toward
You bringing them to pass. We declare that our dreams
are in Your hands in Jesus' Name. Amen.*

Help the Hurting

TODAY'S SCRIPTURE

May all kings bow down to him and all nations serve him. For he will deliver the needy who cry out, the afflicted who have no one to help.

Psalm 72:11–12 NIV

n Psalm 72, Solomon prayed what seemed to be a self-centered prayer. He asked God that his fame would spread throughout the land and that kings and queens would bow down before him. You would think God would say, "Solomon, you need to learn some humility." But God did exactly what he asked for. Solomon became one of the most famous people of his day. The queen of Sheba came, bowed down before him, and brought him gold and silver.

The reason God answered that bold prayer is that Solomon went on to pray, "God, I will use that influence and wealth to help the widows and orphans, to bring justice to the oppressed and afflicted." He asked big so he could lift the fallen, restore the broken, and help the hurting to advance God's kingdom. God has no problem giving you influence, honor, wealth, and even fame, as long as your dream is connected to helping others. Be among the couples who have the boldness to pray, "God, let our gifts and talents stand out. Let our work be so excellent, so inspiring, that people all around us know who we are, not for our glory, but so we can use our influence to advance Your kingdom."

A PRAYER FOR TODAY

Father, thank You that You want us to lift the fallen, to restore the broken, and to help the hurting. We want in every way possible to advance Your kingdom. We ask You to use and increase our influence to make a difference in people's lives in Jesus' Name. Amen.

Zip It

TODAY'S SCRIPTURE

*"Before I formed you in the womb I knew you,
before you were born I set you apart; I appointed
you as a prophet to the nations."*

Jeremiah 1:5 NIV

When God gave Jeremiah a promise that he would become a great prophet, he was very young and unsure of himself. He instead listened to the voice of doubt and said, "God, I can't speak to the nations. I'm too young." God said, "Jeremiah, say not that you are too young." The first thing God did was to stop his negative words, because He knew that if Jeremiah went around saying, "I don't have what it takes," he would become exactly what he was saying. So God said in effect, "Jeremiah, zip it up. You may think it, but don't speak it out." It goes on to tell how Jeremiah changed what he was saying, and he became a prophet. The promise came to pass.

In the same way, God has called every one of us to do something great. He's put dreams, desires on the inside, but it's easy to acquiesce as Jeremiah did and say, "We can't do that. We've made too many mistakes. We don't have the education or the experience." We can all make excuses, but God is saying to us what He said to Jeremiah, "Stop saying that." Negative words stop God's promises. Don't curse your future. Those negative words can keep you from your best life together.

A PRAYER FOR TODAY

Father, thank You that You have given us the free choice to zip our lips when we have negative thoughts. Help us to not just stop speaking negative words that stop Your promises, but help us use our words wisely to prophesy victory and success for our lives in Jesus' Name. Amen.

Growing Up

TODAY'S SCRIPTURE

As long as an heir is underage, he is no different from
a slave, although he owns the whole estate.

Galatians 4:1 NLT

t's easy to make excuses in relationships. "I was rude to her because she was rude to me. I shouldn't have said that to him, but I was so tired." No, you have God's grace to not be rude, to not say hurtful things, and to always treat each other with love. You can either feed your flesh and say and do what you feel, or you can feed your spirit and keep your mouth closed and do the right thing. The problem is that if you keep saying everything you want, being argumentative and disrespectful, you'll never grow. You'll stay a child. The Scripture says that even though you're an heir of God with an incredible inheritance that belongs to you—joy, peace, favor, promotion, and abundance—if you remain a child, it won't be released.

Taming the tongue is not just about being disciplined, it's about growing up and receiving the inheritance that belongs to you. Sometimes we let small things keep us from the big things God has in store. In the big picture, it's a small thing to not argue with or put down your spouse. God is simply asking you to use your words and actions to bless and not curse, to build up and not tear down.

A PRAYER FOR TODAY

Father, we bless and lift You up because You are worthy to be praised. We desire to obey You in the small things and to stop excusing any hurtful things we say or do to each other. We declare that we will walk in the incredible inheritance You have for us in Jesus' Name. Amen.

Out of Winter into Spring

TODAY'S SCRIPTURE

*And let us not grow weary while doing good, for in
due season we shall reap if we do not lose heart.*

Galatians 6:9 NKJV

Every season is not springtime, with beautiful flowers,
gorgeous sunshine, and cool breezes. There has to be
planting seasons, watering seasons, and seasons when
you're pulling weeds. Those are important seasons.
Without going through that process, you're not going to come
into a season of harvest.

Instead of being frustrated by life's difficulties, have a new
perspective. That season is getting you prepared for promotion.
It may look as though you're stuck, but at the right time the
season will change. Winter always gives way to spring. There is
contentment to be found not only in the harvest season but in the
pulling weeds season.

You may be in one of those difficult seasons right now. It's
easy to think, *As soon as we get through this tough time, we'll get
our joy back*. No, this is the day the Lord has made. You have to
choose to rejoice today. God has given you not only the grace to
endure this season but to enjoy the season. When you're content,
you see each day as a gift, appreciate the people in your lives, and
are grateful for what God has given you. That not only is developing your characters, but you're passing the test. You will come out
of winter and into your springtime.

A PRAYER FOR TODAY

*Father, thank You that You are our faithful God. We stand
believing that You are working in our present season, preparing
us for promotion. Our faith and trust and contentment are
in You. We declare that our due season is coming and we
will reap a harvest in Jesus' Name. Amen.*

Water Walking

TODAY'S SCRIPTURE

"Yes, come," Jesus said. So Peter went over the side of the boat and walked on the water toward Jesus.

Matthew 14:29 NLT

When Jesus came walking across the stormy sea in the darkness of night, Peter was the only disciple who had the courage to walk on the water to Him. One can imagine the other disciples saying, "Peter, it's too dangerous! You could drown." But when Jesus told him to come, Peter stepped out into the unknown and walked on the water. He showed that although what is familiar is comfortable—what you're used to, how you were raised, the job you've had for years—it can keep you from your destiny. Don't let your comfort keep you from getting out of the boat and becoming who you were created to be.

For every major victory and significant accomplishment in our lives, we've had to step into the unknown...and so will you. You can't play it safe your whole lives and reach the fullness of your destiny. Don't let the what-ifs talk you out of it. "What if we fail or they say no?" You'll never know unless you try. What God has in store for your future together is going to boggle your minds—the places He's going to take you, the people you're going to influence, the dreams you're going to accomplish. It's going to be bigger than you've imagined. You know where it is—it's in the unknown.

A PRAYER FOR TODAY

Father, thank You that the stormy seas of our lives are no difficulty for You. We choose to obey You quickly. Help us not to overthink things, but to trust Your leading in our lives. We declare that we are willing to step out of our comfort zones in Jesus' Name. Amen.

We Declare

we are people builders. We
will look for opportunities to
encourage others to bring
out the best in them and
to help them accomplish
their dreams. We will speak
words of faith and victory,
affirming them, approving
them, letting them know
they are valued. We will call
out their seeds of greatness,
helping them to rise higher
and become all that God
created them to be.

Never Forgotten

TODAY'S SCRIPTURE

*So Boaz took Ruth and she became his wife...
and she gave birth to a son...Obed. He was the
father of Jesse, the father of David.*

Ruth 4:13, 17 NIV

A young widow named Ruth left her country and moved to her elderly mother-in-law's home to care for her. They barely had enough food to survive. She would go out in the fields and pick up the wheat the workers missed. One day Boaz, the wealthy owner of the field, told his workers to leave handfuls of wheat on purpose for Ruth. God was meeting their needs, and she was so grateful. But God is full of surprises. Just when you're satisfied and think you've reached your limits, God has something bigger in mind. Boaz fell in love with Ruth, and they got married. Instead of working in the field, Ruth owned the field!

Ruth had gone through great heartache and pain and could have easily thought, *Life's not fair. Why me?* You may feel that way, but God hasn't forgotten about you. He's seen your sleepless nights and the unfair situations. You may have accepted where you are as a couple, but God has not accepted it. He has some explosive blessings that will make up for the difficulties you've been through.

Here's how amazing God is. Ruth went from barely surviving to being the great grandmother of David, ending up in the family line of Jesus. God has something big coming your way!

A PRAYER FOR TODAY

*Father, thank You that You know every unfair and difficult
situation we have faced, and You never forget us. We choose to
believe that You have more blessings and favor for us than we
could dream. We declare that explosive blessings are
coming our way in Jesus' Name. Amen.*

A Cheerful Heart

TODAY'S SCRIPTURE

A cheerful heart is good medicine,
but a crushed spirit dries up the bones.

Proverbs 17:22 NIV

When people are stressed out, headaches, digestive problems, and lack of energy are just some of the results. Much of this would go away if they learn how to properly deal with stress. One of the greatest stress relievers God has given us is laughter. It's like medicine. Laughing makes us feel better and releases healing throughout our systems. When we laugh, the pressures of life fade and we feel restored and rejuvenated.

Many couples are too stressed to have fun. They need to restore balance. All work and no play is not healthy. When was the last time you had a good hearty laugh together? If it's been awhile, maybe your laughers are rusted and need to be overhauled! You don't know how much better you would feel and the energy you'd pick up if you'd just lighten up and learn to laugh more often every single day. Developing a sense of humor and looking for opportunities to laugh can make a big difference in the quality of your lives and relationship. We suggest that at least three times a day you find something funny that makes you laugh out loud. No chuckling. No laughing on the inside. Release that joy into the atmosphere so everyone can hear it. Take the time to laugh and enjoy each other.

A PRAYER FOR TODAY

Father, we praise You that we are fearfully and wonderfully made.
Thank You for the healing power of laughter. Help us to have
cheerful hearts and learn to laugh and enjoy each and every day.
We declare that we are letting go of stress and heaviness
of the heart in Jesus' Name. Amen.

Don't Be Moved

TODAY'S SCRIPTURE

"None of these things move me."

Acts 20:24 NKJV

When you study the life of the apostle Paul, he went through all kinds of difficulties and unfair situations. He was falsely accused of crimes, beaten with rods, lied about, put in prison for years, and shipwrecked. In Acts 20, he gives us a secret of living a victorious life: "None of these things move me." He was saying, "Yes, there were setbacks, disappointments, and not all my plans worked out, but I didn't lose my joy or complain. God is still on the throne. Even the time in prison gave me the opportunity to write about half of the books of the New Testament."

As a couple, there's always something trying to pull us out of peace. Are you allowing these things to move you? You can't pray them away. These are tests we all have to pass. Jesus said, "Don't let your hearts be troubled." He didn't say, "If you stay in faith, I'll take away all the difficulties." He said troubles will be there, but you don't have to get upset. Look at that negative medical report and say, "You don't move us. We're not going to live worried." Look at the bank account and say, "You don't move us. You may be low right now, but we know increase is coming." Stay in peace. Quit letting these things trouble your relationship.

A PRAYER FOR TODAY

Father, thank You for Your mighty power at work in our lives. We are not moved by the tests and troubles we face because we know that You are still on the throne. Our faith and trust are in You. We declare that You will work Your good plan for our future in Jesus' Name. Amen.

Created to Soar

TODAY'S SCRIPTURE

Awake, awake, Zion, clothe yourself with strength!
Put on your garments of splendor.

Isaiah 52:1 NIV

There is a story about an eagle that was raised with a brood of chickens and acted like a chicken. That's all he'd ever seen. But one day he saw an eagle soaring overhead, and deep down something said, "This is not who I am. I was created to soar." Flapping his wings as fast as he could, the eagle barely lifted off the ground and crashed into the side of the chicken coop. His chicken friends laughed and said, "See, you're just one of us." But he didn't let that failure or the ridicule keep him from trying, and one day he lifted up out of that chicken coop and began to soar up. With every breath he declared, "This is who I really am. I knew I was an eagle!"

Perhaps you've been in a chicken coop way too long. Let us tell you what you already know. You're not chickens. You are eagles. Don't let a limited environment rub off on you. Don't let how you were raised or what others say keep you from knowing who you really are. You've been made in the image of Almighty God. He has crowned you with favor. You were created to soar. Abundance, opportunity, and good breaks are yours. Now get rid of a chicken mentality and start having an eagle mentality.

A PRAYER FOR TODAY

Father, thank You that You created us to soar like eagles rather than sit in a chicken coop. You've given us talents, abilities, and skills to use for Your glory. We believe that we are going to soar to new heights and become everything You have created us to be in Jesus' Name. Amen.

Uncommon Faith

TODAY'S SCRIPTURE

The sun stopped in the middle of the sky and
delayed going down about a full day.

Joshua 10:13 NIV

J oshua was in the midst of a great battle. The sun was going down, and Joshua knew that if he couldn't get the enemy's army totally defeated, they would rise up later and cause problems. So he asked God to stop the sun, something that had never been done before. God said in effect, "Joshua, if you're bold enough to ask it, I'm bold enough to do it." His uncommon faith brought a smile to God's face. God interrupted the entire universe just because one man had uncommon faith.

Uncommon faith is not average faith. It's above and beyond. It gives you a boldness and a confidence to believe for the extraordinary. It's radical faith. You believe God can do anything. Average faith says, "God, help us to survive this recession." Uncommon faith says, "God, we believe You will prosper us in the midst of this recession." Uncommon faith says, "We're not only coming out of this problem, we're coming out better off than we were before." You may say, "That's kind of bold. Who do you think you are?" Here's who we are: we are children of the Most High God, full of uncommon faith.

Have you ever asked God for something out of the ordinary? Don't you think it's time to do so?

A PRAYER FOR TODAY

Father, we want to put a smile on Your face by releasing our faith
in uncommon ways. We want to believe You for the extraordinary
and to believe that You will increase us above and beyond.
We believe that You are taking us forward into the fullness
of our destiny in Jesus' Name. Amen.

Remember the Right Things

TODAY'S SCRIPTURE

"Yours, O LORD, is the greatness, the power,
the glory, the victory, and the majesty.... We adore
you as the one who is over all things."

1 Chronicles 29:11 NLT

Many couples spend a lot of time talking about and reliving their past mistakes and hurts. Here's the problem. You're remembering the wrong things. Nowhere in the Scripture are we told to remember our defeats, failures, or bad breaks. Start remembering your victories—the times God healed you, promoted you, stopped the accidents, and turned the problems around. When you're remembering the right things, you're going to move forward in faith.

David says in Psalm 34, "Let all who are discouraged take heart." He goes on to tell us how to do it. "Come, let's talk about God's goodness. I prayed and the Lord answered my prayer." He was saying, "When you're discouraged, talk about God's greatness—not about your problems. Talk about your answered prayers. Talk about the Red Seas that have been parted."

What you're saying in your tough times will make or break you. If you go around saying, "We'll never get out of this problem," you'll get stuck. Turn it around and say, "God, thank You for Your greatness in our lives and every victory You've given us." When you're always talking about God's goodness, you'll know that God has done it for you in the past, and He'll do it for you again in the future.

A PRAYER FOR TODAY

Father, thank You that Your hand has been upon our lives in
so many ways, answering our prayers and doing what we could
never do on our own. We declare Your greatness, power,
glory, and victory in Jesus' Name. Amen.

Get Up!

TODAY'S SCRIPTURE

*There was a certain man there who had suffered
with a deep-seated and lingering disorder
for thirty-eight years.*

John 5:5 AMPC

Today's Scripture describes this man's condition as a "lingering disorder." It's not just physical, but it's when we dwell on the negative things of the past and make excuses to settle where we are. When Jesus asked this crippled man, "Do you want to get well?" the man responded with one excuse after another for why he hadn't been healed, showing us that he'd used those excuses for so long that they'd become a crutch. Jesus didn't respond by saying, "I feel sorry for you. You've had a rough time." No, Jesus said in effect, "If you're serious about getting well, get up!"

One wonders how many couples would get out of defeat, mediocrity, and the hurtful ways they treat each other, if they would quit making excuses, quit feeling sorry for themselves, and start pressing forward. We've all had unfair things happen that we can allow to become lingering disorders. But God is asking us, "Are you serious about getting well? Are you serious about breaking that bad attitude, getting past that disappointment?" Then there's something you have to do. Get up in your spirits, in your attitudes, in how you talk. Quit making excuses. You're waiting on God, but God's waiting on you. When you get up, so to speak, you'll see things begin to change.

A PRAYER FOR TODAY

Father, today we choose to release any old thinking, old habits, any excuses, and any lingering disorder that would keep us from being our best together. We are serious about getting well and letting go of the old and embracing the new in Jesus' Name. Amen.

When You Need It

TODAY'S SCRIPTURE

Those who trust in the LORD *will lack no good thing.*

Psalm 34:10 NLT

So often we think, *If we had more money, we could accomplish our dreams. If we had a bigger house, we'd be happy. If we knew the right people, we could do something great.* But as long as you feel as though you're lacking something, you'll make excuses to be less than your best together. You have to get a new perspective. God has given you exactly what you need for the season you're in as a couple. You have the talents, the friends, the connections, the resources, and the experience you need for right now. It doesn't mean that's all you're ever going to have. When you need more, God will make sure that you have it.

Psalm 34 says that because your trust is in the Lord, you don't have to worry. Whatever you need, God will make sure you won't "lack any good thing." This means that if you don't have it right now, you don't need it right now. Our attitude should be, *We're equipped, empowered, and anointed for this moment. We are not lacking, shortchanged, inadequate, or missing out. We have what we need for today.* This is an empowering way to live. You take what you have and make the most of it. As long as you keep honoring God, He will give what you need when you need it.

A PRAYER FOR TODAY

Father, we praise You for Your faithfulness. Thank You for providing us with exactly what we need for the season we are in. Thank You that You have equipped and empowered us with every good thing. We believe You will keep providing for us as we need it in Jesus' Name. Amen.

OUR
BEST
LIFE
TOGETHER

We Declare

we will speak only positive
words of faith and victory
over ourselves, our family,
and our future. We will not
use our words to describe
the situation. We will use
our words to change our
situation. We will call in favor,
good breaks, healing, and
restoration. We will not talk
to God about how big our
problems are. We will talk to
our problems about how
big our God is.

Your Seventh Year

TODAY'S SCRIPTURE

If any of your people...sell themselves to you
and serve you six years, in the seventh year
you must let them go free.

Deuteronomy 15:12 NIV

In the Old Testament times, if you were Hebrew and owed someone money that you couldn't pay, they could take you in as a slave and make you work until you paid them back. But every seventh year, no matter how much you still owed, God's people were set free. All the pain, struggling, and suffering was gone in one day. This tells us God never intended His people to be a permanent slave to anything. It is only temporary.

As with the Hebrew slaves, the seventh year is when you break free from limitations that are holding you back—sickness, addictions, debt, constant struggles. It looked as though it would never change. It looked permanent, but then one touch of God's favor and it suddenly turns around. Suddenly you get a good break. Suddenly your health improves. Suddenly a dream comes to pass. What happened? You came into a seventh year.

Quit telling yourselves, "This sickness or financial struggle is permanent." You are children of the Most High God. You are not going to be permanent slaves to anything. Get in agreement with God and affirm, "We're coming into our seventh year. It is our time to break free. Every chain has been loosed. Every stronghold has come down. We know we have been released into increase."

A PRAYER FOR TODAY

Father, thank You for the promise that we are coming into
our seventh year, that You are bringing us freedom and
breaking the yokes of any limitations that have held us back.
We declare that we are free in Christ and coming into
breakthroughs in Jesus' Name. Amen.

Be Compassionate

TODAY'S SCRIPTURE

*Finally, all of you be of one mind, having
compassion for one another; love as brothers,
be tenderhearted, be courteous.*

1 Peter 3:8 NKJV

Everywhere you go these days people are hurting and discouraged; many have broken dreams. They've made mistakes; their lives are in a mess. They need to feel God's compassion and His unconditional love. They don't need somebody to judge and criticize them. They need somebody to bring hope, to bring healing, to show God's mercy. Really, they are looking for a friend, somebody who will be there to encourage them, who will take the time to listen and genuinely care.

Our world is crying out for people with compassion, people who love unconditionally, people who will take some time to help others. When God created us in His image, He put His supernatural love in all our hearts. He's placed in you the potential to have a kind, caring, gentle, loving spirit. But too often, because of our own selfishness, we close our hearts to compassion.

If you want to live your best life together, you must keep your hearts of compassion open. You need to be on the lookout for people you can bless. You have the opportunity to make a difference in someone's life. When God puts love and compassion in your heart toward someone, follow that love. Don't ignore it. Act on it. Somebody needs what you have. Be persons of compassion.

A PRAYER FOR TODAY

*Father, thank You that we are made in Your image to be
compassionate to others. Help us not to be so busy, so caught
up in our own lives that we miss opportunities to serve others.
We want to do the things that are on Your heart
for others in Jesus' Name. Amen.*

Something Great in You

TODAY'S SCRIPTURE

"Here comes that dreamer!"
they said to each other.

Genesis 37:19 NIV

As a young man, God gave Joseph a dream that one day his family would bow down before him. Joseph should have used more wisdom and not told them about his dream. Some people can't handle what God has put inside your lives; rather, as it was with Joseph's brothers, they'll get jealous of you and start finding fault. They would have been fine if Joseph was content to be average. But when you stir up what God has put in you, when you believe that you have seeds of greatness, not everybody will celebrate you.

When you have a dream, you're going to have some detractors. When you believe that you can overcome an illness, pay off your house, start a business, or be successful in spite of past mistakes, sometimes the people closest to you will be the least supportive. They'll ask, "Do you *really* think you'll...?" Let that go in one ear and out the other. The critics don't control your destiny. God does. They can't keep you from your dreams. Here's the key: don't get distracted with fighting battles that don't matter, trying to prove to them who you are, trying to convince them to believe in you. You don't need their approval. You have Almighty God's approval. Let them go. You wouldn't have that opposition if you didn't have something great in you.

A PRAYER FOR TODAY

Father, thank You that You put a dream in Joseph's heart and brought it to pass despite his family's jealousy, and that You've put a dream in our hearts as well. We believe that You alone control our destiny and that we are moving forward with Your approval in Jesus' Name. Amen.

Like a Flood

TODAY'S SCRIPTURE

Then David said, God has broken my enemies...like the
bursting forth of waters. Therefore they called the name
of that place Baal-perazim [Lord of breaking through].

1 Chronicles 14:11 AMPC

After King David experienced a great victory over a huge army, he was so overwhelmed by it that he said, "God has broken through to my enemies like the bursting forth of water." He named the place *Baal-perazim*, which means, "the God of the breakthrough." David likened God's power to an unstoppable flood that moves everything out of its path. He was saying that when the God of the breakthrough releases His power, it will be like a flood of His goodness, a flood of His favor, a flood of healing, a flood of new opportunity.

You may have difficulties that look extremely large and dreams that appear unobtainable as a couple. But know this: when the God of the breakthrough releases a flood of His divine power, nothing can stop it. What's opposing you may look powerful, but it doesn't have a chance when God opens up the floodgates of His favor. Dare to stretch your faith. You may be thinking a *trickle* of His increase when God has an entire ocean to work with. You're thinking *stream* of goodness when God has a tidal wave. Enlarge your vision. Get ready for a tsunami of God's favor. He wants to overwhelm you with His greatness.

A PRAYER FOR TODAY

Father, thank You for Your mighty power at work in our lives.
We are not moved by any obstacles in our way because we
know You are greater than anything we face. We believe
that a tidal wave of Your goodness is coming
in Jesus' Name. Amen.

The Laugh of Faith

TODAY'S SCRIPTURE

He Who sits in the heavens laughs;
the Lord has them in derision.

Psalm 2:4 AMPC

Envision that right now God is on the throne. He's not mad. He's not worried about the economy. He's not upset with the two of you. God is on the throne, full of joy. Psalm 37 explains why He's laughing: "The Lord laughs at the wicked, for He sees that their own day of defeat is coming." In other words, the reason God laughs is that He knows the end of the story. He knows the final outcome. The good news is that you win. God always causes us to triumph!

God gave Abraham a promise that he would father a child. In the natural he was much too old. But the first thing Abraham did when he heard God's promise was to laugh (see Gen. 17:17). His was the laugh of faith. He said, in effect, "Ha, ha! God, I know You can bring this to pass. I know You are a supernatural God."

So often when God puts a promise in our hearts it looks impossible. Perhaps your family is pulled apart. Yet you have God's promise that He will heal the bonds. Your minds may have doubts. But remember to laugh in faith as Abraham did, because it's just a matter of time before those promises come to pass. You are in a fixed fight. God has already recorded the victory in your favor.

A PRAYER FOR TODAY

Father, thank You that You always lead us in triumph in
Jesus. Just as You laugh knowing the outcome, we choose to
laugh by faith. We choose joy, we choose peace, and we
choose trust, knowing You've already recorded our
victory in Jesus' Name. Amen.

Power Up

TODAY'S SCRIPTURE

*You have armed me with strength for the battle;
you have subdued my enemies under my feet.*

2 Samuel 22:40 NLT

God knows every temptation and every obstacle you will ever face. He has armed you with strength for that battle. The greatest force in the universe is breathing in your direction. Tap into that power. Start declaring, "We are well able. We can do all things through Christ. We are strong in the Lord." When you do that, you're getting stronger and gaining energy.

The first thing you should do every morning is power up. Get your minds going in the right direction. Remind yourselves: "We're equipped and empowered for this day. We have our armor on. We're not going to get upset and let people steal our joy. We're not going to fight battles that aren't between us and our destiny. We have our helmets of salvation. We know we're forgiven, redeemed, and approved by Almighty God. We have our shields of faith." Power up and get prepared for a blessed, victorious, faith-filled day.

You may be facing things that could easily steal your joy—a challenge in your relationship, a child not doing right, or an unfair situation at work. You could live stressed and uptight. All through the day, you need to remind yourselves: "God is in control. It is not going to keep us from our destiny." Come back to that place of peace and strength.

A PRAYER FOR TODAY

Father, You are the Almighty God. Thank You for empowering us with strength for every battle, to subdue our enemies under our feet. We receive Your strength, grace, and mercy to help us today. We declare we have our shields of faith up and can do all things in Jesus' Name. Amen.

It's Your Birthday

TODAY'S SCRIPTURE

"You're my son, and today is your birthday. What do you want? Name it: Nations as a present? Continents as a prize? You can command them all to dance for you."

Psalm 2:7-9 MSG

What does that mean, "Today is your birthday"? On your birthday, more than at any other time, you feel entitled to ask for something out of the ordinary. On your birthday, you think, *Okay, I'm going to ask for that favor. I'm going to ask for a new outfit or for a set of golf clubs.* Think back to when you were a child. You knew that was your special day. You had the boldness to ask for what you really wanted.

Did you notice how big God thinks? Sometimes we're praying for a three dollar-an-hour raise; God's talking about giving you nations. We're praying to pay our bills; God's talking about continents as prizes. God is saying, "When you pray, act as though it's your birthday and I am your Heavenly Father. Come to Me with a boldness. Ask Me for what you really want as a couple. Don't hold back. Tell Me your dreams. Tell Me what you're believing for. Ask for the secret things I placed in your heart." You're not inconveniencing God. You're the apple of His eye. God will move heaven and earth to bring about His destiny in your lives. Dare to ask big.

A PRAYER FOR TODAY

Father, thank You for declaring that this day is our birthdays and for inviting us to come to You with boldness and to ask for what we want. Help us to think big. We open our hearts and believe You will move heaven and earth to bring about Your destiny for us in Jesus' Name. Amen.

Release Any Toxins

TODAY'S SCRIPTURE

*Jesus said, "Father, forgive them, for they do
not know what they are doing."*

Luke 23:34 NIV

As Jesus was hanging on the cross, having been betrayed, falsely accused of crimes, beaten and mocked by soldiers, wearing a crown of thorns, and about to breathe His last breath, He did something significant. He could have died and went on to heaven. That would have been it. But He said, "Father, before I go, I need to take care of one last thing. Forgive them, for they know not what they do." They didn't ask for forgiveness or deserve it. But Jesus said in effect, "I'm not leaving this earth with anything negative in Me." He was showing us by example to release the poisonous toxins of unforgiveness, so that nothing will hold us back.

Sometimes it's not easy to empty out the negative in a relationship. If your spouse does something wrong to you, human nature wants to hold on to the hurt and anger, to carry around a bitter grudge. We think, *They don't deserve forgiveness*. But you're not forgiving for their sake; you're forgiving for your sake. Unforgiveness is a toxin that will contaminate your lives. When you forgive, as Jesus forgave us, you're not excusing their behavior or lessening the offense. You're simply getting the poison out of you. You have to forgive so that you can be free. If you let it go, you'll have peace that goes beyond what you can understand.

A PRAYER FOR TODAY

*Father, thank You that because we were freely forgiven by
Jesus on the cross, we can also forgive each other for anything
that we've done wrong. We declare that we're letting it
go and receiving Your peace that goes beyond
understanding in Jesus' Name. Amen.*

OUR
BEST
LIFE
TOGETHER

We Declare

we will not just survive;
we will thrive! We will
prosper despite every
difficulty that may come
our way. We know every
setback is a setup for a
comeback. We will not get
stagnant, give up on our
dreams, or settle where we
are. We know one touch
of God's favor can change
everything. We're ready for
a year of blessings and a
year of thriving!

Maintaining Your Peace

TODAY'S SCRIPTURE

*Make every effort to keep yourselves united in the Spirit,
binding yourselves together with peace.*

Ephesians 4:3 NLT

When we allow strife into our lives and our relationship, it damages our attitudes, our dreams, our energy, and our creativity. You make better decisions and are more productive, more creative, and more successful if you take steps to have peace in your relationship. Where there's unity, God's favor, blessing, and anointing are on your home, your lives, your marriage, and your finances. The peace you bring will have such an anointing, such a favor on it, that it will override the negative forces that are trying to bring your family down.

The Scripture says, "Blessed are the makers and maintainers of peace." We know what it means to make peace. After an argument, we apologize, forgive each other, and get over it. That's important, but we need to be more aware of maintaining the peace. That means staying on the high road—biting your tongue, not arguing, not being sarcastic, doing the right thing when the wrong thing is happening. Maintaining your peace is much easier than always having to make peace. Instead of getting offended and upset, start maintaining your peace. Don't open the door to strife. When you make the extra effort to keep unity in the home, you're going to have not only God's anointing and blessing, but you'll have His protection. He'll keep you from unnecessary trouble.

A PRAYER FOR TODAY

*Father, thank You that because we are united in Your Spirit,
we commit ourselves to peace. Thank You that Your favor
covers our relationship and home from any negative forces
that come against us. We declare that Your protection
is over us in Jesus' Name. Amen.*

Much, Much More

TODAY'S SCRIPTURE

*"[David,] if that had not been enough,
I would have given you much, much more."*

2 Samuel 12:8 NLT

n the book of 2 Samuel is the story of how King David got off course with his life. The prophet Nathan was correcting him. In doing so, he reminded David of the ways he had experienced God's goodness, favor, protection, and provision down through the years. God made an interesting statement through Nathan: "David, if you were ever lacking, I would have given you much, much more."

That tells us that what we have right now is what we need to fulfill our destiny. The moment it becomes insufficient is the moment God will give us more. The moment it begins to stop God's plan for our lives together is the moment God will intervene. So if it hasn't happened yet, don't be discouraged, thinking that it's never going to work out. If it hasn't happened, you haven't needed it. When you need it, it won't be late.

The moment you need new friends, the moment you need a good break, the moment you need an idea, it will show up. God is closely watching your lives. You are His most prized possessions. He is saying to the two of you what He said to David: "If it's ever not enough, you can count on Me. I will always be there to give you more."

A PRAYER FOR TODAY

Father, thank You for the "much, much more" promise that You made to David and to us as well. Thank You that we have everything we need right now to fulfill our destiny, to live lives that bring pleasure to You. We believe that nothing we need will be a second late in Jesus' Name. Amen.

Drop It

TODAY'S SCRIPTURE

*"Do not remember the former things, or ponder
the things of the past. Listen carefully,
I am about to do a new thing..."*

Isaiah 43:18-19 AMP

We've all had negative things happen to us. People did us wrong, the company let us go, we spoke unkind words and hurt each other. It's easy to go through life carrying offenses, trapped in self-pity, blaming ourselves, blaming our family, even blaming God. Because we're always looking back, reliving the negative, we end up carrying around emotional baggage that weighs us down. One of the best things you can learn to do is drop it. Whether it happened twenty years ago or twenty minutes ago, don't carry negative baggage from yesterday into today. You won't have a healthy relationship if you're always reliving what didn't work out, who hurt who, the mistakes you made.

Past hurts occurred once. Don't let them continue to hurt you by always thinking about them. That's going to keep you down and discouraged. As long as you're dwelling on the past, you're going to miss "the new things" God said He would do. You need to be looking forward to new beginnings. You have to do your part and quit remembering the past, quit reliving it, and move forward. The reason it's called "the past" is that it's done, it's over, it's history. Now do your part and let it go.

A PRAYER FOR TODAY

*Father, thank You that we can be free from all the negative
baggage that comes from carrying past offenses, guilt, and blame.
Help us to treat the past as the past. We believe and look
forward to the new things that You're doing in our lives
and relationship in Jesus' Name. Amen.*

Be Encouragers

TODAY'S SCRIPTURE

Therefore encourage one another
and build each other up.

1 Thessalonians 5:11 NIV

The first time young Robert met his uncle, out of the blue the uncle said, "Robert, I think one day you will be a great minister." Why did the uncle say this? There were no ministers in this family. He simply felt something inside, and he was bold enough to speak it out by faith. He planted a seed in little Robert's heart. That night Robert secretly prayed, "God, let what my uncle said be true one day." As you may know, Robert Schuller became one of the great ministers of our time. Isn't it amazing what a simple word of encouragement can do?

The word *encourage* means "to urge forward." Every one of us should have someone we're urging forward, someone we're helping to achieve goals and dreams. Certainly, that "someone" starts with your spouse. How do you encourage someone? You study that person and identify what he or she does well. What excites him? What are her strengths? An encourager sees things in others that they often can't see in themselves. You have the ability to speak faith into the heart of another and stir up someone's dreams by giving them permission to succeed. When you take time to believe in someone, you can light a fire on the inside that glows joyfully for a lifetime. Your words can become the seed God nourishes.

A PRAYER FOR TODAY

Father, help us to see and believe the best about others. Help us to always use our words to speak life and blessing over each other and the people around us. Thank You for choosing us and using us to stir up others' dreams and give them permission to succeed in Jesus' Name. Amen.

With All Your Heart

TODAY'S SCRIPTURE

And whatever you do, do it heartily,
as to the Lord and not to men.

Colossians 3:23 NKJV

When you give 100 percent effort, you do it to the best of your ability; because you're honoring God, you will have His blessing. That means it will go better, and you will accomplish more together. When you do the dishes, for instance, don't complain; do it with all your heart and you honor God. When you mow the lawn, don't drag around all sour. Mow it with enthusiasm, as though you're on a mission from God. Don't give a halfhearted effort to making a meal. Do it with all your heart. Give it your very best.

Years ago, there was a police officer who directed traffic on one of the busiest intersections in Houston. He didn't just direct traffic like normal; he practically danced while he directed. Both hands would be constantly moving. He had his whistle and held his head like a drum major. His feet would dance here and there. He could direct traffic and moonwalk at the same time. Drivers pulled over just to watch him. He was passionate.

That's the way you should be. Don't drag through the day. Whatever you do, put your heart into it. Put a spring in your step. Wear a smile on your face. You honor God when you do it with all your heart.

A PRAYER FOR TODAY

Father, thank You that because Your joy is our strength,
we can enjoy our lives to the fullest and do everything with all
our hearts. We want to give You pleasure in all that we do and say.
We declare that we're shaking off the blahs and getting our
passion back in Jesus' Name. Amen.

Into Your Promised Land

TODAY'S SCRIPTURE

*Now the people complained about their hardships
in the hearing of the Lord and when he heard
them his anger was aroused.*

Numbers 11:1 NIV

This was one of the reasons the Israelites never made it to the Promised Land. God brought them out of slavery, they were headed to the land flowing with milk and honey, but along the way they got under pressure and started complaining. It was an eleven-day journey to the Promised Land, but because of their negative words, they went around the same mountain for forty years.

In your relationship, if what you're about to say isn't good, beneficial, and edifying, do yourself a favor and zip it up. You're not just affecting your spouse; you're keeping yourself from your destiny. God will put us in situations to test us. If you're critical, harsh, and condescending, you have to go around the same mountain.

The next time you're tempted to say something you know you shouldn't, pause for thirty seconds. Under your breath, say, "God, help me to control my tongue." If you do that, you will start passing these tests. You'll see more of His favor. The point is, you can't be critical and disrespectful to your spouse and make it into your promised land. This is why Proverbs says, "Life and death are in the power of the tongue." Our question is, are you speaking life to your spouse?

A PRAYER FOR TODAY

*Father, we praise You for speaking to our hearts. Thank You
that You are leading us to our promised land. Help us to be quick
to control our tongues and speak words of life to each other.
We declare that we will reach the fullness of our destiny
together in Jesus' Name. Amen.*

Anointing of Ease

TODAY'S SCRIPTURE

"Take my yoke upon you. Let me teach you...
and you will find rest for your souls.
For my yoke is easy to bear..."

Matthew 11:29-30 NLT

God wants to make your lives easier. He wants to help you when you're shopping at the grocery store, raising your children, and dealing with problems at home. Every day His favor and blessing are lightening your load and taking the pressure off. David declared in Psalm 23, "God anoints my head with oil." Whenever there is friction or things are stuck, oil is used to lubricate it and make it more fluid. That's what God is doing with you when He anoints your head with oil.

David went on to say, "Because God has anointed me, surely goodness and mercy will follow me wherever I go." That means things will be easier. What you used to struggle with will no longer be a struggle. For no reason, people will want to be good to you. You will have good ideas, wisdom, creativity, and you won't know where it came from. That is God's anointing of ease.

God is directing every one of your steps as a couple. He has already lined up solutions to your problems. He has lined up the breaks you need. We want you to go out each day knowing there is favor, restoration, and healing in your future. If you stay in faith, you will see favor that will make your lives easier.

A PRAYER FOR TODAY

Father, thank You for destroying every yoke of bondage off our
lives. We choose to take Jesus' yoke upon us and to live by Your
Word, which is rest for our souls. Thank You for Your anointing
of ease that lightens every burden in Jesus' Name. Amen.

True Fulfillment

TODAY'S SCRIPTURE

*"Here is a boy with five small barley loaves
and two small fish, but how far will
they go among so many?"*

John 6:9 NIV

This little boy had a sack lunch—five loaves of bread, two fish. Nothing much. But Jesus took his lunch, multiplied it, and fed thousands of hungry people. Think about the boy's mother who got up early that morning to make the lunch. She was a homemaker raising a child, without a title or acclaim. But titles don't bring fulfillment. Keeping up with your neighbors doesn't bring happiness, but understanding your assignment and being comfortable with who God made you to be are what bring true fulfillment.

Don't discount the gift God has given you. It may seem small just making a lunch for your child, but raising your child is a great calling. Are you secure enough to play the role that God has given you? Are you comfortable enough to not have to be number one, to have the title, the position? We put so much emphasis on rising to the top. And yes, we believe in excelling and having big gifts and big dreams, but not everyone is gifted to be the leader or on the platform. You may be gifted to teach children or sing or play an instrument. The beauty of our God is that He has given every one of us a specific gift and purpose.

A PRAYER FOR TODAY

Father, thank You that the gifts You have given us are custom-made for us alone. Thank You that You have matched us for what You want us to do and that we have exactly what we need to fulfill Your plan for our lives. We declare that we are content with our assignments in Jesus' Name. Amen.

OUR
BEST
LIFE
TOGETHER

We Declare

we will choose faith over fear!
We will meditate on what is
positive and what is good
about our situation. We will
use our energy not to worry
but to believe. Fear has no part
in our lives. We will not dwell
on negative, discouraging
thoughts. Our minds are set
on what God says about us.
We know His plan for us is
for success, victory,
and abundance.

Ordinary to Extraordinary

TODAY'S SCRIPTURE

"If you knew [about] God's gift [of eternal life],
and who it is who says, 'Give Me a drink,'
you would have asked...and He would have
given you living water (eternal life)."

John 4:10 AMP

Jesus surprised a Samaritan woman at a well when He offered to give her "living water," meaning eternal life. But she immediately began to view the circumstances from a human perspective. She said, "You don't even have anything to draw water with from the well." I wonder how many times we do the same thing. God tells us He is going to do something great in our lives, in our relationship, in our health. But we start looking at what we don't have, the obstacles in our path. Before long, we talk ourselves out of it even though we serve a supernatural God. He can take something that is ordinary, breathe on it, and turn it into something that's extraordinary. Don't talk yourselves out of it.

Don't underestimate what you have. It may look small and insignificant. Compared to what you're facing, perhaps it seems useless. All the odds are against you. But when God breathes on your lives, the odds dramatically change. You and God are a majority. God can open doors that never should have opened in the natural. God can take you beyond where your talents and your education say you should be. God can always make a way.

A PRAYER FOR TODAY

Father, we praise You that You give us the living water that
so satisfies us that we never thirst again. Thank You that You
are breathing into our lives and turning the ordinary into the
extraordinary. We believe that You and the two of us
are a majority in Jesus' Name. Amen.

Guard Your Mind

TODAY'S SCRIPTURE

Above all else, guard your heart,
for everything you do flows from it.

Proverbs 4:23 NIV

We hear a lot about certain chemicals, hormones, and bacteria in our food that can build up in our bodies and be harmful. Many experts recommend you go through a deep cleansing fast and then eat a certain diet, staying away from harmful foods. They say that over time you'll rid yourself of the toxins and feel better.

In the same way, there are all kinds of toxic thoughts that can build up in your mind—bitter, cynical, negative thoughts—that can do as much damage as toxins in your body. They become part of who you are. That's why the Scripture says to make guarding your mind a top priority. If you've allowed those thoughts to take root, they will poison your future and sour your relationship.

You need to go through a mental cleansing. The only way you will be free is to detox the mind of the bitterness, the low self-esteem, the negative words spoken over you, the condemnation from past mistakes, and the discouragement that's trying to become a part of you. To detox, you make a decision that rather than dwelling on those thoughts anymore, you will dwell on what God says about you. If you keep your mind filled with thoughts of hope and faith, those toxic thoughts will grow weaker, and before long they won't have any effect on you.

A PRAYER FOR TODAY

Father, thank You that our minds can be cleansed and
renewed by Your Word. We declare that we will no longer
meditate on negative, condemning thoughts, but we will
dwell on what You say about us, which is the truth
that sets us free in Jesus' Name. Amen.

Closed Doors

TODAY'S SCRIPTURE

*"What he opens no one can shut,
and what he shuts no one can open."*
Revelation 3:7 NIV

We all know that God opens doors. We've seen Him give us favor, good breaks, promotion. That's the hand of God opening the door. But He will also close doors. Maybe you prayed, but you didn't get a promotion you wanted. Your house loan application didn't go through. A relationship you enjoyed didn't work out. So often we can become discouraged and feel as though God has let us down.

But God can see the big picture for your lives. God knows where every road is leading. He knows the dead ends and short-cuts. We could go for years and end up right back where we started. We can't see what God can see. A big part of faith is trusting God when you don't understand why things happen the way they do. God may close a door because you're believing too small. If He opened the door, it would limit what He wants to do in your lives. Another door may close because it's not the right time, or there are other people involved and they're not ready yet.

The bottom line is: God has your best interests at heart. When a door closes, you don't know what God is saving you from. If your prayers aren't answered the way you want, instead of being discouraged, have a bigger perspective: God has something better in store.

A PRAYER FOR TODAY

Father, thank You that You love us so much that You haven't answered certain prayers. You haven't allowed certain people or situations into our lives because they would have limited our growth. We believe that closed doors mean You have something better for us in Jesus' Name. Amen.

People of Excellence

TODAY'S SCRIPTURE

*...that your love may abound more and more, with
knowledge and all discernment, so that you may approve
what is excellent, and so be pure and blameless...*

Philippians 1:9-10 ESV

For many people, mediocrity is the norm; they do as little as they possibly can to just get by. But God did not create us to be mediocre. He has called us to be people of excellence and integrity, and anything less will cause us to be unhappy as a couple. Any hint of compromise will taint our greatest victories or our grandest achievements as well as keep us from God's best.

People of excellence and integrity go the extra mile to do what's right. They keep their word even when it's difficult. They give their employers a full day's work and don't call in sick when they are not. When you have an excellent spirit, it shows up in the quality of everything you do and the attitude with which you do it.

God's people are people of excellence. Remember that you represent Almighty God. How you live together, how you conduct your business and do your work, is all a reflection on our God. The Scripture says that whatever you do, you should give your best effort and do it as if you were doing it for God. If you want to live your best life together, start aiming for excellence in everything you do.

A PRAYER FOR TODAY

*Father, we love You and dedicate every area of our lives to You.
Thank You for calling us to live lives of excellence and for the
privilege of representing You to our loved ones and friends.
We want our excellence to flow out of our hearts of love
for You in Jesus' Name. Amen.*

Silence Is Golden

TODAY'S SCRIPTURE

"Do not even talk," Joshua commanded.
"Not a single word from any of you
until I tell you to shout."

Joshua 6:10 NLT

When Joshua was leading the people of Israel into the Promised Land, they had to conquer the city of Jericho with its thick, tall wall. They had no way to get in. God told them for six days to march around that wall once a day, and on the seventh day to march around it seven times. If that wasn't odd enough, God said, "While you're marching, keep totally silent." He knew they would be saying, "This wall is never going to fall." Negative words would have defeated them.

Could it be that negative words are keeping you out of your promised land? Could it be that if you would not talk about how big the problem is, not tell friends how you're never going to be successful, maybe the walls that are holding you back would come down? Imagine behind that wall is your healing, your promotion, your dream coming to pass. Every day, so to speak, you're walking around the wall. What are the two of you saying?

God is saying to us, "If you can't say anything full of faith, don't say a word." Don't let your negative words keep you from God's best. If you simply remain silent, God can bring those walls down.

A PRAYER FOR TODAY

Father, today we choose to take captive every thought that is
contrary to Your Word. Strengthen us and help us focus on
Your promises and not our problems. We believe that
as we speak words of faith that we will see You release
Your promises in Jesus' Name. Amen.

Live by What You Know

TODAY'S SCRIPTURE

Why are you down in the dumps, dear soul?
Why are you crying the blues? Fix my eyes on God—
soon I'll be praising again. He puts a smile
on my face. He's my God.

Psalm 43:5 MSG

We all have times when we feel the blahs. Just the thought of an emotionally difficult situation we're facing as a couple can give us the blues. But just because we feel those emotions doesn't mean we have to give in to them.

King David had to fight being moody and depressed even though he had great wealth and success. That tells us that everyone has to choose to deal with negative feelings. Sometimes the best thing we can do is talk to ourselves as David did. He was saying, "David, stop looking at your problems and start looking at your God." That tells us that true joy is found only in God. Take your eyes off how you feel and your circumstances and place them on Him and His Word.

Start living by what you know. You know God is in control. You know He has a great plan for your lives and His power is greater than any other power. Shake off those old discouraging feelings. Decide not to live by how you feel. Fix your eyes toward Him instead of your situation, and you'll live the lives of victory He has in store for you!

A PRAYER FOR TODAY

Father, thank You that the joy of the Lord is our strength.
We choose to take our eyes off our circumstances and put
a smile on our faces and live joy-filled lives because we know
You are in control. We declare that our eyes are fixed
on You and Your Word in Jesus' Name. Amen.

Put on Love

TODAY'S SCRIPTURE

*And over all these virtues put on love, which binds
them all together in perfect unity.*

Colossians 3:14 NIV

A husband and wife were so upset after a big argument
that they refused to speak to each other before going
to bed. He left a note on his wife's side of the bed that
read, "Wake me up at six." When he woke up at eight
o'clock, he found a note on his side of the bed: "It's six o'clock.
Wake up."

In many relationships, over time, couples neglect to walk in
love. One day they realize that their hearts have changed. We hear
it all the time: "We just grew apart." If we're going to live in love,
the Scripture says, "Do not let the sun go down while you are still
angry, and do not give the devil a foothold." The only way to do
that is to forgive and above having your own way, choose to put
on love and keep peace in your home. Be the first to apologize.
Be quick to forgive.

God has a good plan for how you can have your best life
together. Remind yourselves that God has put the two of you
together. If you will do your part by being kind, respecting each
other, treating each other the way you want to be treated, God
will do His part, and you will live in love!

A PRAYER FOR TODAY

*Father, thank You for another day to praise You and live for You.
We invite Your love and forgiveness to flow through us. We choose
to show Your love and kindness through our actions and words.
Help us to always take the high road and put on love and
peace with each other in Jesus' Name. Amen.*

Prune to Grow

TODAY'S SCRIPTURE

*"...every branch that continues to bear fruit,
He [repeatedly] prunes, so that it will bear
more fruit [even richer and finer fruit]."*

John 15:2 AMP

At home, we have green plants that look like tall grass lining the sidewalk. One day we were shocked to see that the gardener had cut these plants down to about three inches. But in just a few weeks those plants were taller, fuller, healthier than ever. Our gardener knows when and how much each plant needs to be pruned.

In the same way God is the master gardener. This means all of us at times are going to experience being cut back. But He's not going to cut anything back unless it's the perfect time. Sometimes we think, *God, we were doing great. Why did You cut back our business, why did we go through that disappointment?* God cut you back for one reason—so you can bear much fruit. That means on a regular basis we're going to experience pruning, sometimes of things we don't understand.

In those tough times we tend to focus on the cutback, what we lost, what didn't work out. You have to remind yourselves that you're being pruned so you can see new growth. That cutting may be uncomfortable, but it's making you better. God's getting you prepared. You may have lost something, but you need to get ready to gain something better.

A PRAYER FOR TODAY

Father, we praise You for being the master gardener of our lives. Thank You for times of pruning when You cut back something in our lives so that we can bear more fruit. We believe that You know what is best for us and that You're bringing something better into our lives in Jesus' Name. Amen.

We Declare

we are equipped for every good work God has planned for us. We are anointed and empowered by the Creator of the universe. Every bondage, every limitation, is being broken off of us. This is our time to shine. We will rise higher, overcome every obstacle, and experience victory like never before!

Reign in Life

TODAY'S SCRIPTURE

*...how much more will those who receive God's
abundant provision of grace and of the gift of
righteousness reign in life through the
one man, Jesus Christ.*

Romans 5:17 NIV

When God looks at you, He doesn't see you defeated, barely getting by, or just taking the leftovers. God sees you as a king and queen. You have His royal blood flowing through your veins. You are to reign in life. "To reign" means "time in power." God said your term to reign in power is for every single day—to be victorious, to rise to new levels, to accomplish great things together. And on those days when you don't feel like a king or queen, remember that you have to do this by faith. You may not feel victorious. It may not look like you're blessed. But by faith you need to walk, talk, think, and smile like a king and queen. Don't go by what you see. Go by what you know. You were created to reign in life.

Too many couples are living below their privileges. Perhaps you don't think you can be successful and accomplish what God has put in your hearts. But strongholds that may have kept you back for years, even right now, are being broken. You need to rise up and say, "That's it. We're not settling where we are. We know it's still our time of power. We are stepping up to who God created us to be."

A PRAYER FOR TODAY

*Father, thank You that we are Your children with royalty in
our blood and destined to reign as a king and queen every
single day. We declare that we are empowered by Your
abundant provision of grace and of the gift of righteousness
in Jesus' Name. Amen.*

Dinner Will Be Served

TODAY'S SCRIPTURE

*You prepare a table before me in the
presence of my enemies.*

Psalm 23:5 NIV

I n the Scripture, a court official named Haman tried to push down Mordecai, who was Queen Esther's cousin. He disrespected Mordecai and tried to make him look bad. But one day the king told Haman to get a royal robe, put it on Mordecai, and announce to everyone in the streets what a great man Mordecai was. The very man who was trying to make Mordecai look bad was chosen to honor him. That's what happens when you let God do it His way.

All the things that come against us to try to get us upset—people talking, gossiping, spreading rumors, not giving us respect—are all distractions. That's the enemy trying to get us to waste valuable time and energy on something that doesn't really matter. Stay in peace. God has your back. He will not only make your wrongs right, but God will give you honor, recognition, and favor in front of the people who try to pull you down. Just imagine that God just turned the oven on. He is getting your dinner prepared. It's not going to be just you. Those people who tried to push you down will watch you get promoted. The ones who said you don't have what it takes as a couple will watch you accomplish your dreams. Stay in peace. Dinner will be served!

A PRAYER FOR TODAY

*Father, thank You for preparing a place of blessing for us
and for arranging things in our favor. We choose to trust You
and Your timing, knowing that You are working behind the
scenes on our behalf. We declare that we are staying in
peace in Jesus' Name. Amen.*

Small Beginnings

TODAY'S SCRIPTURE

*Do not despise these small beginnings, for the
LORD rejoices to see the work begin.*
Zechariah 4:10 NLT

When David went out to face Goliath, he had no armor, so King Saul tried to get David to wear his armor. But David was much smaller than Saul and the armor swallowed him. It didn't help him. That's because what God has given other people is not going to work for you. Don't try to be like somebody else or some other couple. "If only we had their talents, their looks, their personalities…" Their armor wasn't designed for you. God has custom-made your armor just for you.

The Scripture says, "Don't despise the day of small beginnings." All David had was a slingshot and five smooth stones. It looked insignificant, ordinary. But God breathed on him, and he defeated Goliath and became the king of Israel. The Creator of the universe is also breathing on your lives. He is breathing on your health, your finances, and your marriage. If you will be confident in what God has given you, He can take what looks like little and turn it into much. Don't look at what you have and say, "We can't do anything great." What God has given you right now may seem small, but when you use what you have, God will multiply it. You will see an explosion of His goodness.

A PRAYER FOR TODAY

*Father, thank You for Your word to never despise small beginnings,
for You rejoice to see us use what You've given us and You
will bring the increase as we trust in You. Thank You that we
don't need to be like anyone else. We believe that we will
bring down giants in Jesus' Name. Amen.*

The 80/20 Rule

TODAY'S SCRIPTURE

*And my God will supply every need of yours according
to his riches in glory in Christ Jesus.*

Philippians 4:19 ESV

n our relationship with each other, when we quit expecting our
spouse to keep us happy, not only will their life be better, but
our relationship will improve greatly. No matter how good they
are, nobody can meet all our needs. A husband can do his best
to love his wife, but there will be times when he lets her down. If
she only looks to him, she'll be disappointed. But when she goes
to God to meet her needs, she'll never be disappointed. No person
has 100 percent. Some people say that in a relationship the most
the other person will have is 80 percent of what you need. There
will always be 20 percent that they cannot give you. Perhaps you're
thinking, *My spouse is missing a lot more than 20 percent!*

The key to a good relationship is to recognize the other person's strengths and weaknesses, and then give them some space
to be who they are. Don't try to make them fit into your mold.
Perhaps you love to talk, but your spouse prefers to be quiet.
Recognize that's part of the 20 percent that they don't have. You're
going to live frustrated if you try to make them into something
they're not. Love them and just let them off the hook.

A PRAYER FOR TODAY

*Father, we praise You for supplying every need. We believe
that means 100 percent of our needs and that it frees
us from looking to each other to meet our needs.
We know that You will never disappoint us
in Jesus' Name. Amen.*

Soar Above

TODAY'S SCRIPTURE

They held him in contempt and refused to congratulate him. But Saul paid them no mind.

1 Samuel 10:27 MSG

When Saul was chosen to be the first king of Israel, most of the people were excited and congratulated him. But many longtime friends were jealous of him and ridiculed him. Saul could have easily lost his focus and wasted time defending himself. What did he do? Saul ignored them.

Remember this phrase: "When people belittle you, they are being little themselves." Small-minded people won't celebrate you as a couple. They will be jealous and gossip to make you look bad. But they are not going where God is taking you. You are called to soar like eagles, to do great things together. If some pesky crows dive-bomb you at times, you can fly at altitudes where the crows cannot fly. Simply rise higher and eventually the crows are left behind.

When someone is pestering you out of jealousy or spite, leave them behind. God hears what your critics say, and if you stay in faith, He will make it up to you. Use your energy to improve your relationship, to be the best that you can be. Follow Saul's wise approach. Pay no mind to jealous people or those who try to bring you down. They don't control your destiny; God does. They are simply distractions. Just stay focused and do what God has called you to do together.

A PRAYER FOR TODAY

Father, thank You for empowering us to rise up higher over the adversities of life. We won't focus on what others say about us, but only on what You say, because Your Word is fixed in heaven. Help us to ignore distractions so that we can move forward in Jesus' Name. Amen.

The Right Way at the Right Time

TODAY'S SCRIPTURE

Avoiding a fight is a mark of honor;
only fools insist on quarreling.

Proverbs 20:3 NLT

Sometimes when we get in an argument with each other, we may both walk away giving ourselves high fives, thinking, *I won that fight. I told them what I thought.* That's not really winning. You may have made yourself feel good, but it didn't strengthen your relationship. You may have won the argument, but how much damage was done? When we say hurtful things and are disrespectful, it exacts a heavy price. The real way to win is to avoid it, to walk away and take the high road. That's a mark of honor. It takes humility. Pride wants to argue, have the last word, and keep it stirred up.

Instead of trying to figure out what you're going to say in order to win an argument, why don't you spend that same time on how you're going to avoid the argument? We're not saying to not address your differences, but there's a right way and a right time. You should do it calmly, express your concerns, and then leave it there. If it starts getting heated and disrespectful, walk away. When you do it God's way, He'll fight your battles. He'll change what needs to be changed. Do what you can to keep the atmosphere in your home loving, kind, and peaceful. Be a person of honor and avoid the fight.

A PRAYER FOR TODAY

Father, thank You for calling us to be people marked by honor
who avoid quarreling. Thank You that there is a right way and
a right time to quietly and calmly address our differences.
Help us to keep the atmosphere in our home loving and
kind and peaceful in Jesus' Name. Amen.

Come Alive

TODAY'S SCRIPTURE

*"Prophesy to these bones and say to them, 'Dry bones,
hear the word of the LORD!... I will make breath
enter you, and you will come to life.'"*

Ezekiel 37:4-5 NIV

Ezekiel saw a vision of a valley filled with bones. It was like a huge graveyard of people's bones. Bones represent things in our lives that look dead, situations that seem impossible and permanently unchanging. God said, "Ezekiel, prophesy to these dead bones." Ezekiel started speaking to the bones, telling them to come back to life. As he was speaking, the bones started rattling and coming together, morphing back into people. Finally, breath came into those bodies, and they stood up as "a vast army."

You may have things in your life that seem dead—a relationship, a business, your health. It's not enough to just pray about it; you need to speak to it. Prophesy to those dead bones. Call in health. Call in abundance. Call in restoration. Prophesy and say, "Son, daughter, come back in. You will fulfill your destiny." Get your checkbook out and prophesy to it. All it looks like is dead bones. Debt. Lack. Struggle. "We prophesy to these dead bones that we will lend and not borrow. We are the head and not the tail. We are coming into overflow." Just as with Ezekiel, if you prophesy to the bones, God will resurrect what looks dead.

A PRAYER FOR TODAY

*Father, we praise You for Your grace and mercy. Thank You
that we can speak to the things in our lives that seem dead,
and You will breathe life into them. We believe that as we speak
words of faith that You will make things happen that we
could never make happen in Jesus' Name. Amen.*

Propelled

TODAY'S SCRIPTURE

*The LORD took hold of me, and I was carried
away by the Spirit of the LORD...*

Ezekiel 37:1 NLT

n today's Scripture, the word *carried* means "to shoot out, to launch forward, to spring forth." It implies acceleration. As God carries you through life, that doesn't mean it's always going to be little by little. There are times when God is going to shoot you out and propel you years down the road. He'll give you a break that you don't deserve. He'll cause you to meet the right person. He'll turn a problem around when you didn't see a way.

"Well, we don't think God is going to shoot us out. We've had too many bad breaks." Think of it like this. When you have a bow and arrow, the more you pull the arrow back, the farther it's going to shoot. God allowed you to be pulled back so far because He's about to shoot you farther than you can imagine. Your destiny is bigger than you've dreamed. You may feel as though you'll never get to where you're supposed to be. When God shoots you out, you're going to make up for lost time. No person, no unfair situation, and no organization can stop you. The doors that are going to open, the people you're going to meet, and the opportunities that are coming your way are going to be bigger, better, more rewarding that you've ever thought possible.

A PRAYER FOR TODAY

Father, we praise You that You make up for lost time. We believe that You will accomplish our dreams faster than we thought possible, and that our future is bright because this is our time for acceleration. We declare that You are blessing us beyond our dreams in Jesus' Name. Amen.

OUR
BEST
LIFE
TOGETHER

We Declare

that we will ask God for big things in our lives. We will pray bold prayers and expect big and believe big. We will ask God to bring to pass those hidden dreams that are deep in our hearts. If certain promises don't look like they will happen, we will not be intimidated and give up. We will pray with boldness, expecting God to show Himself strong, knowing that nothing is too difficult for Him.

JOEL & VICTORIA OSTEEN

Words of Life

TODAY'S SCRIPTURE

*Hide me from...[those] who have sharpened
their tongues like a sword. They aim
venomous words as arrows.*

Psalm 64:2-3 AMP

David referred to some people's mouths as sharp swords and words as venomous arrows. Are you building each other up or are you cutting each other up with your words? Are you encouraging each other, making each other stronger and more confident, or are you putting each other down? Many times we can recover from a physical wound quicker than an emotional wound.

As parents, we have a responsibility to speak words of life, faith, and encouragement into our children. Yes, you must correct them, but don't do it in an angry, disrespectful way. Don't say derogatory things that are going to damage their self-esteem. Don't tell a child, "You're a bad boy. You're a bad girl." Don't get that down in their spirit. Your child is made in the image of God. They may have bad behavior, but they are good. Correct them in love, with a kind spirit. Don't cut them up with negative, hurtful words at any age. Let's be parents who speak words of life, who push our children into their destiny, who help release their dreams. Our children are a gift from God. With that gift comes a responsibility. God is counting on you to guide them, to nurture them, and to encourage them to become who they were created to be.

A PRAYER FOR TODAY

*Father, we love You and come to You with open and humble
hearts. We commit our words to You. Show us when we speak
negative words so we can change. We believe that You will
help us to speak words of life and faith to each other
and to our children in Jesus' Name. Amen.*

Rejoice

TODAY'S SCRIPTURE

Even though...there are no grapes on the vines...
yet will I rejoice in the LORD! I will be joyful
in the God of my salvation.

Habakkuk 3:17–18 NLT

The prophet Habakkuk was saying, "There's no reason in the natural to be happy, nothing is going my way, yet will I rejoice in the Lord." We can hear him going through the day, saying, "God, I praise You for Your greatness. You're bigger than this cancer, bigger than this financial struggle. I rejoice in the God of my salvation."

Life is too short for you to go through it weighed down by pressure. In the midst of your difficulties as a couple, have a song of praise on the inside. That's what not only keeps you full of faith, but that's what allows God to turn things around. If you can't find any reason to be grateful, do as Habakkuk did and rejoice in the God of your salvation. Go through the day thanking God for Who He is. "Lord, thank You that You are our savior, our healer, our deliverer, our protector, our provider, and our way maker."

When you complain, you leak out your joy; when you're negative, it's making you weaker. If you develop this habit of being joyful in your hearts, your lives are going to overflow with joy, with peace, with victory. You will have the strength you need to overcome obstacles, defeat enemies, and become everything you were created to be.

A PRAYER FOR TODAY

Father, we choose to rejoice in You, knowing that You are the
God of our salvation and that victory is on the way. No matter
what our circumstances look like, we know You are greater
than our circumstances. We declare that You are greater
than all in Jesus' Name. Amen.

File It Away

TODAY'S SCRIPTURE

Trust God from the bottom of your heart;
don't try to figure out everything on your own.

Proverbs 3:5 MSG

n 1881, President James Garfield was shot in the back. Focused on finding and removing the bullet, the doctors stuck their unsanitary fingers in the wound, probing all around, but couldn't find it. Two months later, he died, not from his original wound, but from the overwhelming infection that came from all the unsanitary probing.

Sometimes it's better to leave things alone. As long as you're probing around your wounds, your hurts, your disappointments, you're keeping it stirred up to the point where you're never going to heal. Give it to God and say, "God, we don't understand it, but we're not going to keep trying to figure it out. You wouldn't allow it if You couldn't bring good out of it, so we're going to let it go and leave it."

The fact is that everything that happens to us is not going to fit perfectly into our theology. We should have a file in our thinking called "We Don't Understand It." When things come up that you can't find an answer as to why, just put it in that file and keep moving forward. If you make the mistake of going through life trying to figure out why something bad happened, why something didn't work out, that's going to poison your lives.

A PRAYER FOR TODAY

Father, thank You that we can trust in You and be free from
trying to figure everything out. We know that You wouldn't allow
it in our lives if You couldn't bring good out of it. We will place
these matters in our "We Don't Understand It" file and
move forward in Jesus' Name. Amen.

Rise Up

TODAY'S SCRIPTURE

Though the righteous fall seven times, they rise again...
Proverbs 24:16 NIV

V ery few couples look in the mirror and say, "You're amazing. You're wonderful. You're good." We think, *No, we have shortcomings. We struggle in some areas.* When you say, "We're amazing. We're good," it's because of Whose you are. You are children of the Most High God and crowned with favor. Don't you dare go around feeling intimidated or insecure, as though you don't measure up. Your performance doesn't determine who you are as a couple; your Heavenly Father determines who you are.

When you fall down and make mistakes, you could be discouraged. Thoughts will whisper, "Look at the two of you! You're hypocrites. God is never going to bless you." Just answer back, "We may have fallen, but we didn't stay down. We got back up again and are on the right track."

Don't live with that heaviness. You could be sitting on the sidelines, feeling depressed and full of self-pity, but you're still in the game. You're restored and moving forward. You can hold your head high and feel good about who you are. You may not be where you want to be, but you can thank God you're not where you used to be. You're growing, you're improving, you're coming up higher. Don't go around focused on how far you have to go. Celebrate where you are. Thank God for where He's brought you so far.

A PRAYER FOR TODAY

Father, thank You that You are the Most High God and that because we are Your children, we have royalty in our blood. Help us when we fall to never stay down in discouragement and condemnation. We declare that we are amazing because of Who You are in Jesus' Name. Amen.

Faith and Patience

TODAY'S SCRIPTURE

*...to imitate those who through faith and patience
inherit what has been promised.*

Hebrews 6:12 NIV

We live in a society that wants everything right now. We've been programmed for immediacy, including our faith. It's easy to have faith. "God, we believe we're going to overcome this obstacle." Let's make sure we also get the patience part down. "And God, we trust Your timing. We're not going to get discouraged if it doesn't happen immediately. We're going to wait with faith and patience because we know that it's on the way."

The Scripture says, "God didn't take the Israelites the shortest route to the Promised Land, because He knew they were not prepared for war." God could see the big picture. So on purpose, God took them on a longer route to protect them and to strengthen them so they could fulfill their destiny.

If something is not happening on your timetable, remind yourselves, "God knows what He is doing. He has our best interests at heart. We wouldn't be having this delay unless God had a very good reason for it." And while you're waiting, don't make the mistake of trying to figure everything out. That's only going to frustrate you. Say with David, "God, our times are in Your hands. We're not going to worry about why something hasn't happened. We know at the set time everything You promised us will come to pass."

A PRAYER FOR TODAY

Father, we trust in Your faithfulness. Thank You that You see the big picture for our lives and You know what we're going to need, who we're going to need, and when they need to show up. We declare that through faith and patience we will receive Your promises in Jesus' Name. Amen.

Complete the Masterpiece

TODAY'S SCRIPTURE

Be kind and compassionate to one another, forgiving
each other, just as in Christ God forgave you.

Ephesians 4:32 NIV

There is an old legend that when Leonardo da Vinci was painting a portrait of Christ, he could not make any progress as he tried to paint the face of Christ. The legend says that da Vinci finally realized that until he forgave a person for whom he held hatred in his heart, he could not complete his masterpiece. That's what happens when we hold on to the negatives in our relationship. It stifles our creativity, we aren't our best for each other, and we don't enjoy our life together as we should.

It takes a lot of emotional energy to hold a grudge, to live with unforgiveness, anger, bitterness, jealousy, and guilt. When you're always thinking about what they did, reliving how wrong it was, you're spending emotional energy that you need for your destiny, for your dreams together, for your children. You won't become all you were created to be. Unforgiveness is an impurity. If you have it, release it. When you let it go, you'll not only feel a new freedom, but God will be your vindicator. He will make your wrongs right. You don't have to pay each other back. You're not the judge; God is. If you leave it to Him, He'll vindicate you better than you can vindicate yourself.

A PRAYER FOR TODAY

Father, we praise You for forgiving us and setting us free.
We invite You to search our hearts and minds, and we choose
to let go of all anger, hurt, and bitterness and to forgive.
We declare that we are moving forward in the abundant
life in store for us in Jesus' Name. Amen.

A Time to Run

TODAY'S SCRIPTURE

*"Watch and pray so that you will not fall
into temptation. The spirit is willing,
but the flesh is weak."*

Matthew 26:41 NIV

When Joseph was tempted to sin with Potiphar's wife, this was a defining moment in his life (see Gen. 39). As a slave, he could have said, "What's it going to hurt to compromise?" But instead he "ran from the house," which led to the false accusations that landed him in prison, from which he eventually was promoted to being in charge of all the affairs of Egypt. What he did in that defining moment opened the way to the throne.

The Scripture tells us to run from temptation. If you don't take off running, you'll give in. God will give you the grace to overcome what you can't get away from, but He won't give you the grace to overcome things you can get away from. When you face *any* temptation, run. When your spouse says something that gets on your nerves, and you feel like telling the other off, run. Rather than watch the wrong thing on the television or the computer, go take a run. And God has a word for you about any person who's making advances, being over friendly toward you. *Run.* Get out of that compromising situation as fast as you can or it will destroy your relationship and you'll miss your destiny. Just run.

A PRAYER FOR TODAY

*Father, thank You that we have the power of Your Spirit in us
to help us be strong to run from temptation. Help us to live lives
of integrity and honor in every area of our lives. We declare that
even in the small things we will do what we know in our
hearts is right in Jesus' Name. Amen.*

Fireproof

TODAY'S SCRIPTURE

"If we are thrown into the blazing furnace, the God
we serve is able to deliver us from it...But even if
he does not, we...will not serve your gods."

Daniel 3:17-18 NIV

The three Hebrew teenagers Shadrach, Meshach, and Abednego were about to be thrown into a fiery furnace because they wouldn't bow before the king's golden idol. We're sure they prayed for deliverance, but God chose to do it another way. Sometimes God will deliver you from the fire. Other times God will make you fireproof and take you through the fire.

There is a delivering faith and there is a sustaining faith. Delivering faith is when God keeps you from the adversity. But most of the time we need sustaining faith. Sustaining faith is when God takes you through the difficulty. You are filled with doubt, anxiety, fear, and bitterness. But when you know that God is in control of the fire, and even if you go through the difficulty, you know He will take care of you. He will make you fireproof.

The same God Who kept them safe in the fiery furnace has put a hedge of protection around you as a couple. Whether you realize it or not, you are fireproof. You are coming out stronger, increased, promoted, and without smelling like smoke, just as those teens did. Why? Almighty God is in control of the furnace.

A PRAYER FOR TODAY

Father, thank You for being in control of the fiery furnaces
of our lives. We know that You will take us through and
get us to where we're supposed to be. We believe that
You will keep us safe in the fiery furnace and bring us
out stronger in Jesus' Name. Amen.

We Declare

that God is working all things together for our good. He has a master plan for our lives. There may be things we don't understand right now, but we're not worried. We know all the pieces aren't here yet. One day it will all come together and everything will make sense. We will see God's amazing plan taking us places we never dreamed of.

Well Pleased

TODAY'S SCRIPTURE

*And behold, a voice from heaven said, "This is my
beloved Son, with whom I am well pleased."*

Matthew 3:17 ESV

When God spoke these words, Jesus hadn't started His ministry yet. He had never opened one blind eye, never raised the dead, never performed a single miracle. His Father was pleased with Jesus because of who He was and not because of anything He had done.

We tell ourselves, "If we prayed more or break these bad habits, we'd feel good about ourselves." You have to learn to accept yourselves while you're in the process of changing. We all have areas we need to improve, but we're not supposed to go around down on ourselves because we haven't arrived. You may not be perfect, but God is not basing your value on your performance. He's looking at your hearts.

When you're against yourselves, it doesn't help you to do better. It makes you do worse. You may have bad habits you need to overcome, but if you go around feeling condemned, thinking about all the times you've blown it, that will not motivate you to go forward. You have to shake off the guilt. You're growing. You're making progress. Do yourselves a big favor and quit listening to the accusing voices. That's the enemy trying to convince you to be against yourselves. He knows that if you don't like yourselves, you will never become who God created you to be.

A PRAYER FOR TODAY

*Father, we praise You that Your amazing love and approval
of us is not based on our performances. We refuse to let guilt
and condemnation keep us from staying close to You. We declare
that we are growing and becoming the persons You created
us to be in Jesus' Name. Amen.*

Just Obey

TODAY'S SCRIPTURE

*And the peace of God, which transcends
all understanding, will guard your hearts
and your minds in Christ Jesus.*

Philippians 4:7 NIV

Many times we feel an inner prompting to be good to someone. That's not random. That's God talking to us. Or maybe you're in a situation that seems fine, but you feel an uneasiness. Something says, "It's not right. Stay away." That's not just your nerves. It's God protecting you. Don't ignore it, don't talk yourself out of it, just obey. The Holy Spirit is in each one of us to guide us. The Scripture talks about being sensitive to our inner ear, listening to His still small voice, the promptings, the suggestions, the alarms. Then God will guide you along the best path for your lives.

When God gave Moses the Ten Commandments, He said, "Do not add or subtract to what I've given you; just obey." He was saying, "Don't debate it, overanalyze it, or try to figure it out. Just do what I'm asking you to do." Too often we feel these inner impressions, but we dismiss them. Or we override it and say, "I don't feel peace about this, but it looks safe." We overanalyze it and think, *I could give them ten dollars, but that doesn't make sense.* Don't talk yourself out of it. Just obey. Anytime you obey, a blessing will always follow.

A PRAYER FOR TODAY

*Father, we praise You for speaking to our hearts. Thank You
for giving us an inner ear to know right from wrong. Help us
to be sensitive to Your still small voice and hear it with clarity,
to hear any alarms, promptings, and suggestions, and to
be quick to obey in Jesus' Name. Amen.*

Rule Your Spirit

TODAY'S SCRIPTURE

He who is slow to anger is better than the mighty,
he who rules his [own] spirit than he who takes a city.

Proverbs 16:32 AMPC

The Scripture tells us to rule our own spirit. It doesn't say to rule somebody else's spirit or to rule your circumstances. You can't control what other people think or say about you. We spend too much time worrying about what they said, trying to convince them to agree with us. If you're dealing with negative circumstances around you, your attempts to control it will only lead to frustration, worry, and discouragement. Part of ruling your spirit is to not let that poison get in you or your relationship. When things come against us, it's very powerful to say, "None of these things move me. God has made a way in the past, and He'll make a way this time." That's ruling your own spirit.

Another part of ruling your spirit is to not believe the enemy's constant whispers, "You've blown it so many times as a couple. God's never going to bless you." You know God's mercy is bigger than any mistake. The Scripture says, "God's gifts and calling are under full warranty—never cancelled and never rescinded." Your mistakes didn't cancel God's plan, and He's not finished with you. Your attitude should be, *We are under a lifetime warranty. God can still get us to where we're supposed to be.*

A PRAYER FOR TODAY

Father, thank You for Your strength in times of difficulty.
We can't control what others say or do or control negative
circumstances around us, but we can rule our spirits. We believe
that You will make a way for us and get us safely to where
we're supposed to be in Jesus' Name. Amen.

Glorious Things

TODAY'S SCRIPTURE

Give us gladness in proportion to our former misery!
Replace the evil years with good. Let us see your miracles
again; let our children see glorious things.

Psalm 90:15-16 TLB

Psalm 90 is a prayer of Moses. Perhaps as a couple you can identify with his request in today's Scripture. He was saying, "God, we're having a tough time. Things aren't going our way, but we're asking for Your second touch." When you face difficulties, do as Moses did and pray, "God, touch us again, strengthen us again, heal us again, show us Your favor again."

You may be facing something at your business, in a relationship, or have a health issue that you don't think could ever work out. But God didn't bring you this far to leave you. There's a second touch coming. The first touch got you to where you are, but the second touch is when it turns around, you see the breakthrough, your health and happiness are restored, your business takes off. The second touch is when you say, "We see glorious things, miracles again, the dream came to pass, the problem was resolved. God finished what He started." It takes a couple with great faith to say, "We don't see a way, but we know God has a way. We're not going to give up. We believe our second touch is coming. God's done it for others, and He can do it for us."

A PRAYER FOR TODAY

Father, we praise You for being the God Who does glorious
things that our children can see. Thank You for the assurance that
the work You've started to do in our lives will be brought
to completion. We will never give up our trust in what
You can do in Jesus' Name. Amen.

Enter into His Rest

TODAY'S SCRIPTURE

*Suddenly there was an angel at his side and
light flooding the room. The angel shook
Peter and got him up: "Hurry!"*

Acts 12:7 MSG

King Herod first killed James for being a follower of
Christ, then he had Peter arrested and chained between
two soldiers in prison. The next day it looked as though
Peter would be put to death. Yet when an angel appeared
in the prison during the night, Peter was sleeping so soundly that
the angel had to shake him to wake him. If you were Peter, would
you be sleeping soundly or would you be wide awake and stressed
out? Peter must have said, "God, I've done my best, believed and
prayed, and now I'm going to rest in You."

Worrying doesn't make anything better. Living frustrated
doesn't get God's attention. Begging God, constantly reminding
Him what's wrong, only makes us depressed. Take the problem
off the throne and put God back on the throne. If you're talking
about your problem more than you're talking about your God, you
have the wrong one on the throne. Try a different approach and
do what Peter did—go to sleep. Enter into His rest. Say together,
"God, we know You're bigger than anything we're facing. You said
You never sleep, so we're going to sleep. Even though things aren't
perfect in our lives, we're going to relax, knowing that You are
fighting our battles." That's a freeing way to live.

A PRAYER FOR TODAY

*Father, we praise You for Your strength and comfort in difficult
times. We refuse to be overwhelmed by problems, because
You will bring us through to victory. We declare that we
rest in a mighty God Who is greater than anything
we face in Jesus' Name. Amen.*

Simple Things

TODAY'S SCRIPTURE

...to put their hope in God, who richly provides us
with everything for our enjoyment.

1 Timothy 6:17 NIV

Don't miss a great season in your lives wishing you had more, complaining about what you don't have. The real joy in life is in the simple things—making memories with your family, riding your bikes together, playing hide-and-seek in the house, watching the sunset and staring up at the stars at night with your spouse.

When our son, Jonathan, was about five and Alexandra was two, we planned a big vacation to Disneyland. We were so excited. But we weren't in the Disneyland park for fifteen minutes when Jonathan said, "I want to go back to the hotel and go swimming." We pled with him over and over, "We can go swimming anytime. We're at Disneyland!" But he sat down on the pavement, crossed his arms, and refused to budge.

Having a big vacation does not guarantee having fun. Learn to enjoy the simple things in life. Could it be that you're at the right place for the season that you're in, but you're not enjoying it? Maybe if you looked at it from a new perspective, you would realize that God is directing your steps. He knows where you are, what you like and don't like. Instead of always wishing you were somewhere else, embrace the place where you are. See the good. Be grateful for what you have together.

A PRAYER FOR TODAY

Father, we praise You that You richly provide us with everything
for our enjoyment. Help us find real joy in the beauty of this
moment in our lives and in life's simple things. We believe that
You have us in the palms of Your hands and are directing
our steps in Jesus' Name. Amen.

Recalculating Route

TODAY'S SCRIPTURE

The steps of good men are directed by the Lord.
He delights in each step they take. If they fall, it isn't
fatal, for the Lord holds them with his hand.

Psalm 37:23–24 TLB

Today's Scripture is saying that even though God is directing our steps, there will be times when we fall as couples, when we make mistakes and go the wrong way. But God doesn't say, "That's it. I'm done with the two of you." He holds us in His hands and helps us get back on the right course.

It's like the GPS system in your car or phone. When you type in an address, it calculates the best route. If you miss a turn, it doesn't say, "You loser! I'm never going to help you again." It says, "Recalculating route." It just keeps recalculating your route no matter how many mistakes you make.

How much more can the Creator of the universe recalculate your route when you make mistakes? The good news is that you haven't made too many wrong turns. Your Heavenly Father isn't mad at you. He's saying, "Recalculating route. I have a way to get you to your destiny. The mistakes didn't stop My plan or cancel your purpose." Why don't you quit beating yourselves up over your failures and get back on the path. God has already calculated a new route. You can still fulfill God's best plan for your lives.

A PRAYER FOR TODAY

Father, we love and praise You that You direct our steps. Thank
You that You delight to lead us and that You always are there to
recalculate our route when we make mistakes. Show us Your
ways and give us the strength and grace to stay on the
right course in Jesus' Name. Amen.

Who Told You That?

TODAY'S SCRIPTURE

*But I am afraid that just as Eve was deceived
by the serpent's cunning, your minds may
somehow be led astray from your sincere
and pure devotion to Christ.*

2 Corinthians 11:3 NIV

n the Garden of Eden, Adam and Eve were living confident and secure. They knew they had God's blessing and favor. But one day the enemy deceived them into eating the forbidden fruit, and immediately they were afraid. They ran and hid. When God called out to Adam, "Where are you?" Adam said, "We're hiding because we're naked." God asked, "Who told you that you were naked?"

God is asking us today, "Who told you there's something wrong with you? That you're just average? That you can't accomplish your dreams? That you're not good enough?" The enemy's main tool is deception. He would love for you to go through life letting people and circumstances convince you that "You don't deserve to be blessed. You can't feel good about yourselves." The Scripture says your Creator has crowned you with glory and honor. Don't you dare give away your crown! It belongs to you. It has nothing to do with how you feel or what other people say. It's based solely on the fact that you are children of the Almighty God. Keep your crown on, keep being your best together, keep honoring God, and He will get you to where you're supposed to be.

A PRAYER FOR TODAY

*Father, we praise You that You gave us crowns of honor and
even the enemy does not have the power to take them from us.
Thank You that as Your children we are covered by Your grace
and made in Your image. We believe that we will reach our
best life together in Jesus' Name. Amen.*

We Declare

that God is going before us making crooked places straight. He has already lined up the right people, the right opportunities and solutions to problems we haven't had. No person, no sickness, no disappointment can stop His plan. What He promised will come to pass.

Your Father's Good Pleasure

TODAY'S SCRIPTURE

"Do not fear, little flock, for it is your Father's good pleasure to give you the kingdom."

Luke 12:32 NKJV

Too often, instead of believing that God will do something special for us as a couple, we do just the opposite. "We can't ask for what we really want. That would be selfish." Yet the Scripture says it is the Father's good pleasure to give you the kingdom. He says that so you'll have the boldness to ask for big things.

When we received word that the Compaq Center was coming available, we knew in our hearts that it was supposed to be ours, but every voice said, "You don't deserve it. Who do you think you are to even ask for it?" Instead of believing those lies, we did what we're asking you to do. We went to God and said, "God, we know this is far out, but we believe this is part of our destiny."

In all the big things you ever ask God for, you won't hear Him say, "Who are you to ask for that?" Just the opposite. God will be whispering, "I love the fact that you come to Me as a couple and dare to believe that I can do the impossible." Of course, everything you'll ask for won't come to pass, but there will be times when you see God show out in your lives in ways greater than you ever imagined.

A PRAYER FOR TODAY

Father, thank You that it is Your good pleasure to give us the kingdom. Thank You for encouraging us to come to You and dare to ask big. We believe and declare that we are asking You to show out through our lives in ways we never imagined in Jesus' Name. Amen.

Beware of the Negative

TODAY'S SCRIPTURE

And they laughed and jeered at Him.
But He put them all out...

Mark 5:40 AMPC

When Jesus entered a home where He was going to pray for a young girl who had died, it was filled with mourners who mocked and doubted Him. What did He do? He put the doubters out of the house before He raised her up.

When people in need come to you, try to help any way you can. But beware of negative, needy people who constantly dump their problems on your doorstep and expect you to clean them up. In truth, they don't want to be helped or encouraged. They just abuse your kindness, bask in the attention, and suck the energy right out of you. Sometimes you are able to love them back to wholeness, but you can't spend your whole lives knee-deep in their troubles. In some cases the best help you can give needy people is to not help them at all. Otherwise, you just enable their dysfunction.

Are your friends making you stronger? Are they challenging you to become better parents, better spouses, better coworkers? You may need to rid yourselves of relationships that drain you or leave you feeling the worse for wear. You have a destiny to fulfill, and you can't make it happen if you are carrying needy and negative people on your backs. The solution is to show them the door. Be kind. Be polite. But pull away.

A PRAYER FOR TODAY

Father, thank You for the people You have brought into our lives. Give us discernment to see them the way You see them. Help us to be loving and kind, but not manipulated by negative people, and empower us to pull away when necessary in Jesus' Name. Amen.

Hope in God

TODAY'S SCRIPTURE

*Why are you cast down, O my soul? And why are
you disquieted within me? Hope in God.*

Psalm 42:5 NKJV

One time David felt overwhelmed by life. Everything
kept getting worse. He was down and discouraged.
He finally realized that he'd let his circumstances
cause him to pull up his anchor of hope. He said in
effect, "I'm going to put my anchor back down. I'm going to hope
in the Lord."

Perhaps it doesn't look as though you'll ever pay off your
house mortgage or travel as the two of you had dreamed. You have
to do as David did and hope in the Lord. Don't put your hope in
your circumstances; they may not work out the way you want.
Don't put your hope in people; they may let you down. Put your
hope in the Lord. When you have your hope in Him, the Scripture
says that you'll never be disappointed. You may have some temporary setbacks, but when it's all said and done, you'll come out
better than you were before.

Maybe your dream looks impossible. Neither of you have the
connections or the resources. Every voice says, "Give up. It's never
going to happen." Most couples would throw in the towel. But
your attitude is, *God is opening doors that no man can shut; favor
is in our future.* When your hope is anchored to God, He will make
things happen that you could never make happen.

A PRAYER FOR TODAY

*Father, we declare that You alone are our hope. You give
us beauty for ashes, and we know that we will never be
disappointed in You. We believe that You will accelerate
our dreams and that explosive blessings are coming
our way in Jesus' Name. Amen.*

Be Real

TODAY'S SCRIPTURE

*Admit your faults to one another and pray for
each other so that you may be healed.*

James 5:16 TLB

f you hide problems and pretend they're not there, you're going
to get stuck. You have to take off the masks. Everybody is struggling with something. Don't be embarrassed by it. The enemy
would love for you to wear masks your whole lives, not dealing
with the issues that are holding you back.

The apostle Paul said, "All of us, with unveiled faces, see God's
glory." As long as your faces are veiled with masks, you won't
see His glory. If you're wearing a mask of perfection, pretending
everything is okay, or wearing a mask of pride, worried about what
others think, or wearing a mask of shame, feeling guilty and condemned, that's going to keep you from God's best. Get honest with
yourselves, and be honest with God. You don't have to pretend.
When you're real, you'll see God's favor.

Paul goes on to say that God changes us from glory to glory,
not from shame to glory. If you're wearing a mask of shame, you're
going to get stuck. He doesn't change us from condemnation to
glory or from pride to glory. He changes us from glory to glory.
When you're not wearing masks, God's glory is on you. When
you're open, honest, and real, God changes you and takes you to
the next level.

A PRAYER FOR TODAY

*Father, we praise You that You allow us to see Your glory and
to be changed from glory to glory. Thank You for the freedom
You bring into our lives when we admit our faults to each other.
We believe that as we pray for each other, we will be
healed in Jesus' Name. Amen.*

Consult the Lord

TODAY'S SCRIPTURE

The Israelites examined their food,
but they did not consult the LORD.

Joshua 9:14 NLT

Joshua and the Israelites had just seen the walls of Jericho come down miraculously. God's favor was on them. When a group of people, who lived just a couple of cities beyond where Joshua had camped, heard how powerful the Israelites were, they knew they would be destroyed as well. So they loaded their donkeys with worn-out sacks and old cracked wine-skins and moldy bread and put on old clothes and patched sandals. They deceived Joshua into believing that they were from a distant land and made a peace treaty with the Israelites, which God had forbidden. It was a big headache that could have been avoided if they had consulted the Lord.

That's why you need to consult with the Lord before you get involved with people, before you sign that contract, before you put the money down. People are not always who they say they are. They will show what they want you to see, but God can see the whole package. You better step back as a couple or you may have a problem you'll have to live with that's not at all what you thought when you agreed to it. You're not going to make the best decisions if you're not consulting with God. He will protect you and take you to the fullness of your destiny.

A PRAYER FOR TODAY

Father, thank You for the hope that rises within us whenever we remember all the ways You have protected us from harm and mistakes. Thank You that You haven't left us on our own to work out our destiny. We choose to consult You for guidance in our decisions in Jesus' Name. Amen.

The Palace Is Coming

TODAY'S SCRIPTURE

Although Joseph recognized his brothers,
they did not recognize him. Then he remembered
his dreams about them.

Genesis 42:8-9 NIV

Many years after being sold into slavery by his brothers and bad breaks and disappointments in an Egyptian prison, Joseph interpreted a dream for the Pharaoh and was put in charge over all the affairs of Egypt. Years later, there was a great famine in the land, and Joseph's brothers showed up at the palace looking to purchase food. You would think Joseph would be bitter and vindictive. But when Joseph saw his brothers, it says he remembered his dream about them. He didn't remember the pain and suffering. He remembered the promise that God had spoken to him and how through all the difficult years God directed his steps to get him to where he was supposed to be. God used it for his good.

When God puts a promise in your hearts, it doesn't mean it's going to come to pass without opposition, delays, and adversities. You'll have plenty of opportunities to get discouraged and frustrated, thinking it's never going to happen. In the tough times you have to remember your dreams. You may not understand it, but God is in control. He's directing your steps. Now do your part, stay in faith, and keep a good attitude. Let God fight your battles. There are detours on the way to your destiny. The palace is coming. The promise is still on track.

A PRAYER FOR TODAY

Father, even when we don't understand our circumstances, we know
that You are working things out for our good and to fulfill our
dreams. We lift our eyes to You and declare that You are directing
our steps on the way to the palace in Jesus' Name. Amen.

Good Fires

TODAY'S SCRIPTURE

The tongue is a small thing, but what enormous damage it can do. A great forest can be set on fire by one tiny spark. And the tongue is a flame of fire.

James 3:5-6 TLB

When Moses' sister, Miriam, didn't like the woman Moses had married, she started talking behind his back, stirring up trouble, and sowing discord. The Scripture says, "The Lord heard it." He heard her disrespectful, critical, hurtful words. All of a sudden Miriam was stricken with leprosy. Because leprosy is contagious, she had to immediately leave the Israelite camp.

We need to realize that God hears what we say. He hears us when we bless people, when we compliment and encourage them. He hears when we criticize and stir up trouble. The prophet Isaiah said that we will eat the fruit of our words. If you sow disrespect, sarcasm, discord, and judgment, you're going to reap those things. But when you sow kindness, encouragement, and mercy, that's what you're going to reap.

James said that our tongue is like a fire. One word can start a major problem or a major blessing. We're asking you to start some good fires in your relationship. Ignite dreams, ignite hope, ignite passion. Your words can breathe new life into your spouse's dreams. Don't be a part of the problem, be a part of the solution. Be a lifter, be an encourager, be a healer.

A PRAYER FOR TODAY

Father, thank You for the people You have placed in our lives. We want to love them and to love each other like You do. Help us to use our words to start some good fires in our relationships. We believe that You are making us into lifters, encouragers, and healers in Jesus' Name. Amen.

It Will Not Prosper

TODAY'S SCRIPTURE

...no weapon turned against you will succeed. You will silence every voice raised up to accuse you.

Isaiah 54:17 NLT

saiah doesn't say that we won't have difficulties or never have a problem. That's not reality. Challenges will come. People may talk. A family member may get off course. God says, "The problem may form, but you can stay in peace, knowing that it's not going to prosper against you." Because you're His child, because you're in the secret place of the Most High, God has a hedge of protection, mercy, and favor around you that the enemy cannot cross. No person, no sickness, and no trouble can stop God's plan for your lives. All the forces of darkness cannot keep you from your destiny.

When you face these challenges and you're tempted to worry, you need to tell yourselves: "We have a promise from Almighty God that it is not going to prosper." In other words, "They may be talking about us, trying to make us look bad, but we know God is our vindicator. He will take care of them." "This medical report may not look good, but we know God made our bodies. He has us in the palms of His hands. Nothing can snatch us away." Whatever you're facing, stay in peace. The two of you and God are a majority. The problem may have formed, but it is not going to prosper.

A PRAYER FOR TODAY

Father, thank You that we have Your promise that nothing that forms against us is going to prosper. We declare that because we are Your children, there is a hedge of protection, mercy, and favor around us that the enemy cannot cross in Jesus' Name. Amen.

OUR
BEST
LIFE
TOGETHER

We Declare

everything that doesn't
line up with God's vision
for our lives is subject to
change. Sickness, trouble,
lack, and mediocrity are not
permanent. They are only
temporary. We will not be
moved by what we see but
by what we know. We are
victors and never victims.
We will become all that God
has created us to be.

Into the Unknown

TODAY'S SCRIPTURE

*"I and my attendants will fast as you do.
When this is done, I will go to the king,
even though it is against the law.
And if I perish, I perish."*

Esther 4:16 NIV

There was a young Jewish orphan girl named Esther, who was living in a foreign country. But God raised her up to become the queen. When a powerful official passed a law that all the Jewish people be killed, Esther's cousin Mordecai told her that she had to go in and plead with the king for their people. In those days, if you approached the king without his holding up his golden rod first, you would be killed. That included Esther. God was asking her to step into the unknown, and we love what Esther did. She put her life on the line, and her heroic actions saved her people.

Like Esther, God will give us opportunities as couples to step into the unknown. When they come your way, don't shrink back, don't let fear talk you out of it, and don't let the what-ifs silence you. Be bold, be courageous, and step into the unknown. You may not see how it's going to work out, but along the way you'll see miracles. If you do this, you're about to step into a new level of favor and reach the fullness of your destiny.

A PRAYER FOR TODAY

*Father, we praise You because nothing is too hard for You.
Thank You for the opportunities You will bring our way to step
into the unknown, and we expect to see Your hand of favor
work powerfully in our behalf. We declare there is no
God like You in Jesus' Name. Amen.*

Keep Digging

TODAY'S SCRIPTURE

"Thus says the LORD, 'Make this valley (the Arabah) full of trenches.' For thus says the LORD, 'You will not see wind or rain, yet that valley will be filled with water.'"
2 Kings 3:16-17 AMP

The armies of Judah and Israel had traveled through the desert for seven days on their way to a battle when they ran out of water for themselves and their animals. Feeling they were doomed, they sent word to the prophet Elisha, asking what they should do. He told them to dig ditches throughout the valley to prepare for the water that was coming. They could have said, "Elisha, it never rains here." But Elijah was saying, "It's going to happen supernaturally. Just dig." So they did, and the next morning, out of nowhere water started flowing into the valley.

Every time you're discouraged and don't know how a promise from God is going to happen, dig a ditch. For instance, when you say together, "Father, thank You that our children make good decisions. Thank You that they will fulfill their destiny," there may not be any sign of it at that moment. Don't be moved by what you see; be moved by what you know. If you do your part and keep digging the ditch, God is saying, "I'll do My part and bring the water. I'll show you favor and open new doors. I will make things happen that you could never make happen."

A PRAYER FOR TODAY

Father, thank You that Your favor is available to us every day. We turn our hearts and minds toward You, knowing that You will fulfill Your promises to us. We declare that we are trusting You to make happen what we could never make happen in Jesus' Name. Amen.

One Step

TODAY'S SCRIPTURE

"I tell you, her sins—and they are many—have been forgiven, so she has shown me much love."

Luke 7:47 NLT

Jesus was at a Pharisee's house when "a certain immoral woman" came in and poured a jar of expensive perfume on Jesus' feet and began to wash them with her tears and her hair. The religious leaders were shocked that Jesus would allow this "sinner" to touch Him. They judged her by her performance. But while her performance was poor, she had her heart turned toward God. She loved and longed to please Him. Jesus told them a parable about how when you've been forgiven much, you will love much. He said to the lady, "Your sins are forgiven."

She had made a mess of her life, but when she took one step toward God, He showed her mercy. He cleaned up the mess and didn't say anything about it. That's the God we serve. It's not about your performance as a couple that matters. God is not judging you based on what you've done. He looks past the outside, past the mistakes and failures, and He looks at your hearts. When your hearts are right, God will show Himself strong in your lives. When you call out to God, He'll turn things around and get you on the right track. As it was with this lady, you're going to see His favor, restoration, mercy, and reach the fullness of your destiny together.

A PRAYER FOR TODAY

Father, thank You for looking beyond the surface and seeing our hearts. Thank You for looking past our mistakes and failures and messes. We break off all the negative and condemning thoughts! We believe that You will show Yourself strong in our lives in Jesus' Name. Amen.

Think Supernatural

TODAY'S SCRIPTURE

And because of their unbelief, he couldn't do any
miracles among them except to place his hands
on a few sick people and heal them.

Mark 6:5 NLT

n today's Scripture, it doesn't say Jesus wouldn't do any miracles; it says He couldn't. God works where there's an attitude of faith. How many times do we stop God from abundantly blessing our lives because we don't believe His promises are going to happen? We let our circumstances and what's happened in the past talk us out of it. Your minds may tell you that you've seen your best days as a couple, but a voice is saying down in your spirits, "Something good is on the way. New levels are coming." It's the seed God has put in you. When you live with this expectancy and you go through the day saying, "God, we believe You can take us where we've never dreamed," you'll see the surpassing greatness of God's favor.

Here's the key: God's idea of blessing you as a couple is very different than what you think being blessed is. We think natural; God thinks supernatural. He's the running-over, the exceed-your-expectations God. He's already decided to bless you. Now it's up to you. Take the limits off Him. Dare to believe what God has already decided. If you do this, God is going to exceed your expectations and take you to the fullness of your destiny.

A PRAYER FOR TODAY

Father, You are the all-powerful and all-knowing God. We ask
You to help us take the limits off what we believe You can do in
and through our lives. We believe Your promise of blessing
and declare that we will see the surpassing greatness of
Your favor in Jesus' Name. Amen.

Fresh Anointings

TODAY'S SCRIPTURE

...there they anointed David king over the tribe of Judah.

2 Samuel 2:4 NIV

D avid was thirty years old and about to take the throne. At this time, Israel was divided into two kingdoms—Judah and Israel. First, Judah anointed David to be their king. He served there seven and a half years, then he brought the two kingdoms together. When he was thirty-seven years old, the men of Israel joined the men of Judah, and they anointed David again to be the king over all Israel. What's interesting is that David had been anointed as a teenager to become the king. He could have declined the subsequent anointings as unnecessary. But David understood the importance of having a fresh anointing. You can't win today's battles on yesterday's anointing. You need to have a fresh anointing.

Too often we are trying to do things in our own strength. It's a struggle. It's weighing us down. The reason things get stale and we just endure our marriage, endure the job, and drag through the day is that we're not stirring up the anointing. We don't realize that on a regular basis we need to pray, "God, we need a fresh anointing in our marriage, on our careers, on our minds and thoughts. Help us to see things from the right perspective. Fill us with new strength, new ideas, new creativity, and new passion." When you do that, God will breathe freshness onto your lives.

A PRAYER FOR TODAY

Father, thank You for fresh anointings on the dry places in our lives. We refuse to let things get stale in our relationship or our minds. We believe we are equipped and empowered to go places and do what we've never done in Jesus' Name. Amen.

Just Remember

TODAY'S SCRIPTURE

...because they had not understood [the miracle of]
the loaves [how it revealed the power and deity of Jesus].

Mark 6:52 AMP

On one occasion, the disciples were in a boat and so stressed out by a nighttime storm that they forgot how earlier that day they had seen one of the greatest miracles ever recorded. If they had just remembered how Jesus had fed some fifteen thousand people, they would have stayed in faith, knowing that everything would be okay despite the high waves. What's interesting is that they were out on the lake because they had done what Jesus asked. They were being faithful. Where they missed it was their not remembering what God had done.

Are you doing what they did? Are you letting your circumstances, a medical report or a financial situation, cause you to live worried, stressed out? Why don't you start considering your miracles? God is saying to you what He said to His disciples: just remember. Look back over your lives. Remember the times God showed up and suddenly turned it around. You have a history with God. Every victory He's given you wasn't just for that time; it was so you could go back and use that as fuel to build your faith. If you are low on faith, go back and get some fuel. It's in your past victories. Don't talk about your problems; talk about the greatness of God.

A PRAYER FOR TODAY

Father, we praise You for all the wonders that You have worked in our lives. Thank You for all that we can point to and say that this is what You've done, and thank You that we can use it as fuel to build our faith. We declare Your amazing greatness in our lives in Jesus' Name. Amen.

A Master Plan

TODAY'S SCRIPTURE

"For I know the plans I have for you," declares the
LORD, *"plans to prosper you and not to harm you,*
plans to give you hope and a future."

Jeremiah 29:11 NIV

Every couple deals with disappointments and challenges that don't seem to make sense. We want you to understand that even though life is not always fair, God is fair. And He promises that all things work together for our good, with the key word being *together*. You cannot isolate a challenge in one area of your lives, one disappointment or setback, and say, "Well, our lives are ruined." The challenge you are facing is simply one piece of your puzzle. God sees the big picture. There is another piece coming that will connect it all. It will work together for your good.

God has promised a great plan for you. You may feel as though your lives are missing something, whether it's in the area of your finances, your careers, or your relationship. But all God has to do is add some pieces to the puzzle, and your lives will feel whole and complete. Those new parts may be the right people, the right opportunities, or the right breaks at just the right time. Keep pressing forward together, and one day you'll look back and see how it all played into a master plan that God designed for your lives. Somehow, someway, He will work it all out to your advantage.

A PRAYER FOR TODAY

Father, thank You that Your plan is to prosper us and to give
us a hope and a future. We know that You see every unexpected
and uncertain circumstance in our lives, and we declare
that You are working all things together for
our good in Jesus' Name. Amen.

Praise from God

TODAY'S SCRIPTURE

"...for they loved human praise more
than praise from God."

John 12:43 NIV

Jesus talked about those who loved the praise of people more than the praise of God. One of the tests we all have to pass is when someone in our lives whom we respect wants us to go one direction, yet we know in our hearts that we should take another path. We want their approval, but if we are to fulfill our destiny, we have to be strong as a couple.

We've learned that if you please God and stay true to what He's put in your hearts, eventually you will have the praise of people. His favor, His anointing, and His blessing will cause the two of you to excel. People may not understand why you don't take their advice, but later they'll see you walking in the fullness of your destiny. If you quit worrying about what everyone else thinks, you will see new opportunities and relationships. God's favor on your lives will increase.

People will tell you how to run your life. If you try to please everyone, we can guarantee you one thing: you'll be confused, frustrated, and miserable. Don't let people control you and go around feeling guilty because you don't fit into their boxes. Look straight ahead together and, as the apostle Paul said, "Run with purpose in every step."

A PRAYER FOR TODAY

Father, we love You for guiding us with Your peace and joy.
Help us to be wise in our relationships and to be free from living
for the approval of others. We declare that we want to stay
true to pleasing You and You alone as we run the race
You've set before us in Jesus' Name. Amen.

The Privilege of Prayer

TODAY'S SCRIPTURE

And by him we cry, "Abba, Father." The Spirit himself testifies with our spirit that we are God's children.

Romans 8:15-16 NIV

When we pray, something supernatural occurs. Prayer is the most powerful posture we can take in this earthly realm. When we pray together, we connect the strongest part of ourselves with the strongest force in the universe—the Spirit of God. We open ourselves to Him, and Scripture says that God's Spirit testifies with our spirit. He confirms His will to our hearts.

Prayer is simply talking to God. When you come to God with an open and humble heart, there's no right or wrong way to pray. The apostle Paul tells us that we are to rejoice and pray in all seasons and on every occasion. That's how we become stronger and stronger. The important part is that you do it. Rather than think you need to commit to an hour of prayer a day, it's so much better to say, "Every day we're going to pray five minutes," then add on to it.

Remember, prayer is a privilege. Without Jesus, we wouldn't be able to come directly to God. We wouldn't be able to make our requests known to Him. We wouldn't be able to know peace that passes understanding. Make prayer a priority. Put Him first and draw strength from the wonderful privilege we have in Him!

A PRAYER FOR TODAY

Father, we humbly come before You to learn from You and listen to You. Thank You for the promise of Your presence when the two of us gather in Your name and that what we agree about and ask You for will be done. We cast all our cares upon You now in Jesus' Name. Amen.

Be Still and Know

TODAY'S SCRIPTURE

*"You need not fight in this battle; take your
positions, stand and witness the salvation
of the Lord who is with you."*

2 Chronicles 20:17 AMP

The Israelites were surrounded by a huge army and greatly
outnumbered. They were so stressed out, and finally they
decided to pray. Notice God's answer: if you will be still
and remain at rest, God will turn it around, restore you,
and vindicate you.

The Scripture says, "Be still and know that I am God." When
you feel overwhelmed and you're tempted to take everything into
your own hands, you have to make yourselves be still. This is
when many couples make quick decisions that end up only making
matters worse. The battle is not yours. The battle is the Lord's.
As long as you're fighting it, God is going to let you do it on your
own. But when you put it into His hands, that's when God will
fight your battles.

Maybe you're facing a big challenge. You're upset and frustrated. God is saying to you, "Be still. I've already set the time to
not only bring you out, but to bring you out better off than you
were before." Now do your part and rest. Trust God's timing. We
may not understand why something is taking so long, but sometimes God will delay an answer so He can show His power in a
greater way.

A PRAYER FOR TODAY

*Father, we praise You for Your hand of protection upon our lives.
We choose to be still before You and listen to You. Give us the
grace to accept Your timing and to rest in the fact that You've
already scheduled things in for us. We believe our times
are in Your hands in Jesus' Name. Amen.*

People of Integrity

TODAY'S SCRIPTURE

Catch all the foxes, those little foxes,
before they ruin the vineyard...

Song of Solomon 2:15 NLT

God wants us to be people of integrity, people of honor, people who are trustworthy. A person of integrity is open and honest and true to her word. He says what he means and means what he says. She doesn't have any hidden agendas or ulterior motives. He doesn't need a legal contract to force him to fulfill his commitments. People of integrity are the same in private as they are in public. They do what's right whether anybody is watching or not.

If you don't have integrity, you will never reach your best life together. Integrity is the foundation on which a truly successful relationship is built. Every time you compromise, every time you are less than honest, you are causing a slight crack in the foundation. If you continue compromising, that foundation will never be able to hold what God wants to build. You may enjoy some temporary success, but you'll never see the fullness of God's favor if you don't take the high road and make the more excellent choices. On the other hand, God's blessings will overtake you if you settle for nothing less than living with integrity.

Remember, our lives are an open book before God. He looks at our hearts and motives. There's no limit to what God will do in your lives when He knows that He can trust you.

A PRAYER FOR TODAY

Father, thank You that You see our hearts and motives
and that You reward integrity. We want to step up to a higher
level of integrity and honesty in our relationship with each
other and with other people. Help us to always do the
right thing in Jesus' Name. Amen.

When God Is Silent

TODAY'S SCRIPTURE

...you know that the testing of your faith
produces perseverance.

James 1:3 NIV

Sometimes when we're being tested by discouragement as a couple, it seems God is silent. We pray and we don't hear anything. We read the Scripture and still come away feeling as though God is a million miles away. But remember, this is a test. When you're in school, teachers never talk during tests, but they have been preparing you in the days prior to the test. On test day, they want to see if you can put into practice what you've learned.

God works the same way. He is right there with you during the test. The silence only means that God has prepared you, and now He's watching to see if you have learned. God is not mad at you when He is silent. He hasn't forsaken you. His silence is a sign that He has great confidence in you. He knows you will come through the test victoriously or He would not have permitted you to be tested. Stay in faith.

Today is a new day. God is breathing new hope into your hearts and new vision into your spirits. He is the glory and the lifter of your heads. Look up with a fresh vision, and God will put a new song in your hearts. You will soar through life full of joy, full of faith, full of victory.

A PRAYER FOR TODAY

Father, You are the glory and the lifter of our heads. Thank
You for the good plan You have for our lives. Even when
we don't understand things, we choose to put our hope
and trust in You. Help us to pass the tests and live
in Your joy in Jesus' Name. Amen.

The Right People

TODAY'S SCRIPTURE

The women said to Naomi: "Blessed is the LORD who has not left you without a redeemer (grandson, an heir)... May he also be to you one who restores life and sustains your old age."

Ruth 4:14-15, AMP

Naomi lost her husband in death, then both her married sons died. She was so discouraged she didn't think she could go on. She even changed her name from Naomi, which means "my joy," to Mara, which means "bitter." She was saying, "Call me bitter." But her friends refused and kept calling her Naomi, "my joy." She was trying to stay in defeat, but they said, "No, you're coming into victory."

Naomi's widowed daughter-in-law Ruth remarried and one day had a baby boy. At this time it didn't seem as though Naomi had any reason to live. But when she saw that baby, she felt a new sense of purpose. Her friends rejoiced, saying, "Naomi, this baby will restore your youth." She took care of that child as though he were her own. Naomi thought she'd never be happy again, but now she was more fulfilled than ever. That was God paying her back for the unfair things that had happened.

If you have been through disappointments and loss, stay close to people who will call you blessed and victorious. You want people in your lives who will remind you that your best days are yet to come.

A PRAYER FOR TODAY

Father, thank You that You are able to take the most unfair situations in our lives and turn them into wonderful positives. And thank You for the people in our lives who call us victorious and blessed. Help us to stay close to those who remind us that we are Yours in Jesus' Name. Amen.

A Hedge of Protection

TODAY'S SCRIPTURE

*"Have you not put a hedge around him and
his household and everything he has?"*

Job 1:10 NIV

Satan was looking for somebody to test. God said to Satan, "Have you seen my servant, Job? There's none like him in all the land." Satan answered back, "Yes, but I can't touch him. You've put a hedge around him. If You will remove the frame around his life and let me get to him, he'll curse You." Job went through a time of testing. He fought the good fight. And in the end, not only did he not curse God, but he came out with double.

What we want you to see is that the enemy can't just do whatever he wants. He has to ask God for permission. God has to allow him to do it. When you go through tough times, you have a bad break, you're facing a sickness, don't get discouraged. Remember, the hedge is still up. You keep moving forward, and you'll not only come out, but God will bring you out better off than you were before.

Don't worry about your future. You've been framed. There are boundaries around your lives put in place by the most powerful force in the universe. Now all through the day, instead of being stressed out, under your breath, say, "Lord, thank You that our lives, our children, our health, our finances, and our dreams are in Your frame. We are protected."

A PRAYER FOR TODAY

*Father, we praise You for Your divine protection in our lives.
Thank You for watching over us and controlling our times
of testing. We believe we are framed and that as we move
forward You will bring us out better off than we were
before in Jesus' Name. Amen.*

Sing a New Song

TODAY'S SCRIPTURE

"Behold, the former things have come to pass, and
new things I declare...Sing to the LORD a new song,
and His praise from the ends of the earth."

Isaiah 42:9-10 NKJV

God is saying that the things you've been struggling with as a couple are coming to an end—the disappointment, the hurt, the withdrawal, the fatigue of familiarity. He's about to put a stop to it. He's going to do a new thing. But there's one requirement. If you're going to see the negative come to an end and God do a new thing, you have to sing a new song. You can't go around with that same old song of who hurt who and how wrong it was. No, get rid of that song of defeat and self-pity, throw out that song of "it will never get better," and start singing a song of victory.

If you want to see the new, there can be no more talking about what you can't do and how it's never going to work out. God knows everything that's happened to you. You don't have to remind Him. If you lose the sad song and start singing the new song, God will turn your mourning into dancing. He'll take that setback and use it as a setup to do something greater. Is there something you need to get over today? Make this decision with us: no more excuses.

A PRAYER FOR TODAY

Father, You are worthy of our worship and our new songs of
praise. Thank You that we can put the old songs of defeat behind
us and start singing songs of victory. We declare that this is a
new day and our dreams and vision and passions are being
renewed in Jesus' Name. Amen.

Peace and Unity

TODAY'S SCRIPTURE

*And those who are peacemakers will plant seeds of
peace and reap a harvest of righteousness.*

James 3:18 NLT

Today, more than ever, we have to be proactive and do whatever we can to stand together for our relationships and our families. Adversity comes. Disagreements happen. But one of the most powerful ways you can strengthen your relationship is by being a peacemaker.

Think about a campfire. It can only burn as long as someone is throwing logs on it. When you stop fueling the fire, eventually it will go out. Maybe you feel as though you have a fire of strife and confusion in your home or in your relationship. If you ask God to help you be a peacemaker, if you will stop throwing logs on the fire, He will supernaturally cause that fire to be extinguished.

Peace and unity are so important because we have an enemy who is after this generation. He targets our families and relationships and brings division. If you stay focused on your differences, there is going to be division. However, if you change your focus and look for the common ground of peace, you can bring harmony into your relationships again. Remember, "blessed are the peacemakers, for they will be called children of God." When we dwell together in unity, we honor God and open the door for His hand of blessing in every area of our lives!

A PRAYER FOR TODAY

*Father, we praise You for being the God of love and peace and
for the promise that You will be with us always. Thank You for
the way You are watching over our lives and keeping us in the
palms of Your hands. We declare that we are moving forward
in peace and unity and into the victory that You have
prepared for us in Jesus' Name. Amen.*

We Want to Hear from You!

Each week, I close our international television broadcast by giving the audience an opportunity to make Jesus the Lord of their lives. I'd like to extend that same opportunity to you.

Are you at peace with God? A void exists in every person's heart that only God can fill. I'm not talking about joining a church or finding religion. I'm talking about finding life and peace and happiness. Would you pray with me today? Just say, "Lord Jesus, I repent of my sins. I ask You to come into my heart. I make You my Lord and Savior."

Friend, if you prayed that simple prayer, I believe you have been "born again." I encourage you to attend a good, Bible-based church and keep God in first place in your life. For free information on how you can grow stronger in your spiritual life, please feel free to contact us.

Victoria and I love you, and we'll be praying for you. We're believing for God's best for you, that you will see your dreams come to pass. We'd love to hear from you!

To contact us, write to:

Joel and Victoria Osteen
P.O. Box 4600
Houston, TX 77210

Or you can reach us online at www.joelosteen.com.

Stay connected, be blessed.

From thoughtful articles to powerful blogs, podcasts and more, JoelOsteen.com is full of inspirations that will give you encouragement and confidence in your daily life.

Visit us today at JoelOsteen.com.